"With the assistance of nine other scholars, Firth and Wilson have provided us with the finest of introductions to the theological reading and research of Old Testament wisdom. Wide ranging in its coverage of the biblical and modern literature and clear in its explanation of major issues and themes, this book will benefit students, teachers, and all who love wisdom."
Richard S. Hess, Denver Seminary

"David Firth and Lindsay Wilson have placed us in their debt by compiling this excellent collection on Old Testament wisdom. Drawing together esteemed senior scholars as well as insightful younger voices in the field, this anthology provides a rich and expansive description of the study of Old Testament wisdom today. Be prepared to be informed, challenged, stretched, and inspired by this superb volume."
Daniel J. Estes, Cedarville University

Interpreting Old Testament Wisdom Literature

Edited by David G. Firth
and Lindsay Wilson

An imprint of InterVarsity Press
Downers Grove, Illinois

InterVarsity Press
P.O. Box 1400, Downers Grove, IL 60515-1426
ivpress.com
email@ivpress.com

US edition of this collection ©Inter-Varsity Press, 2017
UK edition of this collection ©Inter-Varsity Press, 2016

Published in the United States of America by InterVarsity Press, Downers Grove, Illinois, with permission from Inter-Varsity Press, England. Published in the United Kingdom as Exploring Old Testament Wisdom Literature.

All rights reserved. No part of this book may be reproduced in any form without written permission from InterVarsity Press.

InterVarsity Press® is the book-publishing division of InterVarsity Christian Fellowship/USA®, a movement of students and faculty active on campus at hundreds of universities, colleges, and schools of nursing in the United States of America, and a member movement of the International Fellowship of Evangelical Students. For information about local and regional activities, visit intervarsity.org.

Scripture quotations from the New Revised Standard Version of the Bible are copyright ©1989 by the Division of Christian Education of the National Council of the Churches of Christ in the USA. Used by permission. All rights reserved.

Scripture quotations from the Revised Standard Version of the Bible are copyright ©1946, 1952, and 1971 by the Division of Christian Education of the National Council of the Churches of Christ in the USA. Used by permission. All rights reserved.

Scripture quotations from The Holy Bible, English Standard Version, are copyright ©2001 by Crossway Bibles, a division of Good News Publishers. Used by permission. All rights reserved.

Scripture quotations from the Holy Bible, New International Version (Anglicized edition) are copyright © 1979, 1984, 2011 by Biblica (formerly International Bible Society). Used by permission of Hodder & Stoughton Publishers, a Hachette UK company. All rights reserved. "NIV" is a registered trademark of Biblica (formerly International Bible Society).

Cover design: Cindy Kiple
Images: harp illustration: © RonyGraphics/iStockphoto
  stained glass window: King Solomon, French School, (13th century) / Chartres Cathedral, Chartres, France / Bridgeman Images

Typeset in Great Britain by CRB Associates, Potterhanworth, Lincolnshire

ISBN 978-0-8308-5178-2 (print)
ISBN 978-0-8308-9112-2 (digital)

Printed in the United States of America ∞

green press *As a member of the Green Press Initiative, InterVarsity Press is committed to protecting the environment and to the responsible use of natural resources. To learn more, visit greenpressinitiative.org.*

Library of Congress Cataloging-in-Publication Data
A catalog record for this book is available from the Library of Congress.

P	22	21	20	19	18	17	16	15	14	13	12	11	10	9	8	7	6	5	4	3	2	1
Y	35	34	33	32	31	30	29	28	27	26	25	24	23	22	21	20	19	18	17			

CONTENTS

List of contributors   vii
List of abbreviations   ix

Introduction   xiii
David G. Firth and Lindsay Wilson

PART 1: THE STUDY OF WISDOM TODAY

1. Old Testament wisdom today   3
   Craig G. Bartholomew

PART 2: THE WISDOM LITERATURE

2. The book of Proverbs: some current issues   37
   Ernest C. Lucas

3. Job as a problematic book   60
   Lindsay Wilson

4. Reading Ecclesiastes with the scholars   81
   Katharine J. Dell

5. Seeking wisdom in the Song of Songs   100
   Rosalind Clarke

PART 3: THEMES

6. Is Ruth also among the wise?   115
   Gregory Goswell

7. Retribution and wisdom literature   134
   Lennart Boström

8. Worrying about the wise: wisdom in Old Testament narrative   155
   David G. Firth

9. Wisdom and biblical theology   174
   Christopher B. Ansberry

10. 'Children, listen to me': the voicing of wisdom in the Psalms   194
    Simon P. Stocks

11. 'Oh, that I knew where I might find him': aspects of divine absence in Proverbs, Job and Ecclesiastes   205
    Brittany N. Melton

    Index of authors   217

    Index of Scripture references   223

CONTRIBUTORS

Christopher B. Ansberry is Tutor in Old Testament and Hebrew, and Director of Postgraduate Studies, Oak Hill College, London. He is author of *Be Wise, My Son, and Make My Heart Glad: An Exploration of the Courtly Nature of the Book of Proverbs* (Walter de Gruyter, 2011) and of a forthcoming commentary on Proverbs (Zondervan).

Craig G. Bartholomew is Professor of Philosophy and Religion & Theology at Redeemer University College, Ontario, Canada, and Adjunct Faculty at Trinity College Bristol. He is the author of numerous books including *Old Testament Wisdom Literature: A Theological Introduction* (with Ryan O'Dowd, IVP Academic/Apollos, 2011), *Christian Philosophy: A Systematic and Narrative Introduction* (with Michael Goheen, Baker Academic, 2013), *When You Want to Yell at God: The Book of Job* (Lexham, 2014), and *Introducing Biblical Hermeneutics: A Comprehensive Framework for Hearing God in Scripture* (Baker Academic, 2015).

Lennart Boström is Lecturer in Old Testament at Örebro School of Theology, Sweden. He is the author of *The God of the Sages: The Portrayal of God in the Book of Proverbs* (Coniectanea Biblica, Old Testament, Almqvist & Wiksell, 1990).

Rosalind Clarke is Online Pastor for the Diocese of Lichfield. When she is not on Facebook and Twitter, her research interests include Hebrew poetry, hermeneutics and especially the Song of Songs. She holds theology degrees from Oak Hill College and Highland Theological College.

Katharine J. Dell is Reader in Old Testament Literature and Theology in the Faculty of Divinity at the University of Cambridge. She is a Fellow and Director of Studies in Theology at St Catharine's College, Cambridge. She is the author of books mainly in the area of wisdom literature, including *Job: Where Shall Wisdom Be Found?* (Phoenix Guides to the Old Testament, 2013) and *Interpreting Ecclesiastes: Readers Old and New* (Critical Studies in the Hebrew Bible 3, Eisenbrauns, 2013), and co-editor with Will Kynes of *Reading Ecclesiastes Intertextually* (LHBOTS 587, Bloomsbury T&T Clark, 2016).

David G. Firth is Old Testament Tutor and Academic Dean at Trinity College, Bristol. He is the author of *1 & 2 Samuel* (AOTC), *The Message of Esther* and *The Message of Joshua* (IVP, 2009, 2010, 2015), and co-editor of *Interpreting the Psalms*, *Interpreting Isaiah*, *Interpreting Deuteronomy*, *Words and the Word* and *Presence, Power and Promise* (all Apollos, 2009, 2009, 2012, 2008, 2011).

Gregory Goswell is Academic Dean and Lecturer in Biblical Studies at Christ College, Sydney. He is the author of *Ezra–Nehemiah* (EP Study Commentary, Evangelical Press, 2014) and numerous journal articles, and co-author with Peter W. H. Lau of *Unceasing Kindness: A Biblical Theology of Ruth* (NSBT, 2016).

Ernest C. Lucas has doctorates in both Old Testament studies and biochemistry. He is Vice-Principal Emeritus of Bristol Baptist College, where he taught Old Testament studies and biblical languages for eighteen years, and an Honorary Research Fellow in Theology and Religious Studies, University of Bristol. His publications include *Exploring the Old Testament, Vol. 3: The Psalms and Wisdom Literature* (SPCK, 2003), and *Proverbs* (The Two Horizons Old Testament Commentary, Eerdmans, 2016).

Brittany N. Melton is a PhD student at the University of Cambridge, researching divine presence and absence in the *Megilloth* under Dr Katharine Dell. She is author of 'Solomon, Wisdom, and Love: Intertextual Resonance Between Ecclesiastes and Song of Songs' in *Reading Ecclesiastes Intertextually* (ed. Dell and Kynes, LHBOTS 587, Bloomsbury T&T Clark, 2016).

Simon P. Stocks is Tutor for Biblical Studies at St Augustine's College of Theology in the south-east of England. His research exploring Hebrew poetic structures was published as *The Form and Function of the Tricolon in the Psalms of Ascents* (Pickwick, 2012). His special interests also include the theology of lament, and he is active in Anglican church ministry.

Lindsay Wilson is Academic Dean and Senior Lecturer in Old Testament at Ridley College, Melbourne, Australia. He is the author of *Job* (THOTC, Eerdmans, 2015).

ABBREVIATIONS

General

ANE	Ancient Near East(ern)
AT	Author's translation
EVV	English versions
Heb.	Hebrew text
mg.	margin
NT	New Testament
OT	Old Testament
tr.	translation, translated

Bible versions

AV	Authorized (King James) Version
ESV	English Standard Version
LXX	Septuagint
MT	Masoretic Text
NIV	New International Version
NRSV	New Revised Standard Version
RSV	Revised Standard Version

Apocrypha and Septuagint

Sir.	Sirach
Wis.	Wisdom of Solomon

Mishnah and Talmud tractates

Ber.   *Berakot*

Modern works

AB	Anchor Bible
ABR	*Australian Biblical Review*
AHw	Wolfram von Soden, *Akkadisches Handwörterbuch*, 3 vols. (Wiesbaden: Harrassowitz Verlag, 1965–81)
AJSL	*American Journal of Semitic Languages and Literatures*
AnaBib	Analecta Biblica
ATD	Das Alte Testament Deutsch
AYB	Anchor Yale Bible Commentaries
BBB	Bonner Biblische Beiträge
BBC	Blackwell Bible Commentary
BCOTWP	Baker Commentary on the Old Testament, Wisdom and Psalms
BETL	Bibliotheca Ephemeridum Theologicarum Lovaniensium
BHT	Beiträge zur historischen Theologie
Bib	*Biblica*
BibInt	*Biblical Interpretation*
BibSac	*Bibliotheca sacra*
BNTC	Black's New Testament Commentary
BST	The Bible Speaks Today
BTB	*Biblical Theology Bulletin*
BZAW	Beihefte zur Zeitschrift für die alttestamentliche Wissenschaft
CBQ	*Catholic Biblical Quarterly*
CD	Karl Barth, *Church Dogmatics*, ed. G. W. Bromiley and T. F. Torrance, tr. G. W. Bromiley, 4 vols. (Edinburgh: T&T Clark, 1956–75)
ConBOT	Coniectanea Biblica Old Testament series
CTJ	*Calvin Theological Journal*
EJT	*European Journal of Theology*
EQ	*Evangelical Quarterly*
ExpTim	*Expository Times*
FAT	Forschungen zum Alten Testament
HAT	Handkommentar zum Alten Testament
HBM	Hebrew Bible Monographs

HBS	Herders Biblische Studien
HCOT	Historical Commentary on the Old Testament
HS	*Hebrew Studies*
HTKAT	Herders Theologischer Kommentar zum Alten Testament
HUCA	*Hebrew Union College Annual*
ICC	International Critical Commentary
IRM	*International Review of Missions*
ITQ	*Irish Theological Quarterly*
JAAR	*Journal of the American Academy of Religion*
JANESCU	*Journal of the Ancient Near Eastern Society of Columbia University*
JBL	*Journal of Biblical Literature*
JESOT	*Journal for the Evangelical Study of the Old Testament*
JPS	Jewish Publication Society
JQR	*Jewish Quarterly Review*
JSOT	*Journal for the Study of the Old Testament*
JSOTSup	Journal for the Study of the Old Testament, Supplement Series
JSS	*Journal of Semitic Studies*
JTS	*Journal of Theological Studies*
LHBOTS	Library of Hebrew Bible/Old Testament Studies
NC	New Criticism
NCB	New Century Bible commentary
NEB	Neue Echter Bibel
NICOT	New International Commentary on the Old Testament
NIDB	*New Interpreter's Dictionary of the Bible*, ed. K. D. Sakenfeld (Nashville: Abingdon, 2006–9)
NIDOTTE	*New International Dictionary of Old Testament Theology and Exegesis*, ed. W. A. VanGemeren (Grand Rapids: Eerdmans, 1997)
NIGTC	New International Greek Testament Commentary
OBO	Orbis Biblicus et Orientalis
OBT	Overtures to Biblical Theology
OTC	Old Testament Commentary
OTL	Old Testament Library
OTS	Oudtestamentische Studiën
PGOT	Phoenix Guides to the Old Testament
RB	*Revue Biblique*
RevExp	*Review and Expositor*
RTR	*Reformed Theological Review*
StBL	Studies in Biblical Literature

SBL	Society of Biblical Literature
SBLDS	Society of Biblical Literature Dissertation Series
SBLMS	Society of Biblical Literature Monograph Series
SBLSymS	Society of Biblical Literature Symposium Series
SBT	Studies in Biblical Theology
SJT	*Scottish Journal of Theology*
SOTSM	Society for Old Testament Study Monographs
TDOT	*Theological Dictionary of the Old Testament*, ed. G. J. Botterweck, H. Ringgren and H.-J. Fabry (Grand Rapids: Eerdmans, 1974–2006)
THOTC	Two Horizons Old Testament Commentary
TOTC	Tyndale Old Testament Commentary
TynB	*Tyndale Bulletin*
USQR	*Union Seminary Quarterly Review*
VT	*Vetus Testamentum*
VTSup	Supplements to Vetus Testamentum
WBC	Word Biblical Commentary
WMANT	Wissenschaftliche Monographien zum Alten und Neuen Testament
ZAW	*Zeitschrift für die Alttestamentliche Wissenschaft*
ZTK	*Zeitschrift für Theologie und Kirche*

INTRODUCTION

David G. Firth and Lindsay Wilson

Wisdom has always been an important part of the Old Testament. Jeremiah mentions three important figures in Israel's national life: the priest, whose task it was to teach the law; the prophet, who proclaimed the word; and the wise person or sage, who gave counsel or advice (Jer. 18:18). The wise counsellor seemed to hold a prominent place in society, most likely as the professional adviser (2 Sam. 16:23), performing a role in Israel similar to that of Joseph in Egypt and Daniel in Babylon. Solomon was a king who, at his best, epitomized wisdom, though he also showed the danger of separating wisdom from the fear of the Lord (1 Kgs 11).

Yet despite this, wisdom has been marginalized by those studying the thought of the Old Testament as a whole (see Chris Ansberry's essay in this volume). Themes that are prominent elsewhere receive only scant attention by the wisdom writers. There is a focus in the wisdom books of Proverbs, Job and Ecclesiastes on *everyday life* rather than on national history. God's special dealings with the nation of Israel – both in judgment and in salvation – are completely absent from wisdom literature, even though they dominate the rest of the Old Testament. Wisdom ignores great national events of religious significance, such as the exodus, the conquest, the giving of the law and the messianic hope. Goldsworthy notes that 'Wisdom's apparent lack of concern for Israel's history, covenant and law is one of its distinctive features'.[1] It concentrates instead on

---

1. G. L. Goldsworthy, *Gospel and Wisdom* (Exeter: Paternoster, 1987), p. 50.

the mundane things of everyday life – buying and selling, bringing up children, eating, and so on. This gives the literature a cosmopolitan or more universal flavour. The sages are primarily aware of their fellows as human beings rather than as Israelites or Gentiles.

The worldview of the wise is now rightly regarded as an aspect of the Israelite worldview, not something totally foreign. The covenant beliefs are presupposed, yes, but they are almost never specifically referred to. As Murphy has suggested, 'The covenant relationship to the Lord does not figure directly in the wisdom experience; it is bracketed but not erased.'[2] Old Testament theology is wider than simply a study of the covenants and the mighty actions of God.

Wisdom must be learnt from parents, teachers and friends, but it is ultimately a gift from God. Contrary to common assumptions, it is not primarily intellectual but rather intensely practical. The chief craftsman in making the tabernacle (Exod. 31:1–5; 35:10, 25–26, 30–35) was given special wisdom by God for the task (ability, intelligence, knowledge). Shipwrights and navigators (Ezek. 27:8–9) needed wisdom, as did farmers (Isa. 28:23–29) who knew how to carry out their tasks. Wisdom is basically skill in living, in how to order one's life so as to achieve desirable goals.

A clearer understanding of the nature of Old Testament wisdom literature has led to something of a revival in academic interest of late. Indeed, its interest in everyday life is seen to have great potential in speaking to new generations of people within and outside the church. The issues dealt with in the wisdom books of Proverbs, Job and Ecclesiastes (and probably Song of Songs and a number of psalms) – justice, faith, wealth, suffering, meaning, sexuality, to name a few – are the very topics the world is talking about. This book is one attempt to bring the wisdom literature into such discussions.

The focus of this volume is on both wisdom books and wisdom ideas. Craig Bartholomew provides a comprehensive study of recent developments in the field of Old Testament wisdom. This is followed by more specific chapters discussing some issues which have arisen in the three main wisdom books of Proverbs (Ernest Lucas), Job (Lindsay Wilson) and Ecclesiastes (Katharine Dell). These chapters cover disputed areas in academic scholarship, as well as the core ideas of these books. Consideration is also given to the inclusion of Song of Songs (Rosalind Clarke) and some psalms (Simon Stocks) as wisdom texts.

In addition to those parts of the Old Testament which may be identified as wisdom writings, there are other books which appear to contain some wisdom influence or flavour. Greg Goswell explores wisdom in the book of Ruth, while

---

2. R. E. Murphy, *The Tree of Life*, 3rd edn (Grand Rapids: Eerdmans, 2002), p. 124.

David Firth looks at the broader field of Old Testament narrative, ranging from Joshua to Esther. Chris Ansberry explores the theological links between wisdom and the rest of the Old Testament as he discusses the topic of wisdom and biblical theology. Some of the key wisdom themes have been drawn out in these discussions, but there are also chapters devoted to the concept of retribution in wisdom (Lennart Boström) and to the vexed issue of divine absence (Brittany Melton).

May this volume help you to see afresh some of the riches that God has offered to us in the wisdom materials of the Old Testament, and to understand the background to Paul's description of Jesus as 'the wisdom of God' (1 Cor. 1:24). We do well to listen to the exhortation of James: 'If any of you lacks wisdom, you should ask God, who gives generously to all without finding fault, and it will be given to you' (Jas 1:5, NIV).

PART 1:

THE STUDY OF WISDOM TODAY

1. OLD TESTAMENT WISDOM TODAY

Craig G. Bartholomew

Introduction

There is an immense amount at stake in our work on Old Testament wisdom. Wisdom is about navigating life individually and corporately amidst its many challenges. If there is something special about *Old Testament* wisdom, namely that it is inspired and fully trustworthy, as Christians believe, then we have a major responsibility to handle it well, and to make its resources available to academy, church and world today.

It is indeed gratifying, albeit somewhat overwhelming, to see how much attention Old Testament wisdom continues to receive. It was not always so. An effect of historical criticism in its early days was to marginalize Old Testament wisdom. Wellhausen, for example, paid virtually no attention to wisdom literature, regarding it as late and secondary.[1] Consequently, the thorough application of the historical-critical method to 'historical' Old Testament literature occurs earlier than it does to wisdom literature. Gunkel's form-critical approach was particularly significant in moving wisdom into the foreground of Old Testament studies.

---

1. Ronald E. Clements, *A Century of Old Testament Study* (Cambridge: Lutterworth, 1976), p. 100.

Since Old Testament wisdom moved back into focus an enormous body of work has been produced,[2] so that today a crucial question is how to orient oneself in relation to it, so as to see the most creative ways forward. By its nature any framework is reductive, but I propose that the most helpful way to see the whole is in relation to *a series of turns*.[3] In the late nineteenth and for most of the twentieth century *historical* criticism with its various methods – source criticism, form criticism, tradition history and redaction criticism – dominated study of the Old Testament wisdom books. From the 1970s onwards Old Testament study was deeply affected by the *literary turn*, with its various methods such as New Criticism, structuralism, narrative analysis, rhetorical analysis, reception history, and so on, leading to fresh new ways of reading the wisdom books. There can be no doubt that the literary turn raised all sorts of important questions about the validity of the 'assured results' of historical criticism, but before the literary turn could be fully appropriated, the *postmodern turn* was upon us. The effect of postmodernism was to usher in an era of wild pluralism with a smorgasbord of readings being done of Old Testament texts, including wisdom. With its wariness of power and totalizing metanarratives postmodernism reinforced a growing emphasis on *ideological critique* of Old Testament texts. More recently, and in important ways related back to Karl Barth, and to Brevard Childs' canonical hermeneutic, we have witnessed a *theological turn* in biblical studies, with an emphasis on reading the Bible as Scripture for the church. This too has manifested itself in studies of Old Testament wisdom.[4]

We can thus think in terms of the following turns:

Historical
   Literary
      Postmodern
         Theological

In terms of this framework it is important to note that one turn does not obliterate (an) earlier one(s). Of necessity they interact with and upon each

---

2. One cannot begin to produce a comprehensive bibliography for a chapter of this nature.
3. There are, of course, other ways of tracking the vicissitudes of OT wisdom. One could, for example, have a close look at the many introductions to OT wisdom and the state of the discourse in books published in recent years.
4. See Craig G. Bartholomew and Ryan P. O'Dowd, *Old Testament Wisdom: A Theological Introduction* (Downers Grove: IVP Academic; Nottingham: Apollos, 2011).

other. Nor is it the case that later turns are not present in earlier ones. Historical criticism, for example, placed great emphasis on 'literary criticism', but the later focus on Old Testament wisdom as literature scrutinized the extent to which historical criticism understood the literary dimension of texts. Historical critics also retain an interest in the theology of wisdom, but theological interpretation makes its *goal* that of reading Old Testament wisdom as Scripture for the church. The postmodern turn may now be running out of steam but it has been so diffusive in its effects that to a large extent historical criticism has remained the default mode for many Old Testament scholars. The theological turn is a minority school and a broad one at that, so its longer-term effects remain to be seen.[5]

In this chapter we will begin by defining wisdom, and we will then examine the journey of the Old Testament wisdom books through the lens of the turns identified above. After that we will assess the current state of Old Testament wisdom studies as a prelude to concluding with an assessment of where work needs to be done today.

Defining wisdom

Crenshaw refers to wisdom as an 'elusive creature' and asserts that 'Each definition captures a significant feature of wisdom, but none of them succeeds in isolating the total phenomenon that gave birth to wisdom literature'.[6] What 'gave birth' to Old Testament wisdom is an *historical* question and we may well not be able to solve this speculative issue. However, it remains worthwhile to try to delineate the contours of Old Testament wisdom.[7] Proverbs is the foundational Old Testament wisdom book and from it, read as a literary whole, we see that wisdom is:

---

5. See Craig G. Bartholomew and Heath Thomas (eds.), *A Manifesto for Theological Interpretation* (Grand Rapids: Baker Academic, 2016).
6. James L. Crenshaw, 'The Wisdom Literature', in Douglas A. Knight and Gene M. Tucker (eds.), *The Hebrew Bible and Its Modern Interpreters* (Chico: Scholars Press, 1985), pp. 369–407, here 369.
7. Cf. Raymond C. Van Leeuwen, 'Wisdom Literature', in Kevin Vanhoozer et al. (eds.), *Dictionary for Theological Interpretation of the Bible* (Grand Rapids: Baker Academic; London: SPCK, 2005), pp. 847–850; and R. N. Whybray, *The Book of Proverbs: A Survey of Modern Study* (Leiden: Brill, 1995), who lists points of agreement and points of discussion. Some of my points fall under his second list.

- an attribute of Yahweh (Prov. 8:22–31);
- the means by which Yahweh created the world (Prov. 3:19–20);
- and thus built into the fabric of creation[8] and crying out to be heard by humans in all areas of life (Prov. 1:20–21);
- needed by humans in every area of life if they are to flourish (Prov. 3:13–18);
- rooted and grounded in the fear of Yahweh (Prov. 1:7 etc.);
- antithetically opposed to folly, an ever-present possibility in the world (cf. Prov. 9 on Lady Wisdom and Lady Folly's houses and invitations);
- developed into a tradition through the experience of living in God's world.

In brief, Old Testament wisdom deals with how to navigate life 'successfully'.

The extent of the Old Testament wisdom corpus is debated. Clearly it includes Proverbs, Job and Ecclesiastes, but some also include Song of Songs, and the Catholic canon includes other wisdom books such as Sirach and the Wisdom of Solomon. Old Testament introductions tend to confine Old Testament wisdom to the three major books of Proverbs, Job and Ecclesiastes, and we will do likewise. An additional issue is the extent of wisdom influence in the rest of the Old Testament. Gunkel, for example, found a number of psalms to be wisdom ones, and this view retains its influence today.[9] Views have waxed and waned regarding the extent of wisdom influence in the Old Testament. Writing in 1985 Crenshaw speaks of the danger of wisdom becoming an 'insatiable "Sheol figure" who swallows the rest of the Hebrew canon'.[10] Debate has centred on developing criteria for such influence without a consensus

---

8. On order and wisdom and the diverse views of scholars, see the useful essay by James A. Loader, *Proverbs 1 – 9*, HCOT (Leeuven: Peeters, 2014), pp. 19–28.
9. See e.g. John Day, *Psalms*, OT Guides (Sheffield: Sheffield Academic Press, 1990), pp. 54ff.; John Kartje, *Wisdom Epistemology in the Psalter: A Study of Psalms 1, 73, 90 and 107* (Berlin: De Gruyter, 2014); Manfred Oeming, 'Wisdom as a Hermeneutical Key to the Book of Psalms', in Leo G. Perdue (ed.), *Scribes, Sages and Seers: The Sage in the Eastern Mediterranean World* (Göttingen: Vandenhoeck & Ruprecht, 2008), pp. 154–162. On the recent history of wisdom influence on the Psalter, see Kartje, *Wisdom Epistemology*, pp. 53–70.
10. Crenshaw, 'Wisdom Literature', p. 373.

emerging.¹¹ Intertextuality, which we will discuss below, holds the possibility of clarifying this debate.

Historical criticism and Old Testament wisdom

Since historical criticism to a significant extent remains the default mode for many biblical scholars, we *do need* to take note of it to orient ourselves in the present and to be sure to retain its lasting contributions. Although the roots of historical criticism go back much earlier than the nineteenth century, it was in the second half of the nineteenth century that this approach came to fruition in Germany and spread to the rest of Europe, the UK and the USA, as noted above.

Initially marginalized by Wellhausen, several factors altered this situation in relation to Old Testament wisdom. In the context of his form-critical approach Gunkel argued that the form and nature of Old Testament wisdom, especially in Proverbs, are so distinctive that they cannot be derived from prophecy and law, and thus be secondary, derivative and late. The *Sitz im Leben* of wisdom in Israel should rather be located in a particular wisdom class of men.¹² Old Testament wisdom also bore an international character and the wise were

---

11. See James L. Crenshaw, 'Method in Determining Wisdom Influence upon "Historical" Literature', *JBL* 88 (1969), pp. 129–142; Donn F. Morgan, *Wisdom in the Old Testament Traditions* (Atlanta: John Knox, 1981); Roger N. Whybray, *The Intellectual Tradition in the Old Testament*, BZAW 135 (Berlin/New York: De Gruyter, 1974).
12. This has been an influential view, but for a notable critique see Roger N. Whybray, *The Intellectual Tradition in the Old Testament*, BZAW 135 (Berlin/New York: De Gruyter, 1974). Whybray argued that there is no evidence for an institution or class of wise men and that wisdom emanated from educated citizens 'who were accustomed to read for edification and pleasure' (Whybray, ibid., p. 69). Cf. also John G. Gammie and Leo G. Perdue (eds.), *The Sage in Israel and the Ancient Near East* (Winona Lake: Eisenbrauns, 1990), pp. 95–181; Leo G. Perdue, 'Sages, Scribes and Seers in Israel and the Ancient Near East: An Introduction', in Perdue, *Scribes, Sages and Seers*, pp. 1–34; Katharine J. Dell, *The Book of Proverbs in Social and Theological Context* (Cambridge: Cambridge University Press, 2006); G. I. Davies, 'Were There Schools in Ancient Israel?', in John Day, Robert Gordon and Hugh G. M. Williamson (eds.), *Wisdom in Ancient Israel: Essays in Honour of J. A. Emerton* (Cambridge: Cambridge University Press, 1995), pp. 199–211.

probably in touch with other Ancient Near Eastern wisdom writings, a view soon confirmed by the discovery of the *Instruction of Amenemope*.[13] Thus the Old Testament wisdom texts might be late but the oral tradition behind them has its roots in Israel's origins. A long historical process of development thus underlies the Old Testament wisdom books, lending itself to tradition-historical analysis which was taken up with vigour by Hugo Gressmann.[14] According to Gunkel the original, basic form was the brief didactic saying and especially that of the proverb. Over time it developed into more extended and written forms with new styles of its own. The later wisdom was more religious than the earlier worldly, pragmatic form.

It was thus only towards the end of the nineteenth and the beginning of the twentieth century that fully historical-critical works on Proverbs, Job and Ecclesiastes appeared.[15] Modern study of Old Testament wisdom is therefore just over 100 years old, and there is surely a book waiting to be written with the title *A Century of Old Testament Wisdom Study: c. 1908–c. 2008*. Also of significance was the realization that Old Testament wisdom is above all else a theology of creation, and thus deeply theological. Zimmerli states categorically, 'Wisdom theology is creation theology.'[16]

Two aspects of the historical-critical hermeneutic as it was applied to the Old Testament need to be borne in mind. One was the developmental view of Israelite religion and the other was the methods applied to Old Testament texts. These two were, of course, intimately related. Writing in 1956 Hahn says,

---

13. William W. Hallo (ed.), *The Context of Scripture, Vol. 1: Canonical Compositions from the Biblical World* (Leiden: Brill, 1997), 1.47.
14. See Hugo Gressmann, 'Die neugefundene Lehre des Amen-em-ope und die vorexilische Spruchdichtung Israels', *ZAW* 42 (1924), pp. 272–296; *Israels Spruchweisheit im Zusammenhang der Weltliteratur* (Berlin: Karl Curtius, 1925).
15. Whybray, *The Book of Proverbs: A Survey of Modern Study*, points out that already by the mid-nineteenth century critical work on Proverbs and OT wisdom was well underway, with the view accepted of multiple authorship over a long period of time. However, he also notes that in 1908 J. Meinhold, *Die Weisheit Israels in Spruch, Sage und Dichtung* (Leipzig: Quelle & Meyer, 1908), published what appears to be the first study devoted entirely to OT wisdom literature.
16. W. Zimmerli, 'The Place and Limit of Wisdom in the Framework of Old Testament Theology', *SJT* 17 (1964), pp. 146–158. For a critical engagement with Zimmerli, see Jamie Grant, 'Wisdom and Covenant: Revisiting Zimmerli', *EJT* 12/2 (2003), pp. 103–111.

No historian of the nineteenth century, trained in the methods of scientific research, undertook to expound a historical development without first examining the available written sources critically. The initial task of the higher critics, accordingly, was a purely technical one: the careful analysis of the composition of the books of the Old Testament. Even in the eighteenth century, J. G. Eichhorn, 'the father of Old Testament criticism', had seen clearly that, before criticism could proceed with its task of investigating the historical circumstances under which the writings had been produced, the problem of defining the textual limits and the special characteristics of the underlying sources must be solved.[17]

Hahn's phrase 'the careful analysis of the composition of the books of the Old Testament' is heuristically useful. Proverbs, Job and Ecclesiastes, albeit in different ways, have all been subjected to historical-critical analysis of their composition.

Different collections and sections with different literary styles are clearly discernible in Proverbs and debate centred on the date, unity and history of development of the different collections,[18] and the context in Israel in which they came into existence. During the course of the nineteenth century Solomonic authorship was increasingly rejected. F. Delitzsch said of Proverbs that 'Critical analysis resolves it into a colourful market of the most manifold intellectual products of at least three epochs of proverbial poetry'.[19] Proverbs also came to be dated late.[20] In 1835 Vatke dated Proverbs and Job to the fifth century BC

---

17. Herbert F. Hahn, *The Old Testament in Modern Research* (London: SCM, 1956), p. 3.
18. Georg Fohrer, *Introduction to the Old Testament*, tr. David Green (London: SPCK, 1968), pp. 316–317, says of the formation of the wisdom books that 'The simplest method is the growth of a book out of various collections. It is easy to see that the book of Proverbs comprises several originally independent collections. They were simply strung together in their primitive form, and still retain their superscriptions ... Some of them in turn represent smaller collections. Thus the process of addition leads from the smallest collections, conceived as mnemonic aids, to larger and larger units.' Cf. R. N. Whybray, *The Book of Proverbs: A Survey of Modern Study*; *The Composition of the Book of Proverbs*, JSOTSup 168 (Sheffield: Sheffield Academic Press, 1994); Daniel C. Snell, *Twice-Told Proverbs and the Composition of the Book of Proverbs* (Winona Lake: Eisenbrauns, 1993).
19. Franz Delitzsch, *Das Salomonische Spruchbuch* (Leipzig: Dörffling & Franke, 1873), p. 3.
20. On nineteenth-century wisdom study see Rudolph Smend, 'The Interpretation of Wisdom in Nineteenth-Century Scholarship', in Day, Gordon and Williamson, *Wisdom in Ancient Israel*, pp. 257–268.

and Ecclesiastes later. C. H. Toy argued for a date of completion around 200 BC, with the earliest part of Proverbs being around 350 BC. With the discovery of the widespread and ancient nature of Ancient Near Eastern wisdom in the early twentieth century such a late date lost favour. As similarities between Israelite and Old Testament wisdom surfaced, the question emerged of the relationship between Israelite wisdom and Ancient Near Eastern wisdom. In the attempt to track the process of development from a simple form of the proverb to the more complex collections we find in Proverbs, some argued that the earliest strata of Old Testament wisdom were secular and that later in Israel's development a theological component seen especially in the Yahweh sections in Proverbs developed. Amongst Proverbs commentaries McKane's is best known for this view and the attempt to separate the different strands.[21] Various views also developed about how wisdom came to be personified in Proverbs 8 in particular.[22]

Carol Newsom observes that many of the issues pre-moderns struggle with in Job are the same issues that moderns struggle with, even if they provide different answers.[23] 'One critical issue, however, is almost entirely the product of the interpretive assumptions of historical criticism – the problem of the "unity" or "integrity" of the book.'[24] In 1678 Richard Simon was the first to dispute the unity of Job, noting the stylistic difference between the prose frame and the dialogue.[25] For Simon the prose frame was an addition to the poetry.

Source-critical and traditio-critical arguments were presented by later scholars to support the view that two very different types of literature were present in Job. In the late nineteenth century the emerging view was crystallized by Karl Budde and Bernhard Duhm. They argued that the prose frame was a *Volksbuch*, a pre-existing popular story, which was appropriated by the poet as a framework. This became the standard view, although occasionally dissenting voices such as those of Karl Kautzsch and Edouard Dhorme were heard. Dhorme acknowledged the differences in style but rejected the majority view that the differences

---

21. For an evaluation see Stuart Weeks, *Early Israelite Wisdom* (Oxford: Oxford University Press, 1994, 1999).
22. See Roland Murphy, *The Tree of Life: An Exploration of Biblical Wisdom Literature*, 3rd edn (Grand Rapids: Eerdmans, 2002), pp. 133–150.
23. Carol A. Newsom, *The Book of Job: A Contest of Moral Imaginations* (Oxford: Oxford University Press, 2003), p. 3.
24. Ibid.
25. Simon, *A Critical History of the Old Testament*, tr. from the French (London: Walter Davis, 1682), bk 1, ch. iv, p. 34.

implied multiple authors: 'One and the same man can tell a story when necessary and sing when necessary.'[26] Nevertheless, by the mid-twentieth century, Marvin Pope expressed the consensus view that 'the Book of Job in its present form can hardly be regarded as a consistent and unified composition by a single author'.[27]

Form criticism did important work in analysing the variety of literary forms found in Proverbs, Job and Ecclesiastes, and such work continues to bear fruit today. One thinks, for example, of Ogden's analysis of the 'better than' proverbial form,[28] and of Noegel's analysis of Janus parallelism in Job.[29]

In terms of *tradition history* views differed over the extent to which Old Testament wisdom, especially in its earliest from, was distinctively Israelite, at least theologically. Preuss is an extreme example of such a position.[30] In his view:

1. Wisdom is marginal to Israel's faith.
2. The God of wisdom is not Yahweh.
3. Wisdom concentrates on the orders in reality.
4. Retribution is one of these orders. The sages sought to discover this mechanical correspondence between action and consequence, as reflected in Proverbs.
5. A deed–consequence viewpoint is the basic dogma of early wisdom.

Job and Ecclesiastes came to be seen as representing a crisis in the sort of mechanical view of wisdom found in Proverbs. Perdue goes so far as to suggest that Qohelet develops an alternative worldview to that of the sages:

> in his writings the foreground is not occupied by the manifold traditional motives; rather, he transforms them in his extremely individualist criticism by shattering the traditional world-view of earlier wisdom, denying a fixed connection between action and result, and proclaiming the absolute inexplicability of the divine action in nature and history.[31]

---

26. Edouard Dhorme, *A Commentary on the Book of Job*, tr. H. Knight (London: Nelson, 1967), p. lxv.
27. Marvin Pope, *Job*, AB (New York: Doubleday, 1965), p. xxviii.
28. Graham S. Ogden, 'The "Better"-Proverb (Tôb-Spruch), Rhetorical Criticism, and Qoheleth', *JBL* 96 (1977), pp. 489–505.
29. S. B. Noegel, *Janus Parallelism in the Book of Job* (Sheffield: Sheffield Academic Press, 1996).
30. Roland E. Murphy, *Ecclesiastes*, WBC (Dallas: Word, 1992), p. lxi.
31. Leo G. Perdue, *Wisdom and Creation: The Theology of the Wisdom Literature* (Nashville: Abingdon, 1994), p. 116.

Crüsemann maintains that '[t]his difference between Koheleth and his predecessors must be taken as the starting point for understanding Koheleth'.[32] Murphy notes that this notion of a wisdom crisis looms almost as large in scholarly discussion as does the exile of 587 BC![33]

In terms of tradition history, it should also be noted that the view developed that Old Testament wisdom was largely a separate tradition in the Old Testament with little or no awareness of the pentateuchal, narrative/historical and prophetic traditions.[34] It was argued that it was only late in its development that wisdom was connected with *torah*, as seen, for example, in the epilogue to Ecclesiastes.

Of the three major Old Testament wisdom books Ecclesiastes was most subjected to the sort of source criticism applied to the Pentateuch. Source/literary criticism of Ecclesiastes was pioneered by Siegfried in Germany.[35] Siegfried thought in terms of a supplementary hypothesis, in which an original and deeply pessimistic text was supplemented with material from different perspectives. This supplementary hypothesis differed from the sort of documentary hypothesis formulated by Wellhausen for the Pentateuch, but the historical methodology was the same, and Siegfried divided the book among nine sources.

Few would follow Siegfried today and in the latter part of the twentieth century there was a strong reassertion of the basic unity of Ecclesiastes, with the significant exception of 12:8–14. Unlike commentaries before Siegfried, however, there are few critical commentaries in the twentieth century which read Ecclesiastes as an integral whole including 12:8–14. In this sense, at least, source criticism continues to influence the reading of Ecclesiastes.

On several issues a consensus has emerged out of historical-critical study of Ecclesiastes. There is wide-ranging agreement that Solomon was not the author and that the book was written in the third century BC or thereabouts. There has been a growing commitment to the basic unity of Ecclesiastes with the exception

---

32. F. Crüsemann, 'The Unchangeable World: The "Crisis of Wisdom" in Qoheleth', in W. Schotroff and W. Stegemann (eds.), *God of the Lowly: Socio-historical Interpretations of the Bible*, tr. M. O'Connell (Maryknoll: Orbis, 1984), p. 61.
33. Murphy, *Ecclesiastes*, p. lxi. Cf. H. Gese, 'The Crisis of Wisdom in Koheleth', in J. L. Crenshaw (ed.), *Theodicy in the Old Testament* (Philadelphia: Fortress, 1983), pp. 141–153; and H. H. Schmid, *Wesen und Geschichte der Weisheit*, BZAW 101 (Berlin: Töpelmann, 1966) on the crisis of wisdom.
34. Cf. Jamie Grant's critique of Zimmerli in this respect ('Wisdom and Covenant: Revisiting Zimmerli').
35. C. Siegfried, *Prediger und Hoheslied*, HAT (Göttingen: Vandenhoeck & Ruprecht, 1898).

of the epilogue. Any idea of strong Greek influence on the book tends to be rejected although broad connections with Greek thought are recognized. Generally, Qohelet is thought to be rooted in Hebraic thought and part of the wisdom movement in Israel.[36] However, there is no agreement about the structure of Ecclesiastes, nor about its message, with scholars divided between seeing Qohelet as pessimistic or finally positive.

Redaction criticism can be seen as a bridge between historical criticism and literary approaches, with its close attention to how books were redacted into wholes. Childs' canonical approach to Ecclesiastes is regarded by some as an example of redaction criticism, and, intriguingly, he discerns canonical shaping in the epilogue of Ecclesiastes: 'Few passages in the OT reflect a more overt consciousness of the canon than does this epilogue.'[37] Like the superscription, the epilogue in its description of Qohelet identifies the book as part of Israel's wisdom. Qohelet is assigned a public and critical role within Israel's wisdom teaching. Ecclesiastes 12:13 holds wisdom and law closely together under the overarching theme of the judgment of God.

The fragmentation of Old Testament wisdom books by historical criticism did not lend itself to rich theological work. However, there are notable exceptions. Ronald Clements' *Wisdom for a Changing World: Wisdom in Old Testament Theology*[38] remains a useful volume, but pride of place, in my view, must go to Gerhard von Rad, who retained a deep interest in the theology of the Old Testament traditions. This is evident in his fine section on wisdom in his *Old Testament Theology, Volume 1*,[39] but pre-eminently in his *Wisdom in Israel*, which remains a standard resource for the study of Old Testament wisdom today.

The literary turn

In the 1970s onwards the literary turn took place in biblical studies. Its implications for Old Testament wisdom were huge and have still to be fully

---

36. Although there are some, like Norbert Lohfink, *Kohelet*, NEB (Würzburg: Echter, 1993), who argue for strong Greek influence upon Ecclesiastes.
37. Brevard S. Childs, *Introduction to the Old Testament as Scripture* (Philadelphia: Fortress, 1979), p. 585.
38. (Berkeley: Bibal, 1990).
39. Gerhard von Rad, *Old Testament Theology, Vol. 1*, tr. D. M. G. Stalker (Edinburgh: Oliver & Boyd, 1962), pp. 418–459.

appropriated. Most of Old Testament wisdom is poetry,[40] and thus it is not surprising that the aesthetic sensibility[41] the literary turn brought had major implications for Old Testament wisdom.[42] The main impetus for the literary turn came from Jewish literary scholars who turned their attention to the Old Testament/Hebrew Bible. Robert Alter attended inter alia to Old Testament poetry as literature and in the process wrote strikingly on Job. Meir Sternberg delivered the most significant book on a literary approach to the Old Testament with his *The Poetics of Hebrew Narrative*, and since both Job and Ecclesiastes have a narrative dimension to them, his work has proved fertile in Old Testament wisdom studies.[43] In the tradition of form criticism the literary turn further enhanced close analysis of the forms of Old Testament wisdom but its major impact was felt at the macro level of the unity and shape of the Old Testament wisdom books. The literary turn enabled scholars to move from a focus on the composition of Old Testament wisdom books to close attention to *the literary shape of the books as we have received them*. In volume 1 of his commentary on Job, C. L. Seow, for example, concludes his discussion of the unity of Job by asserting,

> There are all sorts of literary tensions within the book. Hence, instead of performing textual strategies to suit modern preconceptions of coherence, it is necessary to give the ancient narrator-poet the benefit of the doubt and

---

40. Note that the extent of poetry in Ecclesiastes is contested. On the poetic forms in OT wisdom literature see Fokkelman's multiple volumes on *Major Poems of the Hebrew Bible* (Assen: Van Gorcum, 1998–2004).
41. There is a significant difference between a literary sensibility and literary methods that can be learnt and applied to OT wisdom texts. The seminal work embodying literary sensibility is Auerbach's *Mimesis*, which ought, in my view, to be compulsory reading for every student of biblical studies.
42. Writing in 1985 Crenshaw noted that 'The current interest in aesthetics – that is, literary artistry – throughout the Hebrew scriptures will naturally extend to wisdom literature . . . There is no more appropriate endeavor, since such analysis takes its cue from ancient sages who labored to master the art of speaking and writing. Perhaps we shall soon understand, among other things, the dynamics of sapiential dialogue' ('Wisdom Literature', p. 390).
43. Alison Lo, *Job 28 as Rhetoric: An Analysis of Job 28 in the Context of Job 22 – 31*, VTSup 97 (Leiden: Brill, 2003); Craig G. Bartholomew, *Reading Ecclesiastes: Old Testament Exegesis and Hermeneutical Theory*, AnaBib 139 (Rome: Editrice Pontificio Istituto Biblico, 1998).

to grapple with those dissonances and asymmetry that may well be part of how the book means.[44]

The effect was radical as a variety of literary methods such as New Criticism and structuralism were appropriated and brought to bear on the Old Testament wisdom books. Thus Wright specifically appeals to New Criticism as providing a methodological key for breaking the deadlock in studies of Ecclesiastes.[45] Plumptre referred to Ecclesiastes as 'the sphinx of Hebrew literature, with its unsolved riddles of history and life';[46] for Wright, New Criticism provides a method for analysing the structure of Ecclesiastes, and thereby breaking this riddle.[47] 'The structure that the author intended to give to this book has finally been recovered.'[48]

Structure is also central to Loader's interpretation of Ecclesiastes.[49] Barton invokes Loader's approach as a possible candidate for a structuralist approach to Ecclesiastes, although he does find it wanting in terms of any precise definition of structuralism.[50] Loader retains historical criticism's emphasis on the

---

44. C. L. Seow, *Job 1 – 21: Interpretation and Commentary*, Illuminations (Grand Rapids: Eerdmans, 2013), p. 38.
45. N. Lohfink is also an important representative of a New Critical approach to Ecclesiastes. Lohfink's indebtedness to NC manifests itself mainly in his commitment to close reading: 'Das ganze Buch durchzieht eine Leitworttechnik, die ihresgleichen im alten Orient sucht. Sie bewirkt, das alles mit allem in einem geheimnisvollen Netz verknüpft ist und alle Ausleger, die einen einlinigen Gedankenfortschritt suchen, sich in dieser subtilieren Sprachwelt rettungslos verheddern' (*Kohelet*, p. 10).
46. E. H. Plumptre, *Ecclesiastes*, The Cambridge Bible for Schools (Cambridge: Cambridge University Press, 1881), p. 7.
47. A. G. Wright, 'The Riddle of the Sphinx: The Structure of the Book of Qoheleth', *CBQ* 30 (1968), pp. 313–334.
48. A. G. Wright, 'Ecclesiastes (Qoheleth)', in R. E. Brown, J. A. Fitzmeyer and R. E. Murphy (eds.), *The New Jerome Biblical Commentary* (Englewood Cliffs: Prentice Hall, 1990), p. 489. This conclusion is, of course, contested. In my view OT scholars make the mistake of constantly looking for a logical structure to books like Ecclesiastes, whereas the book's structure is more of an organic, literary one which resists easy categorization but is none the less real.
49. J. A. Loader, *Polar Structures in the Book of Qohelet* (Hawthorne: De Gruyter, 1979); idem, *Ecclesiastes: A Practical Commentary* (Grand Rapids: Eerdmans, 1986).
50. J. Barton, *Reading the Old Testament: Method in Biblical Study* (London: DLT, 1984), p. 130.

development of wisdom. He discerns three phases in its development. First, there is a strong appreciation for the relationship between action and the opportune time for action. Second, there is a loss of the sense of temporal relevance so that a dogmatic system originates. Third, there is protest against this ossification. For the first see Proverbs 10 – 29. Job's three friends are an example of the second, and Qohelet is an example of the third. Qohelet never comes to a happy ending; the tension and protest structure Loader discerns in Ecclesiastes continue to the end.

Polzin's work on Job is a fine example of how structuralist concern with deep structure can illumine the surface structure and overall interpretation of the message of the text. Polzin correctly comments that '[f]ormulas, methodologies, formal analyses may all have their place in such an enterprise. But they are valuable only insofar as they help to make what one studies a little more intelligible to whoever employs them.'[51]

For Polzin, discrepancy and contradiction are at the heart of Job. He discerns three major contradictions. First, there is that between what one is taught to believe about divine justice and what one experiences. Second, Job's friends affirm divine retribution for ten chapters, but following God's words in 42:7–8 they sacrifice to God for not speaking of God what is right. Third, some of God's words appear to contradict his actions. His statement in 42:7 that Job spoke right of him appears to contradict Yahweh's speeches in chapters 38–41 and the reaffirmation of the principle of retribution in the epilogue.

For Polzin, confrontation of these inconsistencies is part of the book's structure and message.

> Attempts to remove these inconsistencies can be characterised as academic 'failure of nerve' just as the platitudes of Job's friends are a 'failure of nerve' in the face of Job's problems. By removing the book's inconsistencies, some scholars have succeeded in removing its message.[52]

Polzin rejects the usual source-critical and form-critical approaches to Job, and works with Job as a unified work. Of form-critical approaches to Job he notes that '[s]uch attempts at analysis seem to me ultimately to destroy the message(s) of the book and moreover make impossible the first step towards

---

51. R. M. Polzin, *Biblical Structuralism: Method and Subjectivity in the Study of Ancient Texts* (Philadelphia: Fortress; Missoula: Scholars Press, 1977), p. 102.
52. R. M. Polzin, 'The Framework of the Book of Job', *Interpretation* 28/2 (1974), pp. 182–200, here 183.

understanding how, *in its present form*, it has affected men so profoundly down through the ages'.[53]

This raises the question of genre at a macro rather than micro level. Polzin is cautious with respect to form-critical analyses of genre.[54] He does, however, recognize the need for a 'full-fledged science of discourse' which would include a typology of discourse.[55] Such an approach would examine Job as *a whole* in relation to different types of discourse.

Polzin discerns four movements in Job which involve a dialectical working out of a series of contradictions by means of four major sequential functions. In the first movement (Job 1 – 37) the sequential function is that of God afflicting Job. This generates a conflict between belief and experience. The friends side with belief, Job with experience. In the second movement (Job 38:1 – 42:6) the first contradiction is resolved by the theophany but a new one is set up: by assenting to the vision Job has to deny the validity of his previous experience. The third movement (Job 42:7–8) resolves the second contradiction (Job spoke what is right) but sets up another: how does God's speech in chapters 38–41 relate to 42:7–9? The fourth movement (42:10–17) resolves the previous conflict and restores equilibrium. By restoring Job's fortunes God confirms his word of 42:7–8 and the affirmation of his power in chapters 38 – 41. 'Far from being a gratuitous "hollywood ending", the final verses in chapter 42 dialectically resolve the subsidiary conflicts which the central event of the entire book, the theophany of God, had engendered.'[56]

For Polzin the framework of Job is the work of a genius.

> The genius of this journey is that insight is conferred not by the avoidance of contradiction and inconsistency but precisely by the courageous integration of contradiction and resolution. In other words the story is a paradigm. What is on the surface a diachronic linear treatment of a problem reveals itself as containing an underlying or latent synchronic structure.[57]

This pattern provides the material for analysis of the code of Job.

It will be clear from Polzin's work just how radically such a literary approach can change an historical-critical reading of Job. In comparable terms the Dutch

---

53. Ibid., p. 186.
54. Ibid., p. 187.
55. Ibid., p. 189.
56. Ibid., p. 198.
57. Ibid., p. 200.

Old Testament scholar Jan P. Fokkelman, who has done so much to deepen our understanding of the forms of Old Testament poetry, says of Job that it 'is an exceptional, eminently literary work'.[58] He asserts that the poets of Psalms, Lamentations, Song of Songs, Job and Proverbs 'were in full command of their craft on all levels of the text'.[59]

Literary analysis allows for different – in my view, far more appropriate – readings of aspects of wisdom texts that have often been seen as contradictory, with its arsenal of approaches to irony, paradox, contradictory juxtaposition, ambiguity and so on. Gladson, for example, persuasively argues that 'retributive paradox' occurs in all strands of Old Testament literature.[60] Such an approach allows one to revisit Proverbs as a whole and to conclude that, taken as a whole, Proverbs by no means presents a mechanical act–consequence understanding of retribution. This has been clearly demonstrated in an excellent article on wealth and poverty in Proverbs by Van Leeuwen.[61]

In terms of literary approaches to Proverbs several works have emerged exploring interconnections between proverbs within sections and within the book as a whole.[62] Van Leeuwen has gone further in arguing for an overarching shape to the book as a whole, with chapters 1–9 as the introduction, setting out the ABCs of wisdom, and with later sections nuancing this overarching perspective; and with the book as a whole moving from the introduction to its climax in the Proverbs 31 acrostic (A–Z) poem of the valiant woman as the embodiment of wisdom.

Van Leeuwen points out that there are large groups of sayings in Proverbs that assert a simple cause–effect relationship whereby righteousness leads to

---

58. Jan P. Fokkelman, *The Book of Job in Form: A Literary Translation and Commentary* (Leiden: Brill, 2012), p. ix.
59. Ibid.
60. J. A. Gladson, 'Retributive Paradoxes in Proverbs 10 – 29' (PhD diss., Vanderbilt University, 1978; Ann Arbor: University Microfilms International, 1979).
61. Raymond Van Leeuwen, 'Wealth and Poverty: System and Contradiction in Proverbs', *Hebrew Studies 33* (1992), pp. 25–36. See also R. N. Whybray, *Wealth and Poverty in the Book of Proverbs*, JSOTSup 99 (Sheffield: Sheffield Academic Press, 1990); Timothy J. Sandoval, *The Discourse of Wealth and Poverty in the Book of Proverbs* (Leiden: Brill, 2006).
62. See Raymond Van Leeuwen, *Context and Meaning in Proverbs 25 – 27*, SBLDS 96 (Atlanta: Scholars Press, 1988); Knut M. Heim, *Like Grapes of Gold Set in Silver: An Interpretation of Proverbial Clusters in Proverbs 10:1 – 22:16* (Berlin: De Gruyter, 2001).

wealth and wickedness to poverty. These are examples of the 'character-consequence-nexus'. However, they do not concern concrete individual acts and their consequences: 'It is the long-term character and direction of a person or group (as "righteous" or "wicked") which determines life consequences and "destiny".'[63]

These proverbs, *when taken by themselves*, are the basis for the view of some scholars that the tidy dogmatism of Proverbs does not correspond to reality and is doomed to collapse under the weight of reality, as happened in Job and Qohelet. Since the foregoing sayings are not always exemplified in human experience, their falsification presumably led to a crisis of faith in Yahweh's maintenance of a just world order.[64]

However, proverbs are by their nature *partial utterances* and this type of mechanical approach does not do justice to the many sayings in Proverbs which manifest a more complex understanding of how God works in creation. Particularly noteworthy in this respect are the 'better than' sayings in Proverbs (see 15:16–17; 16:16, 19, etc.). The overall picture is a complex one which Van Leeuwen sums up as follows:

> *In general*, the sages clearly believed that wise and righteous behaviour did make life better and richer, though virtue did not *guarantee* those consequences. Conversely, injustice, sloth, and the like generally have bad consequences. The editor-sages who structured Proverbs sought first to teach these basic 'rules of life', thus the heavy emphasis on character-consequence patterns in both Proverbs 1–9 and 10–15. We must first learn the basic rules; the exceptions can come later. Though very aware of exceptions to the character-consequence rule, the sages insisted that righteousness is better than wickedness. The most fundamental and profound reason for this is that they believed that God loves the one and hates the other. For Israel's sages that sometimes seems the only answer . . . the sages knew that there are limits to human wisdom. General patterns may be discerned, but many particular events may be unjust, irrational, and ultimately inscrutable.[65]

Van Leeuwen also notes that there is a future orientation to retribution in Proverbs. Proverbs lacks a doctrine of resurrection and yet insists on the triumph of God's justice. For Van Leeuwen this is a hallmark of Yahwistic faith.

---

63. Van Leeuwen, 'Wealth and Poverty', p. 27; cf. Michael V. Fox, *Qoheleth and His Contradictions*, JSOTSup 71 (Sheffield: Almond Press, 1989), pp. 132–133.
64. Van Leeuwen, 'Wealth and Poverty', pp. 28–29.
65. Ibid., pp. 32–33.

The sages' stance is to maintain faith in God's justice, even when they personally cannot see it or touch it, even when the recorded past does not verify it. Here religion provides no escape from the pain or absurdities of existence. The book of Job was inevitable, not because Proverbs was too simplistic, but because life's inequities, as reflected in Proverbs, drive faith to argue with the Deity.[66]

In relation to Ecclesiastes, in my view, the seminal contribution has come from Michael Fox. Fox rightly maintains that Ecclesiastes is wisdom literature *and* narration.

> It tells something that happened to someone. I would like to take some first steps in the investigation of the literary characteristics of *Qoheleth* as narrative: Who is speaking (the question of *voice*), how do the voices speak, and how do they relate to each other? I will argue that the *Book of Qoheleth* is to be taken as a whole, as a single, well-integrated composition, the product not of editorship but of authorship, which uses interplay of voice as a deliberate literary device for rhetorical and artistic purposes.[67]

Fox argues that while modern scholarship correctly recognizes more than one voice in Ecclesiastes, its presuppositions prevent the voice that is not Qohelet's from being attended to. This other voice is the one we hear speaking in 1:2; 7:27; and 12:8 for example. This third-person voice is not that of Qohelet, as is made particularly clear by the way the voices interact in 7:27. As we attend to these voices,

> we should not ask what Qoheleth or an editor *could* have written, but rather – what are the literary implications of the words? What are we *meant* to hear in the third-person sections? . . . I believe the questions raised can best be answered by the following understanding of that voice and its relation to Qoheleth. That certain words are in a different voice does not mean that they are by a different hand . . . I suggest that all of 1:2 – 12:14 is by the same hand – not that the epilogue is by Qoheleth, but that *Qoheleth* is 'by' the epilogist. In other words, the speaker we hear from time to time in the background saying 'Qoheleth said' . . . this speaker is the teller of the tale, the external narrator of the story of Qoheleth. That is to say, the epic situation of the third-person voice in the epilogue and elsewhere is that of a man looking back and telling his son the story of the ancient wise-man Qoheleth, passing on to him words

---

66. Ibid., p. 34.
67. Michael Fox, 'Frame Narrative and Composition in the Book of Qoheleth', *HUCA* 48 (1977), p. 83.

he knew Qoheleth to have said, appreciatively but cautiously evaluating his work in retrospect. Virtually all the 'story' he tells is a quotation of the words of the wise-man he is telling about. The speaker, whom I will call the *frame-narrator*, keeps himself well in the background, but he does not make himself disappear. He presents himself not as the creator of Qoheleth's words but as their transmitter.[68]

Fox thus sees Ecclesiastes as operating on three levels: first, that of the frame-narrator, who tells about the second, Qohelet-the-reporter, the narrating 'I', who looks back from old age and speaks about the third level, Qohelet-the-seeker, the younger Qohelet who made the investigation in 1:12–18. Level one is a different person from levels two and three; levels two and three are different perspectives from the same person.

Fox's approach leads him to explore in detail the meaning of the epilogue in terms of its relationship to the main body of Ecclesiastes.[69] The frame-narrator's first function in the epilogue is to testify to Qohelet as a real person so that we respond to him as having lived. The second function of the frame-narrator in the epilogue is to convey a certain stance towards Qohelet. Qohelet is acknowledged as a wise man and his goals are praised but the frame-narrator is, according to Fox, subtly non-committal about the truth of Qohelet's words. Finally, Fox considers the relationship between the frame-narrator and the implied author, 'the voice behind the voices'.[70] By ending such an unorthodox book with an orthodox epilogue, for Fox the author creates an ambiguity which allows readers freedom to choose which position they will align themselves with.

Fox's understanding of the epilogue and of the frame-narrator/implied-author relationship is questionable.[71] However, he has demonstrated the value of a literary approach to Ecclesiastes and, in my opinion, raised one of the most important questions in the interpretation of Ecclesiastes, namely how, in a final-form approach, one understands the epilogue to relate to the main body of the text.

Comparisons of the Old Testament wisdom literature to Ancient Near Eastern literature have continued apace,[72] with varying degrees of light cast on our biblical texts.

---

68. Ibid., pp. 90–91.
69. Ibid., pp. 96–106.
70. Ibid., p. 104.
71. See Bartholomew, *Reading Ecclesiastes*, pp. 161–171, for a detailed critique.
72. See e.g. Kenton L. Sparks, *Ancient Texts for the Study of the Hebrew Bible: A Guide to the Background Literature* (Peabody: Hendrickson, 2005), pp. 56–83; Carl S. Ehrlich (ed.), *From an Antique Land: An Introduction to Ancient Near Eastern Literature* (New York: Rowman and Littlefield, 2009), pp. 205–213, 250–252, 375–376, 421–422.

Crenshaw rightly notes that an immense amount of material continues to pour out from Ancient Near Eastern circles and 'Rare indeed are the biblical critics who make themselves at home in this alien world'.[73] While there is undoubtedly a circular hermeneutic operating between Ancient Near Eastern studies and Old Testament wisdom studies, it is imperative that the Old Testament wisdom books be studied as literary wholes in order for genuinely comparative work to take place.[74] There is also a great need to penetrate to the worldview of Old Testament wisdom so that the sort of comparative work done by Frankfort et al. can be done anew in our day, enabling us to see the similarities and differences between Old Testament and Ancient Near Eastern wisdom.[75] Textual criticism has also resurfaced with a vengeance in our day and students of Old Testament wisdom will need to be aware of LXX and Old Greek versions of Old Testament wisdom texts as well as the studies in the Dead Sea Scrolls and wisdom.[76]

A literary approach that is proving fertile in biblical studies is *intertextuality*.[77] Katharine Dell and Will Kynes have recently edited two fine volumes on intertextuality: one on Job and one on Ecclesiastes. A further volume on Proverbs is forthcoming. Intertextuality opens up the questions of:

- the relationship between Proverbs, Job and Ecclesiastes;
- the relationship between these wisdom books and the rest of the Old Testament;[78]

---

73. Crenshaw, 'Wisdom Literature', p. 371.
74. On Ecclesiastes, see Bartholomew, *Reading Ecclesiastes*, pp. 146–157.
75. Henri Frankfort, H. A. Frankfort, John A. Wilson, Thorkild Jacobsen and William A. Irwin, *The Intellectual Adventure of Ancient Man: An Essay on Speculative Thought in the Ancient Near East* (Chicago and London: University of Chicago Press, 1946).
76. See e.g. C. Hempel, A. Lange and H. Lichtenberger (eds.), *The Wisdom Texts from Qumran and the Development of Sapiential Thought* (Leuven: Peeters, 2002).
77. The literature on intertextuality and on intertextuality and the Bible is vast. I find Mary Orr's introduction, *Intertextuality: Debates and Contexts* (Cambridge: Polity, 2003), very helpful.
78. See e.g. Ch. Fevel, 'Eine kleine Theologie der Menschenwürde: Ps 8 und seine Rezeption im Buch Ijob', in F.-L. Hossfeld and L. Schwienhorst-Schönberger (eds.), *Das Manna fällt auch heute noch: Beiträge zur Geschichte und Theologie des Alten, Ersten Testaments*, Festschrift für Erich Zenger, HBS 44 (Freiburg: Herder, 2004), pp. 244–272.

- the relationship between Old Testament wisdom and the New Testament;
- the reception history of Old Testament wisdom; etc.

This is a vast and vital area of research and we can only make initial comments here.

As we noted above, the view that Job and Ecclesiastes represent a crisis in Old Testament wisdom has been central to historical-critical scholarship. In my view recent studies mean that this view should now be put to rest. Read as a whole Proverbs is well aware that the wise can undergo trials and suffering, and both Job and Ecclesiastes should be seen as explorations of this theme. Job's suffering is more existential whereas Qohelet's is more intellectual; both, I suggest, are excruciating. Both make a crucial contribution, not in correcting Proverbs, but in alerting us to the fact that becoming wise involves far more than intellectual knowledge and technique, but depth formation.

Another intertextual issue that has featured centrally in the interpretation of Ecclesiastes is the relationship between wisdom and law, especially as this is focused in chapter 12:13b. For many scholars the introduction of law is alien to the wisdom tradition in which Ecclesiastes is situated, thus indicating that the epilogue, or at least this part of it, is a later attempt to make Qohelet appear orthodox or to open up a relationship between wisdom and the commandments in the law.[79]

However, there is clear evidence that the reference to law is not as alien to Ecclesiastes as some suggest. As Lohfink, for example, points out, law is not alien to the fear of God in Qohelet.[80] He makes the point that 5:6 concludes the section 4:17 – 5:6 (Heb.). Indeed 4:17 – 5:6 contains a restatement of the law of Deuteronomy 23:22–24 in 5:3–4 and the background to 5:5 is Numbers 15:22–31. And this section with its allusions to the Torah concludes with the exhortation to 'fear God'.[81]

This evidence of awareness of pentateuchal cultic legislation needs to be combined with the vocabulary in Ecclesiastes that also appears to relate to the domain of *torah*, namely 'judgment' (3:17; 11:9), 'sinner', 'sin' (2:26; 5:5 [5:6 EVV]; 8:12), 'wicked' and 'righteous' (3:17). These factors, combined with the

---

79. See G. T. Sheppard, *Wisdom as a Hermeneutical Construct* (Berlin/New York: De Gruyter, 1980), pp. 121–129.
80. N. Lohfink, 'Qoheleth 5:17–19: Revelation by Joy', *CBQ* 52/4 (1990), p. 633.
81. There is, however, considerable disagreement as to how to understand Qohelet's view of the cult.

indications that Ecclesiastes has a strong link with Genesis and several strong links with Deuteronomy, make it increasingly difficult to see that the reference to law means that the epilogue *must* be a later addition.[82]

In Old Testament theology the relationship between law and wisdom remains a controversial issue.[83] Murphy has helpfully suggested that '[t]he problem of the relationship between wisdom literature and other portions of the Old Testament needs to be reformulated in terms of a shared approach to reality'.[84] This becomes particularly clear when one notes that '[a] relationship between religious and secular is not applicable to OT wisdom teaching'.[85] Neither is it applicable to *torah*, which also orders all areas of life. How then might these two approaches have been understood to relate to each other?

The wisdom and legal traditions in the Old Testament are clearly distinct and yet they manifest awareness of each other, as we have seen with Ecclesiastes.[86] They have in common the ordering of the life of God's people.[87] Van Leeuwen has analysed the root metaphors of Proverbs 1 – 9 and argues persuasively that

> underlying the bipolar metaphorical system of positive and negative youths, invitations/calls, 'ways', 'women', and 'houses' in Proverbs 1 – 9, is a yet more

---

82. It is, of course, possible to argue that Qohelet knows the Torah but is very negative towards it. This will depend upon one's understanding of the passages in which this vocabulary occurs.
83. For a useful discussion of the relationship of these two traditions which both seek to order the lives of God's people see J. Blenkinsopp, *Wisdom and Law in the Old Testament: The Ordering of Life in Israel and Early Judaism* (Oxford: Oxford University Press, 1983).
84. Roland E. Murphy, 'Wisdom: Theses and Hypotheses', in J. G. Gammie et al. (eds.), *Israelite Wisdom: Theological and Literary Essays in Honor of Samuel Terrien* (Missoula: Scholars Press, 1978), pp. 35–42, here 38.
85. Ibid., p. 40.
86. See R. Van Leeuwen, 'Liminality and Worldview in Proverbs 1 – 9', *Semeia* 50 (1990), pp. 111–144, 122, for some of the links between Proverbs and Job and the Pentateuch. Van Leeuwen argues that certain texts in Proverbs and Job presuppose the historical tradition of the gift of the land.
87. Murphy, 'Wisdom: Theses and Hypotheses', is critical of the close association of wisdom with the search for order, arguing that this question is a modern one which focuses on a presupposition of Israel's wisdom approach. However, see Van Leeuwen, 'Liminality and Worldview in Proverbs 1 – 9', for a powerful defence of taking seriously the tacit presupposition of cosmic order in wisdom literature.

fundamental reality which these images together portray. These chapters depict the world as the arena of human existence. This world possesses two fundamental characteristics. First is its structure of boundaries or limits. Second is the bipolar human *eros* for the beauty of Wisdom, who prescribes life within limits, or for the seeming beauty of Folly, who offers bogus delights in defiance of created limits.[88]

Van Leeuwen argues that the worldview which Proverbs embodies is a 'carved' one in that 'cultural and personal exhortation is grounded in the reality of the created word with its inbuilt normativity'.[89] Justice and righteousness are built into the world.

This link of wisdom with creation has long been recognized. What is often not noted, though, is that the order that Proverbs finds in the 'carved' creation is not and cannot simply be read out of the creation. This is the point that Fox makes about Israelite wisdom; it is not empirical like that of Qohelet, but assumes ethical principles which it uses observation to support. This is the sort of position we find in Genesis 1 – 2. The ordering of creation is not antithetical to instruction from Elohim/Yahweh Elohim. Order and instruction/*torah* go hand-in-hand, and obedience requires both a good creation and instruction. The point is that wisdom literature assumes certain ethical principles which are not just read off the creation but are often very similar, if not identical, to the principles found in the law. Van Leeuwen, for example, argues that Proverbs 1 – 9 indicates that it is in 'the liquid abandonment of married love' that healthy *communitas* takes place. As Van Leeuwen notes, 'This reality has its parallel at Sinai.'[90]

Thus it can be argued that while wisdom is most closely related to creation it presupposes instruction or *torah*. Similarly, when the narrative frame within which law always occurs in the final form of the Old Testament is foregrounded, it becomes clear that the law of Yahweh the redeemer is also the law of the creator God. This link between Yahweh as creator and redeemer is central to covenant in the Old Testament,[91] and alerts us to the link between law and creation.

My suggestion therefore is that law and wisdom share an underlying and often tacit presupposition of a 'carved' creation order. Instruction from Yahweh would therefore not be seen to conflict with the way he ordered his creation,

---

88. Van Leeuwen, 'Liminality and Worldview in Proverbs 1 – 9', p. 116.
89. Ibid., p. 118.
90. Ibid., p. 132.
91. See Craig G. Bartholomew, 'Covenant and Creation: Covenant Overload or Covenantal Deconstruction', *CTJ* 30/1 (1995), pp. 11–33.

but would provide the ethical principles for discovery of that liminality. Literary scholars often show a refreshing freedom to go where biblical scholars fear to tread. Thus, the well-known Canadian literary scholar Northrop Frye argues, 'The conception of wisdom in the Bible, as we see most clearly in some of the psalms, starts with the individualizing of the law, with allowing the law, in its human and moral aspect, to permeate and inform all one's personal life.'[92] If this is even close to the situation that prevailed in Israel, it would confirm our argument for caution about insisting that the epilogue of Ecclesiastes must be an addition because it mentions 'keeping commandments'.

Many other aspects of biblical intertextuality in relation to the Old Testament wisdom books could be considered. For example, in his evocative discussion of Proverbs 7:1–27, under the heading of 'The Educational Theatre of Proverbs',[93] Levy notes the intertextual echoes of the Torah in verses 1–5 and rightly argues that the *shema* of Deuteronomy 6:1–4 is clearly alluded to: 'The father reuses the original Pentateuch text in a sophisticated way.'[94] According to the *shema* God's commandments (cf. 'my commandments' of Prov. 7:2) are to be discussed in the home, presumably the context for the instruction of Proverbs 7. They are to be bound on the fingers (cf. Prov. 3:3); in Deuteronomy 6 they are to be bound on the hand. Furthermore, 'the tablet of your heart' alludes to 'the heart' of Deuteronomy 6:6 and 'tablet' evokes the tablets of the law. Although Job is set outside Israel with all the main characters – apart from Yahweh – being 'non-Israelite', it is written from an Israelite perspective, and has many links with the Psalter, for example.

Work remains to be done, too, on the relationship between Old Testament wisdom and Old Testament prophecy. In the culminating vision of death in Ecclesiastes 12, for example, there appear to be links with prophetic apocalyptic visions.[95]

As regards the intertextuality between the Old Testament wisdom books and the New Testament, much work remains to be done.[96] Wisdom motifs,

---

92. Northrop Frye, *The Great Code: The Bible and Literature* (Toronto: Penguin, 1981, 1982), p. 121.
93. S. Levy, *The Bible as Theatre* (Brighton: Sussex Academic Press, 2000, 2002), pp. 135–142.
94. Ibid., p. 136.
95. T. Krüger, *Qoheleth: A Commentary*, tr. O. C. Dean Jr, Continental Commentary (Minneapolis: Fortress, 2004); Craig G. Bartholomew, *Ecclesiastes*, BCOTWP (Grand Rapids: Baker Academic, 2009).
96. See Ben Witherington's *Jesus the Sage: The Pilgrimage of Wisdom* (Edinburgh: T&T Clark, 1994). OT wisdom is also a major background for James in the NT.

for example, play a larger role in Jesus' ministry than is often recognized. For example, he concludes the Sermon on the Mount with the story of two houses (Matt. 7:24–27) with imagery that appears to come directly from Proverbs (9; 12:7; 24:3–4). Of course wisdom is now defined as obedience to Jesus' teaching. However, as Jesus himself teaches in the Sermon, he has not come to abolish the Old Testament but to fulfil it. In the dawning of the new age believers still require wisdom, and Paul especially, in his letters, not only locates wisdom in Jesus but prays that believers might be filled with wisdom. The dynamic is the same as that in the Old Testament but now in the fullness of time. And it is hard not to see Job as somehow a type of Jesus.[97]

Reception history has now entered biblical studies in a major way, and Old Testament wisdom is no exception. I still remember the exhilaration I felt, having wrestled with how to understand Ecclesiastes as a whole, to discover that my reading was in line with that of the Lutheran Reformers, who, with their strong doctrine of creation, broke the back of Jerome's *contemptus mundi* reading of Ecclesiastes which had dominated the book's interpretation for a thousand years. Especially if we seek to move beyond historical criticism to post-critical biblical studies, the resources of our rich tradition are indispensable. Prior to the rise of historical criticism Scripture was read almost entirely to discern the voice of God and those of us who share this concern need to immerse ourselves in the tradition. A feast beckons, with poignant insights waiting to be transfused into the present. Old Testament wisdom is not yet as well served as are other parts of the Bible. We need histories to be written of the reception of Old Testament wisdom, and of the history of interpretation of Proverbs, Job and Ecclesiastes. Al Wolters' sterling work on the history of reception of the Proverbs 31 valiant woman provides a taste of what is waiting.[98]

It will be obvious from this section that the literary turn has radical implications for historical criticism. What, in my view, has not been adequately done

---

97. See Barth, *CD*; Susannah Ticciati, *Job and the Disruption of Identity: Reading Beyond Barth* (London: T&T Clark, 2005); Craig Bartholomew, *When You Want to Yell at God: Reading Job* (Bellingham: Lexham, 2014).

98. Al Wolters, *The Song of the Valiant Woman: Studies in the Interpretation of Proverbs 31:10–31* (Carlisle: Paternoster, 2001). See also Eric Christianson, *Ecclesiastes Through the Centuries*, BBC (Oxford: Wiley-Blackwell, 2012); Mark Larrimore, *The Book of Job: A Biography*, Lives of Great Books (Princeton: Princeton University Press, 2013); Stuart Weeks, *The Making of Many Books: Printed Works on Ecclesiastes 1523–1875* (Winona Lake: Eisenbrauns, 2014).

is to rethink historical criticism in the light of the literary turn.[99] Recall our quote from Hahn above, who insists that before any historical reconstruction of the history of Israel's religion can take place, 'the problem of defining the textual limits and the special characteristics of the underlying sources must be solved'. The literary turn throws a huge spanner in the works of historical criticism *precisely at this point*, and the implications have yet to be fully explored. Thus the two approaches continue to operate, often in unresolved tension with each other. A major reason for this is that before the literary turn could be fully appropriated, postmodernism was upon us with its smorgasbord of readings.

Old Testament wisdom and postmodernism

From the 1980s postmodernism emerged and affected almost every discipline, including Old Testament wisdom studies. The literature on postmodernism and Old Testament wisdom studies is not huge but is certainly present. Among UK scholars David Clines has been an advocate of postmodernism and inter alia he has produced multiple studies on Job and postmodernism.[100] The effect of postmodernism has been felt in Old Testament studies by the bewildering variety of readings it has spawned. What has been less noticed are the philosophical presuppositions of postmodernism. Coming at the end of the most brutal century in history postmodernism has savaged modernity without actually moving beyond modernity. Historical criticism is a product of modernity and thus it is not surprising that postmodern scholars have tended to ignore historical criticism and to get on with reading texts *as they desire*.

David Harvey in his *Condition of Postmodernity*[101] provides a helpful way to understand postmodernism. Modernity – speaking generally – rejected tradition and religion as ways to truth and espoused autonomous reason as

---

99. Newsom, *The Book of Job*, is exemplary in exploring the various turns and their implications for her reading of Job. More of this sort of work is required.
100. David J. A. Clines, *On the Way to the Postmodern: Old Testament Essays 1967–1998*, JSOTSup 292 (Sheffield: Sheffield Academic Press, 1998), pp. 719–822. Cf. Newsom's *The Book of Job*, critique of Clines.
101. David Harvey, *The Condition of Postmodernity: An Enquiry into the Origin of Cultural Change* (Oxford: Wiley-Blackwell, 1990).

the path there. Postmodernism no longer believes that autonomous reason can get us to the truth about the world but resists recovering tradition and orthodox religion. The result is that we are left with a sort of cheerful nihilism and a wild pluralism of methodologies, akin to the days of the judges when all the people did what was right in their own eyes. 'The more readings, the better!' has become the virtual shibboleth of postmodernism. This itself is a value-laden position and simply untrue, in my view. Indeed, as I have argued elsewhere, I think that Ecclesiastes provides us with a profound critique of postmodernism.[102]

Closely connected with postmodernism are the *ideological readings* of the Bible, approaches such as feminist readings, post-colonial readings, queer readings and so on. Such approaches should, however, not be subsumed under postmodernism since they often depend on reading texts objectively along the grain in order to engage in ideological critique. Feminist readings, for example, have been applied to all three major Old Testament wisdom books.[103] Such approaches are valuable insofar as they push us to engage with the details of the text, but less helpful for Christian interpretation insofar as they impose alien ideologies on the wisdom books.

Postmodernism has, in my view, been valuable in pushing us to look carefully at the worldviews and philosophies informing modern biblical interpretation. With all its diversity historical criticism is not a neutral, scientific approach as many would have us believe, but has its own ideological and often non-Christian presuppositions. However, postmodernism has produced little that is constructive. The great casualty of postmodernism has been truth, replaced in postmodern circles by desire and play. We are now living amidst the demise of postmodernism and Christian scholars need to be ahead of the game in proposing ways of reading Old Testament wisdom texts aimed at truth, and insisting that there is a thick sense in which reading *is* objective. Part of such a thick objectivity will involve reading as Christians, and this leads us on to theological interpretation.

---

102. Bartholomew, *Ecclesiastes*.
103. Athalya Brenner and Carol Fontaine (eds.), *Wisdom and Psalms: A Feminist Companion to the Bible* (Sheffield: Sheffield Academic Press, 1998); Claudia Camp, *Wisdom and the Feminine in the Book of Proverbs*, Bible and Literature 11 (Sheffield: Almond Press, 1985); *Wise, Strange and Holy: The Strange Woman and the Making of the Bible* (Sheffield: Sheffield Academic Press, 2000); Diane Bergant, *Israel's Wisdom Literature: A Liberation-Critical Reading* (Minneapolis: Fortress, 1997); etc.

Theological interpretation

The recent renaissance of theological interpretation has its background in Barth[104] and Childs and seeks to concentrate on reading the Bible *for the church as Scripture*.[105] In my view the exciting developments in missional and liturgical hermeneutics should be seen as subsets of theological interpretation, which concentrates on reading *for God's address today*. As it has emerged theological interpretation is a broad church with a variety of approaches. At its best it has the potential to move biblical studies forward in highly creative ways. Unfortunately, most biblical scholars were not trained for this sort of work. It is ironic that large amounts of literature are produced on the social location and origin of Old Testament wisdom but far too little on the religious, indeed divine, origins. And yet, as we noted under our definition of wisdom, Proverbs, and in different ways Job and Ecclesiastes, are relentless in refusing to allow us to ignore God as the author of wisdom.

Dialogue between Old Testament wisdom and *systematic theology* has great potential. Years ago John McKenna published an extremely important article on *hebel* in Ecclesiastes making use of Barth's notion of creation as contingent.[106] Alas, his article went largely unnoticed by Old Testament wisdom scholars and needs to be retrieved today. In my view, McKenna's article gets at the essence of what is going on with *hebel* in Ecclesiastes.

I have referred above to missional hermeneutics and to liturgical hermeneutics as subsets of theological interpretation.[107] An *ethical hermeneutic* could also be seen as such a subset. Missional hermeneutics is revitalizing biblical interpretation in surprising ways and there is room for creative work on Old Testament wisdom from this perspective, as a major way of equipping God's people to be a royal priesthood and a holy nation amidst the nations. In my opinion an ethical hermeneutic offers tremendous possibilities for Old Testament wisdom. As I have noted elsewhere, for example, if Qohelet does reach resolution of his quest for meaning, then retrospectively all the areas of created life he has

---

104. The amount of exegesis in Barth's *CD* is staggering. Note e.g. his discussions of Job and compare Ticciati, *Job and the Disruption of Identity*.
105. See Bartholomew and Thomas, *Manifesto for Theological Interpretation*.
106. John E. McKenna, 'The Concept of *Hebel* in the Book of Ecclesiastes', *SJT* 45/1 (1992), pp. 19–28.
107. See Craig G. Bartholomew, 'Theological Interpretation and Missional Hermeneutics', in Michael W. Goheen (ed.), *Missional Hermeneutic* (Grand Rapids: Eerdmans, forthcoming).

attended to come into renewed focus. As is well known his search for meaning ranges across the different spheres of life and thus there is in Ecclesiastes an immense resource of largely untapped ethical data. The same is true of Proverbs. Job has always been connected with suffering and theodicy and remains a fertile source for such reflection.

Both Job and Ecclesiastes are important sources for *pastoral theology* today, and much work remains to be done in mining them in this regard with the same rigour scholars bring to structural and other forms of analysis.[108] In my view, a biblical hermeneutic is inadequate if its goal is not to hear God's address today through his Word. If this is correct, serious attention needs to be given to how to preach Old Testament wisdom today, a complex topic and one much neglected.[109] In our *Old Testament Wisdom*, O'Dowd and I also foreground the contribution of Old Testament wisdom to Christian *spirituality*. There is some work in this area being published,[110] but rigorous work remains to be done.

Old Testament wisdom and philosophy

Old Testament wisdom is wonderfully comprehensive in its scope and lends itself to engagement with a range of academic and practical disciplines.[111] An area where signs of this engagement are present is amidst the renaissance of Christian philosophy. Peter Kreeft begins his *Three Philosophies of Life*, on Job, Ecclesiastes and Song of Songs, by noting,

> I have been a philosopher for all of my adult life, and the three most profound books of philosophy that I have ever read are Ecclesiastes, Job, and Song of Songs. In fact, the book that first made me a philosopher, at about age fifteen, was Ecclesiastes.[112]

---

108. See Bartholomew, 'Postscript', in *Ecclesiastes*.
109. But see the series by Sidney Greidanus with Eerdmans.
110. See e.g. Carlo M. Martini, *Perseverance in Trials: Reflections on Job* (Collegeville: Liturgical Press, 1992); Richard Rohr, *Job and the Mystery of Suffering: Spiritual Reflections* (Leominster: Gracewing, 1996); J. Gerald Janzen, *At the Scent of Water: The Ground of Hope in the Book of Job* (Grand Rapids: Eerdmans, 2009).
111. Mention should also be made of *psychological readings*, especially of Job and Ecclesiastes. See Bartholomew, *Ecclesiastes*; 'Hearing the Old Testament Wisdom Literature: The Wit of One, and the Wisdom of Many', in Craig G. Bartholomew and David J. H. Beldman (eds.), *Hearing the Old Testament* (Grand Rapids: Eerdmans, 2012).
112. Peter Kreeft, *Three Philosophies of Life* (San Francisco: Ignatius, 2009), p. 7.

In his classic, *Warranted Christian Belief*, Alvin Plantinga deals with Job in his treatment of theodicy as a potential defeater for Christian faith.[113] Eleonore Stump has attended to Job in her studies of second-person approaches to suffering and also deals with Job extensively in her *Wandering in Darkness*.[114] Fingarette concludes his *Mapping Responsibility* with a chapter on Job.[115] Nemo focuses on Job in his *Job and the Excess of Evil*.[116]

In analytic philosophy an exciting development over the last twenty-five years has been a recovery of interest in the question of the meaning of life. Joshua W. Seachris, in his edited reader *Exploring the Meaning of Life: An Anthology and Guide*,[117] includes the text of Ecclesiastes as a chapter, and in a book project published as *God and Meaning*, Seachris and Goetz[118] included Ecclesiastes on the agenda and invited Tremper Longman and myself to contribute chapters. One hopes that we will see a great expansion of such interdisciplinary work.

Conclusion

The sheer mass of publications on Old Testament wisdom requires a map with which to navigate it, and my hope is that approaching the subject through a series of turns is illuminating. However, we need to move beyond such navigation to a focus on where future work on Old Testament wisdom most needs to be done. The postmodern turn is, in my opinion, running out of steam and a danger is that we will relapse into historical criticism and virulent forms of secular readings.

Old Testament wisdom invites us to a feast of interpretation, but what do we need to do in order to partake of this feast and to open it to others? Historical criticism remains influential as the default mode of many scholars and major

---

113. Alvin Plantinga, *Warranted Christian Belief* (Oxford/New York: Oxford University Press, 2000), pp. 494–498.
114. Eleonore Stump, *Wandering in Darkness: Narrative and the Problem of Suffering* (Oxford/New York: Oxford University Press, 2010), part 3, ch. 9.
115. H. Fingarette, *Mapping Responsibility: Explorations in Mind, Law, Myth, and Culture* (Peru, IL: Carus, 2004).
116. Philippe Nemo, *Job and the Excess of Evil* (Pittsburgh: Duquesne University Press, 1998).
117. (Oxford: Wiley, 2012).
118. Joshua Seachris and Stewart Goetz (eds.), *God and Meaning: New Essays* (London: Bloomsbury, 2016).

work needs to be done in reassessing historical criticism today, especially in the light of the literary *and* theological turns, with a view to retaining its insights and rejecting its unhelpful baggage. We need a reconfigured historical hermeneutic for Old Testament wisdom. Indeed, there is great need for an integrated hermeneutic that will enable us to attend to the historical, literary and theological dimensions of Old Testament wisdom texts, all in the service of listening to their powerful messages for today. The literary turn proved to be fertile and there is a need to return to its best work and ensure that we develop literary readings to their full potential.

What Christian scholars should not do is continue to work away at sites in wisdom studies determined by others who have no interest in reading Old Testament wisdom as Scripture. We always need to be in dialogue with scholars of diverse views, but a Christian perspective will alert us to particular work sites crying out for hard labour if we are to retrieve Old Testament wisdom as Scripture today. Such sites should include intertextuality, biblical theology and wisdom, the theology of the individual wisdom books, wisdom and preaching, wisdom and spirituality, and the public dimensions of wisdom.

In her *Scripture, Culture, and Agriculture*, for example, Ellen Davis opens up a fertile dialogue between the new agrarianism – Wendell Berry in particular – and the Old Testament. Such is the visceral, comprehensive nature of Old Testament wisdom that it too cries out for such treatments. To conclude with one example, the well-known writer and environmental activist Bill McKibben has written on Job, and here I suggest is a fertile dialogue waiting to be developed by Old Testament wisdom scholars.[119]

© Craig G. Bartholomew, 2016

---

119. Bill McKibben, *The Comforting Whirlwind: God, Job, and the Scale of Creation* (Grand Rapids: Eerdmans, 1994); 'Job and Matthew', in *The Bill McKibben Reader: Pieces from an Active Life* (New York: Holt, 2008), pp. 183–193. See also McKibben, 'Will Evangelicals Help Save the Earth?' in ibid., pp. 226–234; 'The Pope and the Planet', *New York Review of Books*, 13 August 2015, pp. 40–42.

PART 2:

THE WISDOM LITERATURE

2. THE BOOK OF PROVERBS: SOME CURRENT ISSUES

Ernest C. Lucas

The limitations of space mean that this survey of current issues in the study of Proverbs has to be very selective. Several important issues get no mention. The selection is subjective, but the issues chosen are relevant to the understanding and use of Proverbs today. They include aspects of hermeneutics, and the basis for that understanding and use. There is consideration of the view that Proverbs presents an unrealistically simplistic take on life, a reason why it is sometimes neglected or gets misused. Its intriguing personification of wisdom and related cast of female figures makes it a centre of debate regarding current gender issues. The book's creation theology has relevance for understanding New Testament Christology and soteriology in a way that has particular relevance today.

Structural units in the sentence literature

Many scholars think that Proverbs 10 – 29 consists of disconnected proverbs arranged haphazardly.[1] However, some have argued for the existence of various

---

1. C. R. Yoder, *Proverbs*, Abingdon OTC (Nashville: Abingdon, 2009), p. 110.

kinds of compositional units in these chapters. Hildebrandt[2] argued for 'proverbial pairs' bound together by various rhetorical devices. Catchword repetition is a common one, being particularly significant when the catchwords are low-frequency words (26:20–21) or when there are multiple catchwords (23:13–14). Bonding by a common theme may result in multiple catchwords. Syntactic bonding is less conclusive, the strongest forms being direct dependence and linking particles or suffixes (22:24–25). Hildebrandt[3] subsequently identified four 'strings' of proverbs in Proverbs 10. Identification of 10:1–5 and 10:6–11 as separate 'strings' is convincing. Both are bounded by *inclusios*. The proposed 'strings' in 10:12–21 and 10:22–30 rely on convoluted proposed structures which are much less convincing. Van Leeuwen[4] used structuralist, rhetorical and semantic approaches to study Proverbs 25 – 27. He identified a 'proverb poem' in chapter 25 and three other 'proverb poems' in chapter 26, but could not find a coherent literary unit in chapter 27, concluding that it is a 'proverb miscellany'.

Proverbial clusters

Heim identified 'proverbial clusters' in Proverbs 10:1 – 22:16.[5] Regarding the criteria for identifying clusters he argued[6] that 'The focus should not be on what *divides* or *separates* groups from their environment, but on features which *link* and *combine* sayings into organic units'. In particular he looked for repetition – such as repetition of consonants, word roots, words and synonyms. The positioning of some linking features makes them boundary markers. Another criterion for distinguishing one cluster from another is the change in linking devices.

Waltke[7] used 'the mostly single-line rearing (or educative) proverbs' as a guide to identifying the beginning of what he calls 'units'. He then divided these into

---

2. T. A. Hildebrandt, 'Proverbial Pairs: Compositional Units in Proverbs 10 – 29', *JBL* 107 (1988), pp. 207–224.
3. T. A. Hildebrandt, 'Proverbial Strings: Cohesion in Proverbs 10', *Grace Theological Journal* 11 (1990), pp. 171–185.
4. R. C. Van Leeuwen, *Context and Meaning in Proverbs 25 – 27*, SBLDS 96 (Atlanta: Scholars Press, 1988).
5. K. M. Heim, *Like Grapes of Gold Set in Silver: An Interpretation of Proverbial Clusters in Proverbs 10:1 – 22:16*, BZAW 273 (Berlin: De Gruyter, 2001).
6. Heim, *Like Grapes of Gold*, p. 107.
7. B. K. Waltke, *The Book of Proverbs 1 – 15*, NICOT (Grand Rapids: Eerdmans, 2004), p. 21.

'subunits' which more or less correspond to Heim's 'clusters'. The criteria he used[8] in linking proverbs together are such things as *inclusio*, catchwords, structural patterns such as a *chiasmus* and logical or thematic connections.

In my commentary[9] I identify 'proverbial clusters' and other structures in the sentence literature using the criteria used by Waltke and Heim. I give a higher priority than Heim does to thematic connections, recognizing that this may introduce more subjectivity, and I do not try as hard as Waltke to find logical or thematic connections. He seems to assume that they must always be there.

Table 1 shows the clusters identified by Heim,[10] Waltke[11] and myself in Proverbs 10. Waltke, and to a lesser extent Heim, tends to see larger units than I do, but then breaks them down into subunits which correspond quite closely with the clusters I identify. This degree of agreement gives encouragement to think that the smaller clusters are not simply subjective creations.

Table 1: Comparing clusters in Proverbs 10

Waltke			Heim			Lucas	
10:1–17							
	10:1		10:1–5			10:1–5	
	10:2–5						
	10:6–14		10:6–11			10:6–11	
						10:12	
	10:15–16		10:12–18			10:13–17	
	10:17						
10:18–32							
	10:18–21		10:19–22			10:18–21	
			10:22–30				
	10:22–26			*10:22–25*		10:22–25	
				10:26		10:26	
	10:27–30			*10:27–30*		10:27–30	
	10:31–32		10:31–32			10:31–32	

---

8. Waltke, *Proverbs 1 – 15*, p. 47.
9. E. C. Lucas, *Proverbs*, THOTC (Grand Rapids/Cambridge: Eerdmans, 2015).
10. Heim, *Like Grapes of Gold*, pp. 111–146.
11. Waltke, *Proverbs 1 – 15*, pp. 447–515.

Fox[12] critiqued Heim's work, finding it unconvincing for a number of reasons.

1. Heim assumes that clusters exist, and this leads to a biased approach. However, it is equally biased to assume that there are no clusters. I have tried to approach the issue without expecting that clusters must exist, but being open to seeing whether any do.
2. Proverbs 10:1 – 22:16 covers a limited number of subjects. Given the terseness of the language, the multivalence of words and the ambiguity of many proverbs, it is not hard to find what may be unintended correspondences between proverbs. Heim is aware of this danger[13] and seeks to guard against it by looking for 'linkages' of sufficient strength to avoid it.
3. Heim's reliance on literary markers rather than thematic connections may seem 'objective'. However, the choice of which repetitions and other patterns are important is somewhat subjective. At times Fox regards Heim's choices as 'idiosyncratic'. I agree that sometimes Heim could be straining to find connections that may not exist. However, this applies in only a minority of cases. One must accept a measure of subjectivity in the choice of criteria for linkages and the application of them. In the natural sciences there is recognition of the importance of 'inter-subjective verification' as a way of ameliorating this. The measure of agreement between Heim, Waltke and myself in identifying the smaller clusters, using somewhat different approaches, is encouraging for this reason.
4. Heim's approach is too esoteric, requiring a 'skilled and equipped analyst' with plenty of time to devote to the task to uncover the patterns which Heim finds. It is unlikely that the compilers of Proverbs would put such patterns there and expect readers to find them. However, the compilers were scholars and, according to the prologue (Prov. 1:2–7), intended to address a readership ranging from fellow scholars ('the wise') to the 'simple' reader. They might have put in patterns that only 'the wise' would be able to perceive, so giving the book different levels of meaning for readers of different reading competency. There is, nevertheless, a danger of being too esoteric and this is why I put more emphasis than Heim on the more obvious criterion of thematic or logical connections of meaning while also recognizing other, less obvious, patterns marking out clusters.

---

12. M. V. Fox, 'Like Grapes of Gold Set in Silver: An Interpretation of Proverbial Clusters in Proverbs 10:1 – 22:16. By Knut Martin Heim', *HS* 44 (2003), pp. 267–272.
13. Heim, *Like Grapes of Gold*, pp. 55–57.

5. Although most commentators have recognized some thematic groups in Proverbs above the level of proverb pairs few have found the preponderance of clusters that Heim does. Heim points out in his survey of scholarship various biases which might lead to scholars not recognizing such clusters. Also, the history of biblical studies provides examples of the appearance of new ways of reading texts that bring to light things which previous scholars have not noticed.
6. Heim's stated goal is to find a way of reading Proverbs that is relevant for a practising pastor and preacher. Fox finds this 'of doubtful appropriateness to scholarly analysis'. This is an unfair criticism. Whatever Heim's goal, the value of it to scholars must be judged by the outcome.

While rejecting Heim's 'totalizing' approach Fox accepts that there is some clustering of proverbs. He says, 'When one thought gives rise to another or one word evokes a related one, the result is an associative sequence.'[14] The result is a (small) group of proverbs on the same theme and/or with similar wording. He regards this as a largely unintentional process. This may explain some, probably looser, clusters. However, there is no reason why there should not also be clusters that are the result of intentional activity by the compilers. It is arguable that good teachers would seek to produce such clusters.

Clusters and hermeneutics

Where structures exist it is worth considering whether they are more than simply literary constructs. They could be hermeneutically significant. Maybe the sentence proverbs in them should not be interpreted atomistically but in the context of the other sentences making up the structure. Some scholars reject such an approach. McKane[15] asserted that any such structures in Proverbs 'are of secondary character' and to be ignored when interpreting a proverb. Schwáb[16] could see no good reason why the reader should ignore or downplay the 'secondary' or editorial activity of the compiler of Proverbs when interpreting it.

Longman[17] suggested that the randomness of the collections in Proverbs is deliberate, reflecting the messiness of life. He admitted that this is 'pure

---

14. M. V. Fox, *Proverbs 10 – 31*, AB (New Haven: Yale University Press, 2009), p. 480.
15. W. McKane, *Proverbs*, OTL (London: SCM, 1970), p. 10.
16. Z. Schwáb, 'The Sayings Clusters in Proverbs: Towards an Associative Reading Strategy', *JSOT* 38 (2013), pp. 59–79.
17. T. Longman III, *Proverbs* (Grand Rapids: Baker, 2006), pp. 40–41.

speculation as to the conscious strategy of the redactors of the book'. I agree with Heim and Waltke that there is evidence which points to a different conscious strategy being used. Because of his 'speculation' Longman thinks that when two or more proverbs do seem to form a group this has come about unintentionally by a kind of magnetic attraction and is not hermeneutically significant. Readers of Waltke's commentary and mine must judge whether or not that is the case when considering the interpretations they give of proverbs within clusters. Finally, Longman says, 'for a proverb to come alive again, it needs to be spoken orally in the right context.' However, a speaker cannot decide what that right context for a proverb is without having some idea about its possible meaning(s), and this has to arise from reading it in Proverbs. It is not unreasonable to consider whether the compiler(s) gave some help with this by the literary context in which a proverb has been put.

Character and consequence in Proverbs

In 1955 Koch[18] published an influential paper arguing that there is in the book of Proverbs, and elsewhere in the Old Testament, the assumption of an 'act–consequence nexus'. It is assumed that actions have an inevitable outcome that is not the result of God stepping in to administer punishments and rewards. Rather, God maintains the act–consequence nexus and ensures that it is 'completed'. Some[19] have argued that the distinction between an impersonal 'nexus' and the personal action of Yahweh would not have made sense in ancient Hebrew thought, which regarded Yahweh's activity as all-pervasive in human affairs. Hatton critiqued Koch's thesis by doing a detailed study of Proverbs 10 – 13, which includes many proverbs cited by Koch. He found tensions in these chapters between different presentations of the relationship between deeds and their outcome. Proverbs which support Koch's thesis are, in his view, 'few and far between'.[20] Many point out that the emphasis in Proverbs is not on concrete, individual acts and their consequences. The sages were concerned with the long-term character of a person

---

18. For an English version see K. Koch, 'Is There a Doctrine of Retribution in the Old Testament?', in J. L. Crenshaw (ed.), *Theodicy in the Old Testament* (London: SPCK, 1983), pp. 57–87.
19. E.g. R. E. Murphy, *Proverbs*, WBC (Nashville: Nelson, 1998), pp. 264–269.
20. P. T. H. Hatton, *Contradiction in the Book of Proverbs* (Aldershot: Ashgate, 2008), pp. 115–116.

or a community.[21] This is seen in the metaphor of 'the two ways' between which people have constantly to make a choice as they determine their life-path. It is also evidenced by the contrasts between antithetical pairs such as the righteous and the wicked, the wise and the foolish, the diligent and the lazy.

There is still a widespread idea that Proverbs presents a simplistic deed–consequence relationship. However, there are types of proverbs which show that this itself is a simplistic understanding of the book.

1. There are seemingly contradictory proverbs. The classic case is Proverbs 26:4–5. Less stark examples are 19:20–21; 21:30–31/24:5–6.
2. The 'better-than' proverbs recognize the complexity of life and that a simple character–consequence nexus does not always hold. Being righteous may lead to having 'little' (16:8). One may have to choose between wisdom and wealth (16:16).
3. Proverbs about what is 'not fitting/becoming' recognize that the character–consequence nexus does not always work out, otherwise these situations would not arise (e.g. 17:7; 19:10; 30:21–23).
4. Some proverbs recognize that the wicked may prosper and the innocent suffer (e.g. 11:16; 13:23; 18:23).
5. Other proverbs recognize incalculables in human existence (e.g. 14:12; 27:1).
6. Very importantly, the sages accepted that human understanding is limited and that we cannot 'second-guess' what Yahweh will do (19:21; 21:30).

This is evidence that the sages recognized that the character–consequence nexus was only a 'rule of thumb' with regard to developing life-skills and had many exceptions. It is often a good approximation to what happens, otherwise proverbs would not have the place they do in most cultures. However, the tensions in the book make its limitations clear to attentive readers. The sages saw it as a pragmatically useful teaching 'model' at the beginning of learning life-skills and character development. This 'rule of thumb' exists because we live in a world created by Yahweh, who is concerned that we should behave with righteousness and justice. For this reason, 'the fear of Yahweh is the beginning of wisdom' (9:10a[22]). However, we cannot expect to understand Yahweh's purposes and actions fully, and so for this reason it is only a 'rule of thumb'.

---

21. E.g. Waltke, *Proverbs 1 – 15*, p. 72.
22. All Bible quotes in this chapter, unless stated otherwise, are the author's own translation.

The prominence of the character–consequence nexus in Proverbs is probably related to its educational purpose. Education in 'life-skills' has to begin with what is *generally the case*. Only when this has been established and understood can the teacher move on to the qualifications and 'hard cases'. Rather than being seen as a 'protest' against the simplistic approach of Proverbs, Job and Qoheleth might be seen as providing the next stage in 'life-skills' education. To some degree Proverbs prepares the attentive reader for this next stage. In his study of contradictions in Proverbs Hatton[23] argues that Proverbs is a truly dialogic text in which different voices address the attentive reader. The difference between it and Job and Qoheleth is a matter of degree, not kind.

The personification of wisdom in Proverbs

There has been much debate about the nature and origin of the personification of wisdom as a woman in Proverbs 1:20–33; 8:1–36; 9:1–6. Some have argued that in Proverbs 8:22–36 Wisdom is not a 'personification' but a 'hypostasis'. A major problem is lack of agreement about the meaning of 'hypostasis' as applied to Wisdom. Ringgren's study is still one of the most comprehensive presentations of the view that Wisdom is a hypostasis, 'a concrete being, self-existent beside God'[24] in Proverbs 8:22–31. However, he does not provide a clear case for his view[25] that in Proverbs 1:20–33; 8:1–21; 9:1–6 wisdom is presented in terms of 'allegories or poetic personifications' while in Proverbs 8:22–31 she is a true hypostasis of Yahweh's attribute of wisdom. It is also questionable whether the concept of 'hypostasis' would have been meaningful or conceivable in ancient Israel given the normative monolatry of Israelite religion. Personification, the personalizing of impersonal things or abstract concepts is, however, well-attested in the Hebrew Bible and other Ancient Near Eastern literature.

Proposed prototypes for personified Wisdom
The Egyptian goddess Ma'at. Kayatz[26] argued that Ma'at, goddess of truth/justice (a single concept in Egyptian thought), was the prototype for the personified

---

23. Hatton, *Contradiction in the Book of Proverbs*, p. 170.
24. H. H. Ringgren, *Word and Wisdom: Studies in the Hypostatization of Divine Qualities and Functions in the Ancient Near East* (Lund: H. Ohlsson, 1947), p. 104.
25. Ibid., p. 99.
26. C. Kayatz, *Studien zu Proverbien 1 – 9*, WMANT 22 (Neukirchen-Vluyn: Neukirchener Verlag, 1966).

figure of Wisdom in Proverbs 8, listing features that they shared. Fox[27] pointed out that none of these features are exclusive to Ma'at. All have parallels in various proclamations of Near Eastern gods and kings. Moreover, there is no recorded speech by Ma'at. As a goddess she was never popular or well known, even in Egypt, and is never personified in Egyptian wisdom literature. Also, Kayatz accepted that in Proverbs 1:20–33 Wisdom speaks more like a Hebrew prophet than a goddess, which led her to see Wisdom here as only a 'poetic personification'.

The goddess Isis became the most popular goddess in the Near East in Hellenistic times. Being consummately wise, she was given the epithet Sophia. Her virtues and powers were proclaimed in 'aretalogies' (hymns praising deities). Knox[28] noted some similarities between these and Wisdom's speech in Proverbs 8 and suggested it was composed as a response to the attractions of Isis worship. However, Hellenistic Isis religion began to spread widely only in the late third century BC, too late for it to have had any influence on even the latest redaction of the book of Proverbs. Moreover, the aretalogies which provided the basis for suggesting a link between Isis and Wisdom are not attested before the first century BC.

A Canaanite goddess. Albright[29] suggested that behind the figure of Wisdom there may lie a Canaanite goddess of wisdom, perhaps a hypostatization of an attribute of the high god El. Whybray[30] critiqued Albright's arguments in some detail. There are far fewer 'Canaanitisms' in Proverbs 8 – 9 than Albright claimed. There is no evidence that Wisdom was regarded as a personal being distinct from El, and no known Canaanite goddess of wisdom.

An Israelite goddess. Lang[31] developed a variant of Albright's thesis. He argues that the origin of the figure of personified Wisdom in Proverbs is an Israelite goddess who was worshipped in the pre-exilic era. She was a daughter of Yahweh. Perhaps Athirat was her mother, but Lang thinks it more likely that

---

27. M. V. Fox, 'World Order and Ma'at: A Crooked Parallel', *JANESCU* 23 (1995), pp. 37–48.
28. W. L. Knox, 'The Divine Wisdom', *JTS* 38 (1937), pp. 230–237.
29. W. F. Albright, 'The Goddess of Life and Wisdom', *AJSL* 36 (1919), pp. 258–294; 'Some Canaanite-Phoenician Sources of Hebrew Wisdom', in M. Noth and D. W. Thomas (eds.), *Wisdom in Israel and the Ancient Near East*, VTSup 3 (Leiden: Brill, 1955), pp. 1–15.
30. R. N. Whybray, *Wisdom in Proverbs* (London: SCM, 1965), pp. 83–87.
31. B. Lang, *Wisdom and the Book of Proverbs: An Israelite Goddess Redefined* (New York: Pilgrim Press, 1986).

she was a 'motherless deity' like the Greek Athena and the Egyptian Thoth. With the rise of the 'Yahweh-alone' party in the late pre-exilic period, the worship of other deities was suppressed. In the post-exilic era it was possible for the orthodox sages to take over poems that were originally about this goddess and apply them to a personification of Yahweh's wisdom. There is virtually no evidence to support Lang's thesis. The deities worshipped by polytheistic Israelites in the Old Testament were members of the Canaanite pantheon. There is no evidence for a Canaanite goddess of wisdom, let alone an Israelite one. The only evidence Lang presents to support the idea that polytheistic texts lie behind the poems about Wisdom in Proverbs 1 – 9 is the use of the plural 'holy ones' in Proverbs 9:10. This is usually taken as a plural of 'majesty' or 'abstraction' and translated as 'the Holy One'. The weakness of Lang's case is that it is built on a series of conjectures.

The Babylonian ummānu. Clifford[32] argues that the personified figure of Wisdom in Proverbs is derived from the pre- and post-flood sages of Babylonian mythology who were the bringers of culture to the human race. A document from Uruk lists seven pre-flood and seven post-flood kings. Each pre-flood king has an associated *apkallu* and each post-flood king an associated *ummānu*. The *apkallu* are divine beings. The post-flood kings are historical rulers and the *ummānu* are human sages, some of whom have the names of known authors. The last of them, from the reign of Esarhaddon, is identified as 'Aba'enlildari, whom the Arameans call Ahiqar'. This identification, Clifford argues, shows that the Babylonian tradition of the 'culture-bringers' was known in Syria–Palestine. As we shall see below, Clifford's suggestion may provide a plausible background for Proverbs 8:22–31. It does not, however, provide much illumination for the other aspects of personified Wisdom presented in Proverbs 1 – 9.

A literary creation. Sinnott[33] argues that the figure of personified Wisdom in Proverbs is primarily a literary creation. Personification is a literary device found in many cultures, especially in poetry. It is fairly common in the Hebrew Bible, including Proverbs. However, in the case of wisdom personification is developed to a far greater extent than anywhere else in the Hebrew Bible. In Sinnott's view, the purpose of the personification of wisdom is to give bodily form, with all its associated physical imagery, to an abstraction. As a result it links the senses with the understanding and presents abstract knowledge in an attractive form. She argues that the creation of the figure of personified Wisdom was a response

---

32. R. J. Clifford, *Proverbs*, OTL (Louisville: Westminster John Knox, 1999), pp. 23–28.
33. A. M. Sinnott, *The Personification of Wisdom* (Aldershot: Ashgate, 2005).

to the fall of Jerusalem in 587 BC, with the loss of the temple, the Davidic kingship and control of the land, and the exile in Babylon. The previous understanding of how Yahweh related to Israel and acted for them did not enable them to address the crisis effectively. Wisdom, personified as the voice of Yahweh, the designer and creator of the world, gave a new focus for their beliefs and relationship to Yahweh. The weakness in this argument is that nothing in Proverbs gives any hint that a serious social and spiritual crisis was a pressing issue for the sages who compiled the book. Most commentators find in it an ethos of social and ideological security, and this includes Wisdom's speeches. While making a good case for personified Wisdom being a literary creation Sinnott has not made a convincing case for the crisis of the exile being the cause of this creative act.

Israelite women and personified Wisdom

Camp[34] has argued that personified Wisdom in Proverbs 1 – 9 is a literary creation based on roles that were actually fulfilled by Israelite women.

1. In Proverbs 1:8; 6:20; 10:1; 15:20; 23:22–25 the mother shares with the father the role of passing on wisdom. The instruction given to King Lemuel by his mother is striking (31:1–9).
2. Camp argues that there are two main recurrent images of the wife in narratives in the Old Testament. The first is of the wife as the manager of the household. This is idealized in Proverbs 31:10–31. The second is that of the wife as a counsellor who can influence her husband in areas where he has decision-making authority. Abigail (1 Sam. 25) and Jezebel (1 Kgs 21) are examples.
3. The stories of the wise women of Tekoa (2 Sam. 14) and of Abel (2 Sam. 20) may indicate a particular leadership role for some women in Israelite society.
4. There were women prophets in Israel. Huldah, who authenticated the newly found book of the law, is an example (2 Kgs 22:11–20). Wisdom sometimes speaks like a prophet and has the function of authenticating the wisdom tradition.
5. Proverbs 1 – 9 contains exhortations to love wisdom. One of the genres of Ancient Near Eastern love poetry is self-description. It is used by the woman in the Song of Songs to justify or defend herself (1:5–6; 8:8–10)

---

34. C. Camp, *Wisdom and the Feminine in the Book of Proverbs* (Sheffield: Almond Press, 1985).

or to provoke the admiration and response of her lover (2:1–2). The self-description of Wisdom in Proverbs 8:6–21 makes no reference to physical beauty, but does serve the same function as these self-descriptions – to justify the speaker and to motivate the hearer's response. Self-presentations by deities or rulers are not the only possible Ancient Near Eastern sources for the origin of that motif as an aspect of the personification of wisdom in Proverbs 1 – 9.

The personification of wisdom as a woman was no doubt due, in part, to the noun for wisdom in Hebrew being feminine in grammatical gender, as are some of the other important nouns used in parallel with it, such as 'understanding' and 'prudence'. Camp makes a plausible case that this was helped by Israelite women fulfilling roles that could appropriately be assigned to Wisdom. As a literary construct personified Wisdom could combine different roles that might never be expected to be found together in any one human person. In Proverbs 8 in particular some of the claims of Wisdom transcend the purely human and here elements from concepts to do with deities and the mythological 'culture-bringers' may be incorporated.

An important consequence of the personification of wisdom is that it enables the presentation of abstract knowledge in an attractive, even sensual, way. This is seen in the use of the language of love and commitment to Wisdom, and probably of marriage (Prov. 4:5–9). As a result Wisdom is presented as more than a 'mediator' between God and humans. Rather, through Wisdom humans can come into a personal relationship with God.

Other female characters in Proverbs

The woman Folly
This character appears only in Proverbs 9:13–18. She is a literary personification created to provide an antithesis to personified Wisdom. The placing together of the vignettes of Wisdom and Folly in Proverbs 9 makes this clear. Both call out from high places in the city to the 'simple' in almost identical words. The change in order from bread/wine (9:5) to water/bread (9:17) forms a chiasmus which links the speeches together. The outcome of accepting the two invitations could not be more different: life (9:6) and death (9:18).

The Strange/Foreign Woman
This figure appears in four passages in Proverbs 1 – 9: 2:16–19; 5:1–23; 6:20–35; 7:1–27. The two Hebrew words used of her, *zārâ* ('strange') and *nokriyyâ*

('foreign'), occur in parallel in 2:16, 5:20 and 7:5. Taking the passages together one can compile a picture of her. She is married and is being unfaithful to her husband (2:17; 6:26, 29; 7:19–20). She is 'guarded of heart' (7:10), usually taken to mean 'wily, crafty'. This indicates secretiveness, hiding her motives. Maybe she is hiding things from her husband, or from her victim. She is described as physically attractive in a general way in 6:25. Her most prominent characteristic is her 'smooth words', her seductive speech (2:16; 5:3; 6:24; 7:21). Her feet wander (5:5–6) and will not stay at home (7:11). They lead to death and Sheol (5:5). The references to her 'lips' and 'feet' have sexual connotations. Lips are used not only for speaking but also for kissing (7:13). In Hebrew 'feet' can be a euphemism for the sexual organs.

Several suggestions have been made about the possible origin of this figure. One is Boström's[35] view that the Strange Woman is a foreign resident, a devotee of Aphrodite-Astarte, who seeks to lure young men into fertility rituals involving sacred prostitution and the 'sacred marriage' ritual at the new moon. If this were so it is surprising that the warning given to the young man says nothing about religious apostasy or idolatry. Blenkinsopp[36] argued that the background to the Strange/Foreign Woman is the issue of marriage to foreign women in post-exilic Judah, with which Ezra (Ezra 9 – 10) and Nehemiah (Neh. 13:23–27) contended and which is also mentioned in Malachi (Mal. 2:10–16). This had social, economic and religious dimensions. The Strange Woman, he suggested, was a literary creation intended to give a warning against such marriages. However, the warnings against the Strange Woman are warnings against adultery, not against marriage with a non-Israelite.

Since the 'lessons' in Proverbs 1 – 9 are teaching from a parent to a son the most obvious background for understanding the figure of the Strange Woman is the age-old temptation to adultery. It might seem a too mundane issue to warrant the repeated severe warnings against the Strange Woman. This, however, fails to understand the significance of adultery in ancient Israel. In discussing the socio-theological reason for the commandment against adultery in the Decalogue Wright[37] has argued that, although the land was the

---

35. G. Boström, *Proverbiastudien: Die Weisheit und das fremde Weib in Sprüche 1 – 9* (Lund: C. W. K. Gleerup, 1935), pp. 103–155.

36. J. Blenkinsopp, 'The Social Context of the "Outsider Woman" in Proverbs 1 – 9', *Bib* 72 (1991), pp. 457–473.

37. C. J. H. Wright, 'The Israelite Household and the Decalogue: The Social Background and Significance of Some Commandments', *TynB* 30 (1979), pp. 101–124.

primary symbol of the covenant relationship between Yahweh and Israel, it was the family that provided the primary tangible locus of realization of that relationship. Therefore Israel's existence as a covenant community in the land depended on the stability of the family for theological as well as socio-economic reasons. Adultery was totally unacceptable because it was a threat to the whole social order of the covenant community. The woman is 'strange' and 'foreign' because she is 'off-limits' morally and socially since she is someone else's wife.

The wife of your youth

This figure is an antithesis to the Strange Woman. This is clear in the lesson in which her description (5:15–19) is preceded (5:3–14) and followed by warnings against the Strange Woman (5:20–23). That she is called 'the wife of your youth' clearly contrasts with the description of the Strange Woman as one who 'forsakes the companion of her youth' (2:17). The contrasting of these two figures strongly suggests that the origin of the figure of the Strange Woman is in the real-life situation of the temptation to adultery and that the purpose of the warnings against her is to protect the stability of the family, and so of society as a whole.

The Woman of Worth

Proverbs is full of human role models, both negative and positive. Yoder[38] argues that the woman of Proverbs 31:10–31 is a composite of real women. She does not represent any particular woman but combines the desired attributes and activities of many. Although intended to be seen as a human person she shares many characteristics with personified Wisdom. This does not mean that the two figures are to be identified with one another. Rather, while Woman Wisdom *personifies* wisdom, the Strong Woman *typifies* wisdom by *incarnating* some of its characteristics. The Woman of Worth can be seen as a filling out of the picture of 'the wife of your youth' (5:18–19) and is the strict antithesis of the Strange Woman, who incarnates some characteristics of Folly. As a result Proverbs 31:10–31 provides a 'bracketing' of the book of Proverbs with the figure of the Woman of Worth resonating with that of personified Wisdom in Proverbs 1 – 9.

---

38. C. R. Yoder, 'The Woman of Substance (אשת־חיל): A Socioeconomic Reading of Proverbs 31:10–31', *JSOT* 122 (2003), pp. 427–447. She uses evidence from the Persian period, but does not establish that it could not be equally valid for other periods of Judean history.

Proverbs and gender issues

Because of its prominent female characters Proverbs has attracted the attention of feminist scholars. The limited portrayal of women as either desirable wife or desirable temptress has troubled some.

Brenner and van Dijk-Hemmes[39] argue that the speaker in parts of Proverbs 1 – 9 is not the father but a female (F) voice. While this might be considered a positive factor from a feminist viewpoint, this is not so for Brenner. She[40] considers that this F voice has internalized male (M) patriarchal values. In Proverbs 7 she sees not just complicity with androcentric values but overzealousness in protecting them. F self-interest is silenced through identification with M interest. She sees the F voice adopting M ideology by recommending control over female sexuality. However, another feminist scholar, Bellis,[41] sees things differently. In her view the voice urging the son to avoid the Strange Woman is countering the 'infamous double standard' which tolerated a degree of male promiscuity in Israelite society. She regards this voice as no more an internalized androcentric one than was the voice of twentieth-century feminists who challenged remnants of the same double standard. The difference is that the teacher in Proverbs seeks to undercut the double standard by limiting male sexual freedom whereas some modern feminists wish to increase female sexual freedom. Either approach could result in a 'more egalitarian ethic'. She notes that, contrary to what Brenner and others assert, the teacher tries to control not *female* sexuality but *male* sexuality. She argues that in the context of ancient Israelite society, it was more in the women's self-interest for men to be monogamous than it was in the men's. It is also worth noting that, despite what some feminists suggest, the father, if he is the 'voice' in Proverbs 1 – 9, does not have any problem with female sexuality in itself, as his advice about enjoying sexual relations with 'the wife of your youth' in Proverbs 5:15–19 shows.

The figure of the Strange Woman is, understandably, offensive to many modern readers of both genders. Yee[42] sees in it a disturbing personification

---

39. A. Brenner and C. van Dijk-Hemmes, *On Gendering Texts* (Leiden: Brill, 1993), pp. 57–62, 117–126. See the critique of their arguments by M. V. Fox, *Proverbs 1 – 9* AB (New York: Doubleday, 2000), p. 258.
40. Brenner, 'Proverbs 1 – 9: An F Voice', in *On Gendering Texts*, pp. 125–126.
41. A. O. Bellis, 'The Gender and Motives of the Wisdom Teacher in Proverbs 7', in A. Brenner and C. Fontaine (eds.), *Wisdom and Psalms* (Sheffield: Sheffield Academic Press, 1998), pp. 79–91.
42. G. A. Yee, '"I Have Perfumed My Bed with Myrrh": The Foreign Woman (*'iššâ zārâ*) in Proverbs 1 – 9', *JSOT* 43 (1989), pp. 53–68.

in a woman's form of all that is evil and destructive. Camp[43] finds some mitigation in considering the literary factors at work here. The figure is not a stereotype of a real person, or class of persons, but an imaginative construct formulated as a contrast to Woman Wisdom. She suggests a need to recognize that the wisdom tradition organizes and patterns perceptions in antithetical terms, especially its moral judgments, and depicts these judgments in vivid and memorable vignettes.

Two other things can be said in response to Yee. The first is that in Proverbs all that is good and life-giving is personified in a woman's form, Wisdom. Second, most of those who have written about the Strange Woman have taken the warnings about her as more or less isolated texts. They have not recognized that she has a male counterpart, or counterparts: different kinds of evil men. The first 'lesson' in Proverbs 1 – 9 is a lengthy warning against such male 'sinners' who use enticing speech to persuade the son into the way that will lead to death (1:8–19). There are resonances here with what is said later in the warnings against the Strange Woman. The first passage about the Strange Woman is preceded by an admonition to seek wisdom because this will provide deliverance from evil men, described in fairly vivid terms (2:12–15), as well as from the Strange Woman (2:16–22). The use of the verb 'delivered' in verses 12 and 16 links the male and female portraits. A warning against 'the wicked' (4:14–19) comes shortly before the second warning about the Strange Woman (5:1–23). Another warning against 'a wicked man' (6:12–15) precedes the warning against the 'evil woman' in 6:24–35. These evil male characters give the lie to Yee's comment that the Strange Woman personifies 'all that is evil and destructive' because they tempt the son in areas that she does not. In Proverbs 1:11–14 they offer the chance to play the role of Sheol rather than becoming its victim, to be the oppressor rather than the oppressed, and they offer wealth of the kind that Wisdom offers later on. Money, sex and power are often linked as the three great motivations to doing evil. The Strange Woman plays on only one of these. The male 'sinners' play on the other two.

Some feminists[44] see in Proverbs an expression of a patriarchal mentality in which woman is the quintessential 'Other'. Fox,[45] rightly, rejects this as a mindset that is foreign to Proverbs in which the only essential 'Other' is evildoers (and

---

43. Camp, *Wisdom and the Feminine*, pp. 116–117.
44. E.g. C. Maier, 'Conflicting Attractions: Parental Wisdom and the "Strange Woman" in Proverbs 1 – 9', in A. Brenner (ed.), *A Feminist Companion to Wisdom Literature* (Sheffield: Sheffield Academic Press, 1995), pp. 92–108.
45. Fox, *Proverbs 1 – 9*, p. 259.

sometimes fools) of both sexes who are beyond influence and redemption, having an inverted and incorrigibly perverse set of values. Women are not the 'Other' in such a radical sense.

The Woman of Worth is sometimes seen as living to advance male interests. In large part this is based on Proverbs 31:23, which implies that her activities contribute to her husband's status in the community. However, it does not follow that his status depends on that alone. The poem is silent about his activities because it is not about him, or even aiming to give a rounded view of family life: it is about the woman. It is true that she does work for others, but it is not to advance male interests, but to advance the interests of her family. If that is of primary importance to her, then she is advancing her own interests. There are feminist scholars who regard this poem as an empowering text for women. Valler[46] argues this in the case of Jewish tradition and Masenya[47] does so with regard to Northern Sotho women in Africa.

Schroer finds positive features in Proverbs.[48] She sees its idea of a just order that embraces the social and cosmic sphere as providing a basis for a feminist theology that would begin with the necessity of a world-encompassing justice and from there develop a theology of relationship. In response to those who suggest that personified Wisdom serves as a figure to bind women into a patriarchal system she points out the significance of the fact that Wisdom never appears as a motherly figure, the crucial role for women from a patriarchal perspective. Schroer thinks Wisdom provides a constructive image for women, as able to promote change. As part of this, the figure of Wisdom as a counsellor provides a non-androcentric image for women. She sees personified Wisdom as in some sense a representation of Yahweh, and therefore providing a helpful feminine aspect of God.

In conclusion, it is worth saying that all readers who want to apply the message of Proverbs (or any part of the Bible) to their lives today have to face the hermeneutic task of 'cultural transposition' of the message. This involves imagining themselves in the place of the original addressee(s) in order to understand what the message of the text is, and then considering how it might apply to their situation today in a different historical and cultural setting. The poem about the Woman of Worth presents men with the challenge of asking what it

---

46. S. Valler, 'Who Is *'ēšet ḥayil* in Rabbinic Literature?', in Brenner, *A Feminist Companion to Wisdom Literature*, pp. 85–97.
47. M. Masenya, 'Proverbs 31:10–31 in a South African Context: A Reading for the Liberation of African (North Sotho) Women', *Semeia* 28 (1997), pp. 55–68.
48. S. Schroer, *Wisdom Has Built Her House* (Collegeville: Liturgical Press, 2000).

would mean to be a Man of Worth today who incarnates the characteristics of wisdom presented in Proverbs. Psalm 112, an acrostic poem about a man who fears Yahweh, provides a possible template for doing such a cultural transposition. The warnings about the Strange Woman present women with an undoubtedly more difficult task of cultural transposition. One feminist scholar, Bellis,[49] provides an example of how this might be done in 'A Letter to My Daughters'.

Wisdom and creation

Although there are few explicit references to creation, or God as Creator/Maker, in Proverbs there is a general consensus that 'creation theology' is a significant element in the book. This is due, in part, to two passages in which Wisdom is spoken of as being involved in some way in the creation of the world. The first passage, Proverbs 8:22–31, is part of a long poem with a clear three-part structure. At first sight the other passage, 3:19–20, may seem an isolated snippet. However, as von Rad noted,[50] it has a context that parallels that of Proverbs 8:22–31, as shown in Table 2.

Table 2: Von Rad's structures for Proverbs 3:13–26 and 8:1–36

3:13–18	8:1–21	In praise of wisdom
3:19–20	8:22–31	The role of wisdom in creation
3:21–26	8:32–36	An appeal to follow wisdom

The use of forms of the root 'šr ('blessed/happy') forming an *inclusio* marks Proverbs 3:13–18 off as a distinct unit. However, the use of the word-pair 'wisdom/understanding' in verses 13 and 19 links this unit with the following one. Although Proverbs 3:21–26 is the introduction to a new 'lesson' given by the father to his son, the placing of the previous two units before it seems to have been done deliberately to give the same pattern as that found in Proverbs 8.

Proverbs 3:13–26

In Proverbs 3:13–18 wisdom is declared to be more valuable than silver, gold and precious stones because she offers life, riches, honour and well-being (*šālôm*). Van

---

49. Bellis, 'Gender and Motives', pp. 90–91.
50. G. von Rad, *Wisdom in Israel* (London: SCM, 1972), p. 151, n. 4.

Leeuwen[51] argued that the use of 'founded', 'established' and 'understanding/ skill' in Proverbs 3:19–20 implies the use of the metaphor of house-building with reference to creation. The role wisdom plays in creation is unclear, though most commentators take the preposition '*b*' in an instrumental sense. It is debatable whether wisdom here is simply an attribute of God or whether the personification of wisdom in the previous unit is meant to be carried over so that she becomes an agent in creation. This seems unlikely. What is clear is that wisdom's involvement in creation provides the reason why wisdom can offer the benefits listed in the previous unit. The way to get the most out of life in this world is to understand how it works and to understand its rhythms and patterns. The best way to do this is to become acquainted with the wisdom that was involved in the creation of the world. Recognizing this provides the basis for the appeal to follow wisdom in Proverbs 3:21–26.

Proverbs 8:1–36

Wisdom is personified in Proverbs 8 and after the initial introduction she speaks in the first person.

In Proverbs 8:4–21 Wisdom speaks about herself. She stresses the value of her instruction (8:4–11), describes her character (8:12–13) and speaks of the benefits she offers to society (8:14–16) and to individuals (8:17–21). There are echoes of Proverbs 3:13–26 in Proverbs 8:10–11, 18. In all this Wisdom speaks in the present tense. Although Wisdom continues to be the subject in Proverbs 8:22–31, the focus shifts to the past and to Yahweh, signalled by his name being the opening word of 8:22. He is the subject of the active verbs in 8:22–29, which refer to his acts of creation. As a result, Wisdom's status is defined in relation to Yahweh and his actions in creation.

Commentators disagree about how Wisdom's origin is depicted here. The meaning of *qānānî* (v. 22) is a key issue. In the Old Testament[52] and in Proverbs the verb *qānâ* nearly always means 'to acquire, to possess' (e.g. 1:5; 4:5, 7), often by purchase (e.g. 20:14). In a few passages the meaning 'to create' is possible[53] (Gen. 4:1; 14:19, 22; Deut. 32:6; Ps. 139:13; Prov. 8:22) and in Psalm 104:24 the derivative *qinyān* seems to mean 'creatures'. Except in Genesis 4:1, God is always the subject of the verb in these examples. Arguably, just as in a number of cases

---

51. R. C. Van Leeuwen, 'Cosmos, Temple, House: Building and Wisdom in Mesopotamia and Israel', in R. J. Clifford (ed.), *Wisdom Literature in Mesopotamia and Israel* (Atlanta: SBL, 2007), pp. 67–90.
52. *NIDOTTE* 3:941.
53. Waltke, *Proverbs 1 – 15*, pp. 408–409.

the context suggests a narrowing of meaning from 'to acquire' to 'to purchase', so in these cases the context suggests the more specific meaning 'to create'. In Genesis 4:1, Deuteronomy 32:6 and Psalm 139:13 the context of parenthood suggests the meaning 'to procreate'. This rendering can be supported by the epithet *qnyt 'lm* ([pro-]creator of the gods) which is applied five times to Asherah in Ugaritic texts.[54]

Subsequent verses in Proverbs 8 use the imagery of procreation. In 8:24–25 Wisdom says 'I was brought forth' (*ḥōllātî*), using a verb denoting a mother's birth labours (Isa. 13:8; 23:4). It is used of Yahweh in Deuteronomy 32:18 and Psalm 90:2 but never of human males. The verb *nissaktî* in 8:23 is problematic. If taken to be from the verb *nsk*, 'to be poured out', giving the literal meaning 'I was poured out', it makes little sense here. So here it may be derived from another verb, *skk*, meaning 'to weave, form'.[55] That verb is used in Psalm 139:13b of God 'knitting together' the embryo in the womb. In context it seems best to translate 8:22 as 'The Lord gave birth to me' and see a consistent birth imagery running through 8:22–25. This imagery is, of course, being used figuratively (cf. Deut. 32:18; Isa. 46:3–4; 66:13).

The description of the creation of the earth uses the imagery of house-building, with terms such as 'shaped' (8:25), 'established' (8:27–28), 'made firm' (8:28), 'foundations' (8:29). The listing of the features of the cosmos begins with the waters of the deep (8:24a) and generally moves upwards to the sky and the clouds (8:27–28) before descending again to the seashore and the foundations of the earth (8:29). This presents the creation as a coherent structure, not an unconnected assemblage of parts. It implies that there is a plan, a pattern, to it all.

Verse 30 is the centre of much debate because the third word in the MT (*'āmôn*) occurs only here in the Old Testament and its meaning is uncertain. The following are the more likely of many suggested possibilities.

1. Most commentators take it as a loanword from Akkadian *ummānu* via Aramaic, meaning 'artisan/craftsman'. They appeal to the word *'ommān* in Song of Songs 7:1 [Heb. 7:2] which probably means 'master craftsman'. However, in the context nothing is said about Wisdom doing anything in the process of creation.
2. Some accept the meaning 'craftsman' but take the word as being in apposition to the pronominal suffix, so that it refers to God, not

---

54. Clifford, *Proverbs*, p. 96.
55. *NIDOTTE* 3:253–254.

Wisdom: 'I was beside him, the craftsman.' This seems odd in context, where some further description of Wisdom would seem appropriate.
3. Clifford[56] accepts that the word is a loanword from the Akkadian *ummānu* and re-vocalizes it as *'ommān* but argues that the background is the Babylonian mythology about the post-flood culture-bringing sages, called *ummānu*. He takes Wisdom to be saying, 'I was at his side as a (heavenly) sage' – that is, as a heavenly figure who mediates to humans the knowledge they need in order to live as the Creator intends. However, Clifford provides only limited evidence that this mythology was widely enough known outside Babylon for a Hebrew author to allude to it.
4. Some take the word to mean something like 'nursling', 'cherished child'. This requires emending the MT to *'amûn*, taking it as a *qal* passive participle. It is argued that this fits the context well, coming after the account of Wisdom's birth and before possible reference to her playing like a child. However, one might expect a feminine form of the passive participle. Also, what follows need not refer to a child's play.

None of these possibilities is totally compelling. On balance, and it is a fine judgment, (3) seems to fit the context best. It prepares the way for what is said about Wisdom's role in instructing humans in 8:32–35. Even if the mythology was unknown, the meaning 'court expert/counsellor', attested in Akkadian[57] for *ummānu*, may have been known and would present much the same picture of Wisdom. As time went on that meaning was forgotten and the word became a puzzle.

The significance of these verses about the origin of Wisdom before the creation of the earth and her presence with the Creator during it is that they support Wisdom's claim to provide the benefits promised in 8:12–21 and give the basis for the appeal to heed her instruction in 8:32–36. They establish her position and authority in various ways:

1. She has an intimate relationship with the Creator as his child.
2. The significance of her origin before anything else and her presence during the creation of the earth is indicated by Eliphaz's taunt to Job, 'Are you the first man who was born, brought forth before the hills? Have you listened in the council of God and does wisdom belong to you alone?' (Job 15:7–8).

---

56. Clifford, *Proverbs*, pp. 23–28.
57. *AHw* III, 1415–1416.

3. Her observation of the plan and process of creation fits her to be the one who teaches humans how to live rightly in that creation. God's questions to Job are relevant here: 'Who is this that darkens counsel with words without knowledge? . . . Where were you when I laid the foundations of the earth?' (Job 38:2–4).
4. For these reasons, plus her delight in the creation and humans, Wisdom is ideally suited to mediate between the Creator and his human creatures.

By relating wisdom to creation Proverbs 3:19–20 and 8:22–31 express something fundamental in the worldview of Israel's sages. What Kidner[58] says of Proverbs 8 is true of both passages: they are 'an exposure of the main framework of [Proverbs'] thought'. They assert the status and authority of wisdom, and so of the wisdom tradition. There is an order and pattern to creation that is known to wisdom. Proverbs 8:24–29 presents this in terms of the physical creation. Because of what Wisdom says about herself in moral terms in 8:7–8, the fact that she delights in the creation implies that there is moral pattern and purpose too. Through coming to know Wisdom and heeding her instruction humans can live in harmony with this order. This will be to live as God intended humans to live in his creation, and so to get the most out of life. However, this does not lead to a straightforward natural theology or to seeking 'oneness with nature' as the basis for a good life. Proverbs insists that 'the fear of Yahweh is the beginning of wisdom, and the knowledge of the Holy One is insight' (9:10). Trust in, and obedience to, Yahweh are preconditions for perceiving and understanding his plans and purposes to be seen in the patterns of his creation.

Wisdom, creation and Christology

The personification of wisdom in Proverbs was developed in later Jewish wisdom literature. These developments influenced how early Christian thinkers, from the New Testament writers onwards, expressed their beliefs about Jesus. In at least three places in the New Testament scholars see evidence of ideas about wisdom influencing what is said about Jesus.

Hebrews 1:1–4. Although wisdom is not explicitly mentioned here, commentators recognize echoes of what is said about personified Wisdom in Wisdom of Solomon 7:25–26. There are also allusions to wider ideas about wisdom in the references to the creation of the world (Wis. 7:22; 8:6; 9:2), the upholding

---

58. D. Kidner, *Proverbs*, TOTC (London: Inter-Varsity Press, 1964), p. 52.

of the universe (Wis. 1:7; 8:1) and 'sitting at the right hand of Majesty on high' (Wis. 9:4, 10).

Colossians 1:15–20. This carefully constructed poem has two strophes (1:15–16, 18b–20), linked by their opening phrases: 'he is . . . the firstborn . . .' The first speaks of the supremacy of Christ over the 'old creation', the cosmos. The second speaks of his supremacy over the 'new creation', the church. The strophes are connected by a 'hinge' consisting of two statements, each beginning, 'He is . . .' Dunn comments on 1:15–17, 'the writer here is taking over language used of divine Wisdom and reusing it to express the significance of Christ.'[59]

John 1:1–18. Scholars have long debated possible backgrounds to John's use of the Logos concept. Jewish wisdom thought is widely accepted as part of that background. Lincoln says, 'The origins of the prologue's use of "the Word" are in all probability to be found in Jewish thought about both Wisdom and the Word of God.'[60]

The reuse and development of Jewish thought about personified Wisdom gave the New Testament writers the concepts and language to speak of Jesus as the incarnation of the pre-existent Word/Son who was the agent in creation. As a result they saw in the mission of Jesus a uniting of God's purposes in creation and salvation. All too often Christians have not held these two things together in their thinking. However, this intimate connection between creation and salvation which arose out of the influence of wisdom thought on the understanding and significance of Jesus and his incarnation, death and resurrection has great significance in the light of the ecological crisis which faces us in the twenty-first century.

© Ernest C. Lucas, 2016

---

59. J. D. G. Dunn, *The Epistle to the Colossians and Philemon*, NIGTC (Carlisle: Paternoster, 1996), p. 89.
60. A. T. Lincoln, *The Gospel According to John*, BNTC (London: Continuum, 2005), p. 95.

3. JOB AS A PROBLEMATIC BOOK

Lindsay Wilson

Introduction

Throughout the dialogue of his book, Job is constantly accused of being a person who has abandoned his former faith in God (Job 1:1, 8; 2:3). Eliphaz, Bildad and Zophar all accuse Job of some form of sin which warrants his present suffering (e.g. 4:17; 8:3–6; 11:4–6). Job's situation of professing faith and extensive suffering was deeply problematic to the tradition represented by the three friends.

Just as the character Job had problems in persuading others that he was a person of faith, so the book of Job has struggled to convince some detractors that it is a book of faith. To some modern commentators, it is greatly troubling. In the light of the words he utters about God, how can he be regarded as a person of faith? Even more vexing for some are the actions of God. If Job is a righteous human being, why does God permit him to suffer so greatly (1:13–19; 2:7)? On the other hand, if Job is not a person of faith, why does God originally commend him, indeed boast about him (1:8; 2:3)? Furthermore, why does God later endorse the stance Job has taken throughout the book, and rebuke the friends (42:7–9)? If the character Job is problematic, then God is also problematic.

There are many issues to explore in connection with the book of Job, and to cover them all would simply be skimming over the surface of a long book which demands to be read slowly.¹ While this chapter will look back over previous scholarship – and around at current approaches – it will mainly look forward to areas where the book of Job can be further and fruitfully explored by God's people.

An overview of previous and current approaches

I do not propose to survey how the book of Job has been interpreted over thousands of years of church history, as this has been done elsewhere.[2] During the first seventy years of the twentieth century, much of the scholarly interest centred on identifying later additions to the book, Ancient Near Eastern parallels and issues of suffering, theodicy and retribution. However, the book of Job was caught up in the broader movement in Old Testament studies to read the book in its final form as a literary whole, with commentaries by Andersen, Habel, Hartley and Janzen, and more recently by Newsom, G. Wilson, Walton and Estes. Of course, during this time there were other readings as well, such as the liberationist reading of Gutiérrez, a deconstructionist reading by the later Clines, studies focusing on genre (e.g. Dell), and approaches to the book based on feminist, psychoanalytical and philosophical readings. There has also been a plethora of literary studies on either the book as a whole or individual parts, often based on the work of particular literary theorists. Many of these issues and approaches have been helpfully outlined by Katharine Dell.[3] Seow has begun to work on reception history and Job, and Clines' massive commentary has explored the use of Job in music, literature and art.[4] The issue of Job and intertexuality has been the subject of a recent volume as well.[5]

---

1. On this, see L. Wilson, *Job*, THOTC (Grand Rapids/Cambridge: Eerdmans, 2015), pp. 26–27.
2. See K. J. Dell, *The Book of Job as Sceptical Literature*, BZAW 197 (Berlin: De Gruyter, 1991), pp. 5–56. For a brief summary see L. Wilson, 'Job, Book of', in K. J. Vanhoozer (ed.), *Dictionary for the Theological Interpretation of the Bible* (Grand Rapids: Baker Academic, 2005), pp. 384–385; and *Job*, pp. 11–13.
3. K. J. Dell, *Job: Where Shall Wisdom Be Found?*, Phoenix Guides to the OT (Sheffield: Sheffield Phoenix, 2013).
4. C.-L. Seow, *Job 1 – 21* (Grand Rapids: Eerdmans, 2013); D. J. A. Clines, *Job 1 – 20*, WBC (Dallas: Word, 1989); *Job 21 – 37*, WBC (Nashville: Nelson, 2006); and *Job 38 – 42*, WBC (Nashville: Nelson, 2011).
5. K. Dell and W. Kynes (eds.), *Reading Job Intertextually*, LHBOTS 574 (New York: Bloomsbury T&T Clark, 2013).

Many of these studies have been insightful, but at times there has been a greater emphasis on the usefulness of the methodology (such as intertextuality) rather than on its interpretive value for the book of Job. This chapter will focus on the issues of human faith and the portrayal of God, drawing out some implications for the contemporary world.

Job and faith

Is Job a person of unblemished faith or not? Two intertwined issues will be explored here. First, is Job's use of laments and complaints consistent with him being regarded as one who is faithful to God? Second, does his pursuit of litigation against God disqualify him from being regarded as righteous?[6]

Lament and complaint

The picture of Job as a person of faith (which God attests to in 42:7–9) is certainly challenged by many today as a result of his strident and even accusing words addressed to God. In 6:4, he complains that

> the arrows of the Almighty are in me;
> > my spirit drinks their poison;
> > the terrors of God are arrayed against me. (ESV)

This does not sound like a typical after-church comment, for he is suggesting that God is firing (metaphorical) poisoned arrows at him and terrifying him. Job accuses God of making him his target (7:20), multiplying his wounds without cause (9:17). He complains that God is oppressing and despising him (10:3), hiding his face from Job and counting him as an enemy (13:24). Indeed, he portrays God as having mounted a full-scale attack on him (16:7–16). Some ministers I know would offer Job a cup of tea in the hope that this might settle him down. For what is often missed about Job's bold words is that he assumes that God is in absolute control of what happens in his world. This big view of God is behind his accusatory words. It may not be 'church-speak' but it is certainly 'God-speak'. The world is not reduced to a secular closed circle from which God is excluded. If it happens in God's world, Job sees God as the one to turn to in the midst of life's struggles.

---

6. This section will draw significantly on my commentary, *Job*, especially pp. 219–257.

Job's wish that he had never been born (3:3–12, 20–23) should be read sympathetically. Though some have understood Job to be calling for an undoing of creation,[7] there is no animosity against God and he even calls on God to be his ally (3:4). Habel comments that 'his curse falls on a past event which would appear to be irreversible'.[8] It is one of many times in the book where Job explores hypothetical possibilities (9:14–20; 13:15; 14:13–17; 19:25–27).[9] None of these are *realistic* possibilities, but Job explores them all as he is backed into one corner after another.

Lament is prevalent throughout the book. Hughes identifies seven laments: 3:11–26; 6:2 – 7:21; chapters 9–10; 13:3 – 14:22; 16:1 – 17:16; chapter 19; and chapters 23–24; but Job's reflection on the prospering of the wicked in chapter 21 and his summary lament of his present life in chapter 30 should also be included.[10] Laments are thus found in Job's speeches right through the dialogue section, and they are a crucial part of the book. In the light of recent scholarship in Psalms and Lamentations,[11] it would be interesting to look for fresh insights in Job.

Yet Job's strong words of protest addressed to God in the dialogue are the ones that seem to sit most awkwardly with his earlier piety. Many Christians have been hesitant to embrace the laments, based on a suspicion that they are sub-Christian. However, a striking feature of Job's laments is that, even in the darkest times of feeling forsaken by God, he still laments and complains *to God*.

---

7. E.g. D. Cox, 'The Desire for Oblivion in Job 3', *Studii biblici franciscani liberannus* 23 (1973), pp. 38, 48.
8. N. C. Habel, *The Book of Job*, OTL (London: SCM, 1985), p. 107.
9. Wilson, *Job*, pp. 351–352.
10. R. A. Hughes, *Lament, Death, and Destiny*, StBL 68 (New York: Peter Lang, 2004), pp. 37–39. See also W. S. Morrow, *Protest Against God: The Eclipse of a Biblical Tradition*, HBM 4 (Sheffield: Sheffield Phoenix, 2006), p. 132.
11. A. Sloane, 'Lament and the Journey of Doubt', *Christian Scholar's Review* 29/1 (1999), pp. 113–127; M. Boulton, 'Forsaking God: A Theological Argument for Christian Lamentation', *SJT* 55 (2002), pp. 58–78; S. A. Brown and P. D. Miller (eds.), *Lament* (Louisville: Westminster John Knox, 2005); M. Card, *A Sacred Sorrow: Reaching Out to God in the Lost Language of Lament* (Colorado Springs: NavPress, 2005); N. C. Lee, *Lyrics of Lament: From Tragedy to Transformation* (Minneapolis: Fortress, 2010). On Lamentations see R. A. Parry and H. A. Thomas, *Great Is Thy Faithfulness? Reading Lamentations as Sacred Scripture* (Eugene: Wipf & Stock, 2011); H. A. Thomas, *Poetry and Theology in the Book of Lamentations: The Aesthetics of an Open Text*, HBM (Sheffield: Sheffield Phoenix, 2013).

He levels bold questions and even accusations against God, but God is still the one he turns to. Andersen comments that 'at least he keeps on talking to the heedless God. His friends talk about God. Job talks to God.'[12] His laments express a faith that is not shaken by God's apparent silence.

Thus the movement within the lament from questioning to a restored relationship is of crucial significance. The lament is, of course, not primarily about the venting of feelings, since it is fundamentally a plea or petition for change or help. Westermann rightly observes that 'petition, or at any rate something like petition, intrinsically belongs to the lament'.[13] Job is not looking for an intellectual solution for his suffering. He wants a way out of the conflict between his faith and his experience, a dilemma neatly summarized by Bergant: 'Job's ... religious beliefs tell him how life should be. His present situation tells him something different.'[14] He refuses to form his ideas solely from his present experience, without reference to his past dealings with, and knowledge of, God. The goal of the lament is thus 'to lay out one's own inner sufferings before the one who alleviates suffering, heals wounds and dries tears'.[15] Though Job's complaints include blame and rebuke, the underlying dynamic is Job's desire to have his relationship with God restored. Simundson suggests that 'the lament gives the sufferer words to use, a way of bringing into the open what is difficult to express, so that it may be acknowledged and worked through in some meaningful process'.[16]

Surely the verdict of God should control our reading of Job's laments, and God concludes that not only was Job blameless and upright at the beginning (1:8; 2:3), but also what Job said about God during the debate was right (42:7–8). Since Job spoke about God in laments, God must therefore be endorsing at least the general thrust of Job's complaints.

Followers of God need a language that will express their deepest feelings to God both in times of joy and in times of great suffering and anguish. The Bible

---

12. F. I. Andersen, *Job*, TOTC (Leicester: Inter-Varsity Press, 1976), p. 98.
13. C. Westermann, *The Structure of the Book of Job*, tr. C. A. Muenchow (Philadelphia: Fortress, 1977), p. 67.
14. D. Bergant, 'Why Do I Suffer?', *The Bible Today* 20 (1982), p. 343.
15. C. Westermann, 'The Role of the Lament in the Theology of the Old Testament', *Interpretation* 28 (1974), p. 32.
16. D. J. Simundson, *Faith Under Fire* (Minneapolis: Augsburg, 1980), pp. 58–59. D. J. Simundson, *The Message of Job: A Theological Commentary*, Augsburg OT Studies (Minneapolis: Augsburg, 1986), p. 107, observes, 'Job had wanted to lament, but his friends wanted to argue theology.'

provides both in songs of praise and thanks, and in laments. It is always appropriate to be honest before the God of the theophany who knows and sustains all things. God will never be 'blown away' by the strength of our language. As Murphy expresses it, 'One of the significant gifts of the book is honest language in conversing with God.'[17]

Hartley has argued that Job has deliberately adapted the lament form.[18] The greatest overlap is in the lament proper and petition. Here, Job has replaced the affirmation of trust or expression of confidence with protestations of innocence (6:29; 16:17; 23:10–12). Hartley also points out a movement within the dialogue from 'despairing laments to determined oaths' (in lieu of a vow to praise) in 27:2–6 and chapter 31.[19]

One way of seeing Job's perseverance (Jas 5:11) more clearly is to look at the options which were open to him but which he did not take. In adopting his twin protests of pursuing litigation and complaining or lamenting, Job has effectively excluded a number of quite foreseeable options which would have been a failure of faith. First, he has resisted the temptation to go through the motions of repenting so that God would have to ease his suffering and restore his blessings. This was the response suggested by his friends. Second, he nowhere contemplates the path of suicide. Third, he does not curse God. Fourth, Job does not take time out from his relationship with God. Job does call on God to leave him alone (7:16; 10:20; 14:6), but this is only part of the picture. He still asks God to 'remember' him and what he is like (7:7; 10:9; 14:13), and it is Job who keeps on initiating conversation with God as he characteristically turns in his speeches from talking to the friends (6:1–30; 12:1 – 13:19) to addressing God (7:1–21; 13:20 – 14:22). His deepest longing is not for God's absence, but for a restored presence (14:15).

What are the implications, then, of this robust faith in God expressed in lament? This is an area where further work is needed, and some writers have begun to explore the book's contribution here. Capps saw that the use of reframing was common to some forms of pastoral counselling and to the book of Job.[20] Hulme and Atkinson have written pastoral commentaries on

---

17. R. E. Murphy, 'The Last Truth about God', *RevExp* 99 (2002), p. 586.
18. J. E. Hartley, 'From Lament to Oath: A Study of Progression in the Speeches of Job', in W. A. M. Beuken (ed.), *The Book of Job*, BETL (Leuven: Leuven University Press, 1994), pp. 89–91.
19. Hartley, 'From Lament to Oath', p. 89.
20. D. Capps, *Reframing: A New Method in Pastoral Care* (Minneapolis: Fortress, 1990), pp. 111–168.

Job.[21] In more recent times, there has been a flurry of articles and books exploring the usefulness of Job for pastoral care.[22] My experience has been that those struggling with life often find it quite liberating to hear Job talking as he does and still receiving the commendation from God that Job has spoken of him what is right (42:7–8).

The book gives helpful perspectives about how to care for others once a crisis has arisen. Job's friends come with the best of intentions, 'to show him sympathy and comfort him' (2:11).[23] However, they soon depart from their considered approach, as they jump to protect God's honour in response to Job's angry words in chapter 3. Eliphaz hears Job questioning God's ruling of his world (4:7–11) and the presence of sin (4:17–19) and discipline (5:17). Bildad is provoked to respond when he understands Job to be questioning God's justice (8:3) and the traditional teachings of the elders (8:8–10). Zophar is exasperated by Job's bold, self-justifying words and implication of sinlessness (11:2–4). Yet the friends respond so quickly to Job's outbursts that they do not take the time to work out the real nature of his dilemma. In responding to Job's apparently wrong understandings, they show that they have moved on from caring for Job as a person to correcting his defective theology. They have reduced his despair to an intellectual problem. Thus, they may say many true words (God is just, God runs the world, God will judge sin), but these were not the words that Job needed to hear, for they did not address his deepest problem. He longed for the presence of a seemingly absent God, but the friends never addressed this longing.

---

21. W. E. Hulme, *Dialogue in Despair: Pastoral Commentary on the Book of Job* (Nashville: Abingdon, 1968); D. Atkinson, *The Message of Job: Suffering and Grace*, BST (Leicester: Inter-Varsity Press, 1991).
22. W. E. Hulme, 'Pastoral Counseling in the Book of Job', *Concordia Journal* 15 (1989), pp. 121–138; G. M. Schwab, 'The Book of Job and Counsel in the Whirlwind', *Journal of Biblical Counseling* 17 (1998), pp. 31–43; P. H. Byrne, 'Give Sorrow Words: Lament – Contemporary Need for Job's Old Time Religion', *Journal of Pastoral Care and Counseling* 56 (2002), pp. 255–264; J. S. Reitman, 'God's "Eye" for the *Imago Dei*: Wise Advocacy amid Disillusionment in Job and Ecclesiastes', *Trinity Journal* 31/1 (Spring 2010), pp. 115–134; J. L. Ramsey, 'First Do No Harm: Pastoral Care Informed by Job', *Word & World* 31/4 (2011), pp. 367–373.
23. D. D. Hopkins and M. S. Koppel, *Grounded in the Living Word: The Old Testament and Pastoral Care Practices* (Grand Rapids: Eerdmans, 2010), p. 21: 'The best thing that Job's friends did for him was to sit with him for seven days and seven nights in empathic silence . . . Listening presence requires a bracketing of our own tendency to judge, explain, or justify.'

There is an increasing defensiveness as the debate progresses. Even in the first cycle there is a progression from the respectful correction of Eliphaz (5:8) to the sterner rebuke of Bildad, who suggests that he is less of a sinner than his children (8:4–6). Zophar even more aggressively claims that Job has been punished less than he deserves (11:6c). Hopkins and Koppel have suggested that 'the repeated use of rhetorical questions by Job's friends serves to shut down any real conversation'.[24] Thus, Zophar turns a pastoral situation into a challenge by asking, 'Can you find out the deep things of God?' (11:7). Hopkins and Koppel claim that 'rhetorical questions . . . encourage defensiveness. Asking them is often the worst thing we can do in a pastoral care situation.'[25] The friends then become stronger in their accusations against Job, so that in the third cycle Eliphaz, the most moderate of the friends, brings out a long list of Job's offences (22:5–9).

Job's bold, forthright words are the fruit of a deep but anguished relationship with God. This 'rhetoric of outrage' consists of words which come from raw pain and need to be understood in that context.[26] Behind the common question 'why' (e.g. 3:11–12, 20) is ultimately a call for God's presence and care. Since God finally endorses Job's words (42:7–8), this has implications for pastoral care. Rather than censor our words to God, there is a need to be honest before him about what we are thinking and feeling, even if it does not reflect reality. The God of the book of Job is big enough to field our accusations and complaints.

God's responses to Job's words – and the corrections of the friends – are telling. He does not respond to each accusation which Job had made, apparently understanding that Job's deepest need was not to have an intellectual answer to his many questions. Yet God's very appearance to Job, and what he chooses to say, does help Job from a pastoral point of view. As Whybray notes, 'it is the loss of his former personal relationship with God that is Job's chief lament.'[27] Job's deepest longing was for the presence of God; for God to remember him and act towards him in care.

---

24. Hopkins and Koppel, *Grounded*, p. 21. They comment that 'the friends' attack simply pushes Job into hurling his own rhetorical questions back at them', such as in 6:12 or 7:17–19.
25. Hopkins and Koppel, *Grounded*, p. 21. They comment, 'Job's friends illustrate the authoritarian use of Scripture in a pastoral care situation.'
26. D. A. Carson, *How Long, O Lord? Reflections on Suffering and Evil*, 2nd edn (Grand Rapids: Baker, 2006), pp. 87–88.
27. R. N. Whybray, *The Good Life in the Old Testament* (London: T&T Clark, 2002), p. 139.

However, God's words in the speeches also help Job to be redirected towards God's more panoramic perspective. He does not need to understand how God runs the world; he needs instead to see that God can be trusted to run the world. Job had confined God to rewarding human righteousness and punishing human wickedness, but God's sovereign ruling of the world involves the wider picture of the entire creation. Seeing something of God's wider plan, Job can trust God in a new way, and resume his former role in society (42:11). God discerned the deeper, underlying issue, addressed this in his words to Job, and this set Job free.

There is a danger in pastoral ministry to respond with advice (even an answer backed up by a Bible verse) to each question asked by someone in pain or confusion. Often there is a need to look beyond the presenting question to the more fundamental issue that needs to be addressed in order to bring lasting healing or change. While the book of Job is not intended as a manual for pastoral care, the way that God treats Job is very instructive.

The laments are a legitimate part of a robust adult faith which knows that God will not be shattered or provoked by strong words of protest. Unlike many of us, God does not avoid conflict, for he knows that the honest expression of where we are at is essential for our transformation. To ask 'Where is God?' in the midst of one's sufferings is based on faith that God could do something about the circumstances if he chose. Desmond Tutu, reflecting on the struggle in South Africa, pointed out that the perplexity which is behind laments comes from a belief that God is good, loving and powerful. This big view of God creates a problem when God does not seem to act in response to those calling out to him.[28]

Complaining to God was better than the path of silent submission, for the latter would neither allow for expression of the loss, nor petition for a restored relationship. The friends, however, misread Job's complaints as 'armchair questions' when they were really 'wheelchair questions'.[29] Their category mistake renders them unable to hear and respond to the real issues in Job's words, and provokes Job into further despair. Andersen appropriately notes that even 'True words may be thin medicine for a man in the depths'.[30]

---

28. Quoted in G. Gutiérrez, *On Job*, tr. M. J. O'Connell (Maryknoll: Orbis, 1987), p. xv.
29. A distinction made by C. Ash, *Out of the Storm: Grappling with God in the Book of Job* (Leicester: Inter-Varsity Press, 2004), pp. 12–13. Andersen, *Job*, p. 190, comments, 'the friends are detached, Job is involved; they are on the balcony, he is in the street.'
30. Andersen, *Job*, pp. 123–124.

The pursuit of litigation

The legal metaphor is often missed by readers who do not naturally think about a relationship with God in litigation categories. There are two distinguishable streams of the book's litigation motif.[31] The first is Job's use of forensic categories such as taking God to court as a way of resolving his present dilemma. It pervades much of the book of Job,[32] and is not entirely surprising, since in both the court setting and the trial of Job's faith, the prologue is relying on an underlying legal analogy. The second is Job's calling on a legal figure, variously described as an arbiter (9:33), witness (16:19), redeemer (19:25) and hearer (31:35), to intervene and settle the dispute. A crucial question is whether these actions are being presented as consistent with Job's piety in the prologue.

Certainly, one of Job's core commitments is to the promotion of justice, which he understands is based on the doctrine of retribution. Clines has suggested that the book of Job deconstructs itself by both affirming and denying the doctrine of retribution.[33] However, Carson rightly insists that 'the book does not disown all forms of retribution; rather, it disowns simplistic, mathematically precise, and instant applications of the doctrine of retribution'.[34] In fact, the book no more denies the idea of retribution than it rejects the notion of God's justice. It is affirming the flexible and partial perspective of retribution which is found in Proverbs, but which had been calcified over the years until it had become a weapon used on sufferers like Job.

Job first contemplates entering into a legal dispute with God in 9:3, but he understands the problems in bringing God to trial (9:3, 14–16) and the difficulty of getting a fair hearing (9:17, 19, 32–34). As chapter 13 begins, Job announces his plan to argue the case he has prepared (13:3, 6, 18), calling for litigation (13:19, 22) and asking for details of the charges against him (13:23). From 13:24 until the end of the speech in chapter 14, he lets the idea of litigation lapse in order to express the depth of his pain.[35] This pattern of floating the possibility of litigation, then letting it go, suggests that the pursuit of litigation is an imaginative exploration of a possibility, rather than a realistic proposal.

---

31. For more detail, see Wilson, *Job*, pp. 230–243.
32. Habel, *The Book of Job*, p. 54.
33. D. J. A. Clines, 'Deconstructing the Book of Job', in *What Does Eve Do to Help? And Other Readerly Questions to the Old Testament*, JSOTSup 94 (Sheffield: Sheffield Academic Press, 1990), pp. 106–123.
34. Carson, *How Long?*, p. 155.
35. Habel, *The Book of Job*, p. 231; Clines, *Job 1 – 20*, p. 316.

Job closes the cycle of speeches in chapter 27 with an insistence that he be vindicated. Here Job resumes his case (27:1) and complains that God has denied him his right (27:2). He asserts with an oath that he has not perjured himself (27:2–4), that he will not concede that God is in the right (27:5), nor will he give up his claim to be a person of integrity (27:5) and righteousness (27:6).

Job also calls for a legal figure on three different occasions in chapters 3–27, using three different terms.[36] Job first considers the possibility of a legal figure in 9:32–35, when he calls for an arbiter or mediator (9:33). In 16:19–22 he looks to a heavenly witness, and in 19:25–27 he envisages a redeemer. The figures mentioned in 9:33, 16:19 and 19:25 are not three separate identities, but the one 'hope' who is variously described. The 'redeemer' of 19:25 is none other than the 'witness' of 16:19 and the 'umpire' of 9:33.

One significant feature of the litigation motif here is that Job is not just making a demand for justice or vindication, but looks forward to seeing God (19:26–27). Thus, underlying the picture of taking God to court is Job's deeper desire for a restored relationship. Job's pursuit of a legal figure is therefore presented as part of genuine piety.

The climax of the developing legal process is Job's summing up of his legal case in chapters 29 – 31. In this comprehensive review, Job rehearses his former righteousness (29:14), set against his present sufferings (ch. 30). This leads to an extended oath of innocence in chapter 31, culminating in a call for a 'hearer', another legal figure. If neither a 'hearer' nor his adversary appears, Job's oath of innocence stands and he is cleared of all charges and vindicated. This summing up begins with a longing for a restored relationship with God (29:2), so that it is clear that Job's aim in pursuing litigation is not to belittle or defeat God.

In response, Elihu attempts to prove to the 'court' that Job's demand for a trial is empty and meaningless (35:13–14). The transcendence of God (35:5–8) implies that God's will is to be discerned through life and nature (35:10–11), not through direct contact. This implies that Job's pursuit of litigation has been a result of his rebellion, not his faith. Ultimately, however, Elihu's human verdict, including his insistence that God will not appear to humans, is overturned by the appearance of Yahweh. The Yahweh speeches make it clear that God's justice is not the only principle on which he runs the world, for God's purposes are wider than justice.

---

36. On this figure, see L. Wilson, 'Realistic Hope or Imaginative Exploration? The Identity of Job's Arbiter', *Pacifica* 9 (1996), pp. 243–252.

The Yahweh speeches are an invitation to cease the process of litigation, rather than the continuation of a 'lawsuit drama'.[37] In the light of an understanding of God's broader purposes in creation, litigation seems futile.

Rowold argues that the purpose clauses show that God's goal is not to win the argument but rather to restore a proper relationship.[38] Yahweh uses so many examples, not to crush Job into submission, but rather to invite him to withdraw his claim. Job's choice to move in a new direction (42:6) involves an informal, but real, renunciation of his legal case. Now that his longings have been satisfied, he no longer needs a litigation process to force God to become present.

However, was Job being unfaithful in thinking of litigation in the first place? O'Connor suggests that the 'conviction of Job that God is the final source of justice is ultimately the factor which stamps Job's pleas as reverent'.[39] Job failed to see that his adopted course of action was flawed because of a wrong presupposition – that a narrow understanding of human retributive justice could bind God. This accounts for Job's acknowledgment in 42:3 that he spoke about what he did not understand fully and which was beyond his knowledge. Yet the fact that Job took both justice and honesty seriously speaks of a genuine, humble submission to God. In refusing to reject God, or to reduce his view of God, Job is confused, but he still perseveres in faith.

This suggests that Job's faith is being stretched and tested, rather than broken. While it appears at times to be a misguided or incomplete faith, the very fact that Job knows he has to deal with God implies that 'righteous' Job has not yet abandoned his God. Job has retained his faith while seeking further understanding. Of course, believers today who have received a fuller understanding of God's ways and purposes can pursue the same goal of a restored relationship by different means. Yet, given Job's limited perspective, he was responding out of faith, not rebellion.

However, the litigation metaphor could be drawn out further in our setting. Litigation is one means used to resolve conflict. Dell has observed that the book of Job has great potential to be applied in contemporary discussion of conflict and conflict resolution. Building on the work of one of her research students

---

37. *Contra* S. Scholnick, 'Poetry in the Courtroom: Job 38 – 41', in E. R. Follis (ed.), *Directions in Biblical Hebrew Poetry*, JSOTSup 40 (Sheffield: Sheffield Academic Press, 1987), pp. 187, 196, 200.
38. H. L. Rowold, 'The Theology of Creation in the Yahweh Speeches of the Book of Job as a Solution to the Problem Posed by the Book of Job' (ThD thesis, Concordia Seminary in Exile, St Louis, 1977), pp. 64–65.
39. D. J. O'Connor, 'Reverence and Irreverence in Job', *ITQ* 51 (1985), p. 101.

(Leon Roper), she shows the value of a conflict-theory reading of the book.[40] The friends try to resolve the conflicts between both Job and God and Job and his friends by making Job acknowledge his guilt and repent. This is in strong contrast to how God later successfully resolves the matter.[41] Dell draws out (from various psychological theories) a number of areas in which the friends fail: the importance of support for the client (a 'joining' attitude); the requirement of new information to break the impasse; the need for those intervening to avoid projecting themselves as 'experts'. She also suggests some positive learnings from God's actions, based on psychoanalytical intervention or interactional theory. I think that this has great potential for providing further insights into Job. Thus, although the pursuit of litigation may not be a model for readers today, there is much that can be gleaned from the book for both conflict resolution and pastoral care more generally.

Job and God

While this chapter has largely focused on the human characters, a number of scholars have claimed that the book is as much about God as it is about Job.[42] Of course, this gives rise to an obvious problem: how palatable to the contemporary world is the picture of God which emerges from this ancient tale? Dell has suggested, 'The book of Job raises in a particularly acute way the problem of "acceptable behaviour" in relation to God.'[43] The prologue is a potentially fruitful source of information as the narrator describes God and his setting, and God both speaks and acts. A number of scholars react against the view of God they discern in these opening chapters. Campbell, for example, complains, 'It may be storytelling, but any sense of human decency is outraged by it ... What is shocking is that God should be presented as responsible for such

---

40. Dell, *Be Found?*, pp. 98–103.
41. Dell, *Be Found?*, p. 99.
42. N. C. Habel, 'In Defense of God the Sage', in L. G. Perdue and W. C. Gilpin (eds.), *The Voice from the Whirlwind: Interpreting the Book of Job* (Nashville: Abingdon, 1992), p. 21; R. J. Clifford, 'The God Who Makes People Wise: The Wisdom Literature', in A. A. Das and F. J. Matera (eds.), *The Forgotten God: Perspectives in Biblical Theology* (Louisville: Westminster John Knox, 2002), p. 65.
43. K. J. Dell, 'Does God Behave Unethically in the Book of Job?', in K. J. Dell (ed.), *Ethical and Unethical in the Old Testament: God and Humans in Dialogue*, LHBOTS 528 (New York: T&T Clark, 2010), p. 170.

fate, apparently motivated by pride, and inflicting such disaster on a faithful follower.'[44] In a similar vein, Clifford observes, 'Perhaps no scene in Job is more disturbing than Yahweh betting with the Satan, handing over Job's family and finally Job himself to malevolent Satan in a wager on whether Job reveres God for love.'[45]

If the book is understood as a wisdom rather than a historical tale, at least some of this difficulty dissipates. The transaction between Yahweh and the accuser is then simply literary artistry designed to draw attention to the issue of whether rightly motivated human faith is possible. On this view, the tests simply serve to raise the opinions and issues which are the subject of the book.

Even if the book is understood more historically, certain observations about the portrayal of God can still be made. First, even in this heavenly court setting, there is no dualism. The accuser is not pictured as a god, and he can act only if Yahweh permits it (1:12; 2:3, 6). God is pictured as the one who is actively ruling his world as the sovereign Lord, who can determine from the heavenly court what will happen on earth.

Second, while many view as arbitrary God's permission to let the accuser act on earth, this view needs to be established rather than simply asserted. To interpret God's actions as accepting a wager, or gambling with Job's life, is based on an unfounded assumption that God is being manipulated by the accuser. Much more likely is the view that God permits this suffering for his own (unexplained, but good) purposes, though it is not clear whether these purposes are good simply for Job or for humanity as a whole. While the extent of Job's suffering does not appear to be in his interests, the refining and confirming of his faith is certainly a long-term benefit. At the very least, the representation of God in the Yahweh speeches and epilogue should lead us to view generously God's motives and purposes in the prologue, rather than to impute shady motives to God, or to picture him as powerless or outmanoeuvred.

Third, the portrayal of God as the one who has absolute freedom is one that many find offensive, but may nonetheless be true. Like the friends, modern men and women often want God to act in predictable and self-evidently good ways, but the book as a whole resists our putting constraints on God. The prologue unsettles us as readers because it depicts God as free to do as he likes.

Thus, while the opening story raises questions for us about the nature of God, the best way to deal with these questions is to read on and see what the

---

44. A. Campbell, 'The Book of Job: Two Questions, One Answer', *ABR* 51 (2003), p. 16.
45. Clifford, 'The God', p. 63.

book as a whole will tell us about God's character and purposes. We are simply not told why God permits these disasters to happen, but we are left in no doubt that God is running the show. The prologue is not so much harmful to our image of God, but rather a challenge to our preconceived ideas.

The friends are also a source for reflecting on the nature of God since they are rebuked for what they have spoken about him (42:7–8). Yet the dialogue works only because so much of what the friends say sounds like truth rather than gross error. Eliphaz, for example, asserts that God's ways and actions cannot be fully known (5:9) but that he is certainly active in and over his creation to both care for the needy and punish the wicked (5:10–16). God can discipline (5:17), but also deliver and restore (5:18–27). His graciousness is seen in his promises of protection and prosperity.[46] Bildad's core belief is that God never perverts justice or rejects a blameless or righteous person (8:3, 20–22). Thus, Bildad insists that God punishes the wicked (18:5–21), though possibly through the agency of others. He depicts God as a powerful ruler over both the cosmos and human armies (25:2–3).

Zophar is less forthcoming in his description of the nature and activity of God. However, he proclaims that God's wisdom and understanding are far beyond human comprehension (11:6–9) and his power is irresistible (11:10). Zophar appears to place greater emphasis on God's judgment on the ungodly (11:13–20; most of ch. 20) rather than on his prospering of the righteous.

How is it that they have not spoken of God what is right (42:7–8)? God's verdict in 42:7–8 is not a condemnation of their largely orthodox beliefs about God and his nature, but rather a rebuke of their pronouncements about God's activity in general and specifically as it touches Job. They have not correctly described how God is acting in his world, for they each assume that God can act only on the basis of rewarding human righteousness and punishing human wickedness, and that this principle exhausts how God can act in his world. Their 'God' is simply 'a God who reacts',[47] or 'the engineer of the mechanisms of retribution'.[48] Thus, the friends are rebuked for strident views about what God is doing in his world, not about what God is like. Parsons expresses it well: 'Though the three friends basically have an orthodox view of God, they often

---

46. D. W. Nam, *Talking about God: Job 42:7–9 and the Nature of God in the Book of Job*, StBL 49 (New York: Peter Lang, 2003), p. 40.
47. Habel, 'In Defense', p. 27.
48. T. N. D. Mettinger, 'The God of Job: Avenger, Tyrant, or Victor?', in Perdue and Gilpin, *Voice from the Whirlwind*, p. 41.

misapply the doctrine to Job's situation.'[49] For this reason, God says that they have not spoken of him what is right.

On the other hand, God says that Job has spoken about him what is right, and this makes Job's words an important source for the book's doctrine of God. Mettinger claims that 'the Job speeches depict a God who is not merely amoral but actively immoral, the omnipotent tyrant, the cosmic thug'.[50] Does Job really view God that way?

Job's initial view of God is very positive. Job sees God as one worthy of respect (1:1) and worship (1:5). After his losses, he acknowledges that God has the power of life and death (1:21), who can send both prosperity and disaster (2:10). Even in his opening self-lament, Job still sees that God has power over birth and death (3:3–4) and is actively working through disasters (3:23). Job's cursing of the day of his birth is not a challenge to God as Creator, but rather an expression of his anguish.[51] In his next speech, Job again acknowledges that God has power over life and death (6:8–9) and the power to send disaster (6:4). So, from the very beginning, Job understands God's active control over the world and his intervention in it. God's goals cannot be blocked (23:13–14). This strong view of God as creator and sustainer of the creation is maintained by Job right through the book.

He regards God as actively involved in the creation (26:7–13), and understands that the various anti-God forces (Rahab, the serpent, Sheol, Abaddon) are powerless before God (26:6, 12b, 13b). Job understands that God is also the one who controls evil, death and destruction. In particular, he is the one who should judge the wicked. This is assumed in chapter 21, as Job complains about how the godless and unrighteous seem to prosper (21:7–18), and he calls on God to judge them (21:19–20).[52] Similarly in chapter 27, he outlines that God is responsible for punishing the wicked (27:7–23).

In his oath of clearance, Job discloses his belief that God is the one to whom he will give account (31:2, 6, 14, 23, 28), the creator of all human beings (31:15) and the God who expects active justice from his people. After the Yahweh speeches, Job voices the view that he has held at all times in the book: that God can do all things and that no purpose of his can be thwarted (42:2). This is not a new understanding for Job, but is simply a restatement of the view he has held throughout.

---

49. G. W. Parsons, 'Job, Theology of', in W. A. Elwell (ed.), *Evangelical Dictionary of Biblical Theology* (Grand Rapids: Baker, 1996), p. 415.
50. Mettinger, 'The God of Job', p. 44.
51. *Contra* Nam, *Talking*, pp. 77–78.
52. Clifford, 'The God', p. 64, suggests that, at this point, Job views God as an enemy.

It is clear from this survey that Job has a big view of God, the creator and sustainer of the cosmos. Even in the midst of his suffering, he refuses to shrink God down to explain his circumstances. He has known what God is like (29:2–5), and he clings to that view of God even when his present situation makes no sense. Job shares the same theological presuppositions as the friends, but draws a different conclusion about God's actions.[53]

Job holds in tension a firm belief that God is a God of justice and that God is not dealing with him justly. God has taken his right to justice (27:2), treating him (wrongly) as an enemy (6:4; 13:24–28; 16:9–14; 19:6–12), oppressing and unfairly condemning him (7:21; 9:19–20, 25–35; 10:14–17; 14:3–4).[54] Yet this represents Job's sense of loss and confusion, not his settled convictions about the character of God.

A key part of Elihu's role is to be a theological foil to what God will disclose about himself when he appears and speaks. Habel rightly notes, 'The reply of God from the whirlwind . . . offers a profound alternative to the various characterizations of God offered in the rest of the book.'[55] In the first Yahweh speech, we see that he is lord over the physical earth (38:4–21), lord over the weather or 'forces of nature' (38:22–38), and lord over the animal world (38:39 – 39:30). The implied answer to most of God's rhetorical questions ('no-one but the Lord') highlights God's sovereignty as the ruler of the universe. McGrath observes, 'Job 38:1 – 42:6 sets out what is unquestionably the most comprehensive understanding of God as creator to be found in the Old Testament.'[56]

The point of the animal section (38:39 – 39:30) is that God is sovereign even over the most remote and apparently useless members of the animal world – in particular, 'the fabulously stupid ostrich'.[57] God's sovereignty is not restrained by his having to act according to an inflexible doctrine of retribution. While God is undoubtedly just, his ordering of the world is broader than a reductionistic concept of human retributive justice in which he can do no more than reward righteousness and punish wickedness. He runs the universe as its creator and sustainer. As Nam observes, 'Yahweh is the patron of life itself in his created world. He facilitates freedom, hilarity, agility, and hostility in the wild animals.'[58]

---

53. Nam, *Talking*, p. 105.
54. Nam, *Talking*, p. 73; Parsons, 'Job', p. 416.
55. Habel, 'In Defense', p. 21. At p. 33, he describes this speech as 'God talking about God'.
56. A. E. McGrath, *Christian Theology: An Introduction*, 5th edn (Chichester: Wiley-Blackwell, 2011), p. 216.
57. Clifford, 'The God', p. 64.
58. Nam, *Talking*, p. 145.

His concerns are wider than humans alone, for he is sovereign over all of creation. The clearest example of this is when he causes rain to fall where there are no humans (38:26–27). The series of impossible questions indicates that God's ordering of his cosmos is beyond human comprehension.

God's dominion also allows for chaotic forces, such as the destructive lightning flashes (38:35) and animals who feed on their prey (38:39, 41; 39:29–30). The ostrich eggs can be crushed (39:15) and the young mistreated (39:16). The wild war horse is involved in battle (39:21–25), which will lead to death and destruction. This is not a sanitized playground, but the real, fallen world over which God is actively ruling.

In 40:8, God raises the issue of 'justice', which is filled out in his second speech. Whether the figures of Behemoth and Leviathan are mythological symbols of cosmic chaos (or even death and Satan), or whether they are natural creatures described hyperbolically, the point of chapters 40–41 is that even the most powerful rival forces are under God's complete control, yet beyond human mastery. Nam rightly points out, 'Yahweh uses Leviathan to demonstrate divine control of even the most awesome forces in the created world.'[59] This picture proclaims that 'God *can* control ultimate cosmic evil'.[60] It is at least clear in the case of Behemoth and Leviathan that there are no powers in the world beyond the control of God.[61]

Overall, the Yahweh speeches depict a God who is far beyond the formulas of the friends, and even the most imaginative hopes of Job. Yahweh is a God without rivals and without peers. He is not bound by human rules, but free and sovereign to implement his goals and design. His activity in his creation cannot be reduced down, not even to the important principle of justice. He is to be treated as the Lord of the universe, which he actively rules and sustains.

Yet, although God is unchanged, he is not in chains. Humans cannot say to God 'you cannot do that' or 'you must act in this way' if that cuts across God's purposes for the whole of creation. Job's friends insist that God can only act to reward human righteousness and punish human wickedness, for that is his character as one committed to retributive justice. However, God can change in his treatment of Job because justice is only one part of God's character, and God must be free to act in accordance with his wider and longer purposes.

In this book, there is no focus on God active in history in rescuing his chosen people, but rather an elaboration of the God who is sovereign over all humanity

---

59. Ibid., p. 158.
60. Clifford, 'The God', p. 65.
61. Nam, *Talking*, p. 163.

and the entire creation. God owns and controls all of the cosmos. This picture peaks in the Yahweh speeches, and is thoroughly consistent with that of the other wisdom books.

A clear contribution of the book is its outline of God's providential workings. The principles on which God bases his activity are not set out, but the assertion of the book is that God is bringing about his purposes, but doing so behind the scenes. God appears in the heavenly court in the prologue, not at all in the dialogue, and only in a whirlwind in the theophany. God's providence is most clearly seen in the prologue, where the events which occur on earth are not directly performed by God himself, but by the agency of the accuser, who also uses both natural forces (lightning, east wind; 1:16, 19) and human actions (Sabeans, Chaldeans; 1:15, 17). Notwithstanding the intermediaries used, what happens on earth is God's doing.

Clifford has observed that 'the book skillfully plays off the portraits of God drawn by Job and by the friends against the portrait of the prologue, divine speeches, and epilogue'.[62] While the friends speak with great authority, the god they describe is only a shadow of the one who reveals himself in the theophany. Their reductionistic views satisfy neither Job nor God himself. In the final chapter, Job concedes that he spoke with limited knowledge of the God who is far beyond his comprehension (42:3), and it is this realization that enables him to move in a new direction.

Yet the book does not just describe God as a majestic creator. Yahweh's endorsement of Job as one who has spoken of him what is right (42:7–8) implies that he also cares for human beings who struggle to cling on to him in faith. Indeed, 'Yahweh proves to be the God of cosmic justice and wisdom and, astonishingly, also of compassionate commitment to Job'.[63] God is big enough to take genuine human hurt and bewilderment, and is not shattered by Job's protests, questions and even accusations. Yahweh is thoroughly committed to the rawness of relationships with humans who trust him. He is not simply a cosmic God, but is also one who draws near to those who draw near to him.

More work needs to be done on drawing out the implications of God's nature for a wide range of other topics such as prayer, the environment, humanity, ethics and mission.[64] Let me illustrate with what is perhaps the most confined

---

62. Clifford, 'The God', p. 65.
63. Ibid., p. 57.
64. See Wilson, *Job*, pp. 355–382, where I introduce some preliminary thoughts on these areas.

of these areas: mission. At first sight, the book of Job does not say much at all about the mission of the people of God.⁶⁵ Van Zyl suggests that the book is 'pre-missional', showing why mission was needed then, and is needed now.⁶⁶ Along a different trajectory, Allen has argued that in a diseased and suffering world, people will not find their way to God unless someone makes the path known to them.⁶⁷ Chris Wright proposes that reading a biblical book missiologically is much wider than asking 'What does the book say explicitly about mission?' It might also include how those 'going on mission' might need to change in their thinking or values in order to be part of God's mission in his world. He notes that the biblical wisdom books call out loudly that any mission endeavour must be carried out with a critical openness to the world, a respect for God's image in humanity, and a humility and modesty in our approach and answers.⁶⁸ Larry Waters has argued that the book has a 'missionary' purpose in that 'a believer's suffering should be viewed . . . as a witness not only to God's sovereignty but also as a witness to His goodness, justice, grace, and love to the nonbelieving world'.⁶⁹ As believers undergo undeserved suffering (like Job), their response will proclaim to the watching, sceptical world that God is still someone worth trusting. Most recently, Tim Davy's PhD has explored a missional hermeneutic of the book of Job, thinking of mission in a holistic sense including care for the poor.⁷⁰

While this gives some sense of where scholarship is at in relation to Job and mission, there is surely more to be said that issues from the doctrine of God in the book. If God is the sole creator and sustainer of all the world, and the one who has shown that it is possible for humans to trust in him without ulterior motives, this provides rich motivation to share this great news with those who do not yet know it.

---

65. D. C. van Zyl, 'Missiological Dimensions in the Book of Job', *IRM* 91 (2002), p. 24, concedes that it 'is on face value probably one of the least likely candidates among all the books of the Bible to contribute to a biblical understanding of mission'.
66. Van Zyl, 'Missiological Dimensions', pp. 24–28.
67. W. A. Allen, 'The Missionary Message of Job: God's Universal Concern for Healing', *Caribbean Journal of Evangelical Theology* 6 (2002), p. 18.
68. C. J. H. Wright, *The Mission of God: Unlocking the Bible's Grand Narrative* (Nottingham: Inter-Varsity Press, 2006), p. 453.
69. L. J. Waters, '*Missio Dei* in the Book of Job', *BibSac* 166 (2009), p. 19.
70. T. J. Davy, 'The Book of Job and the Mission of God: An Application of a Missional Hermeneutic to the Book of Job' (PhD thesis, University of Gloucestershire, 2014).

If God is sovereignly free to bring about his purposes in the creation, his people must be prepared to move beyond their cultural assumptions in order to proclaim God as he is. If God has shown what he values by commending Job, then we know how to trust and live out this faith before a watching world. If God is even concerned with the untamed animals and uninhabited land, then we need to have a more panoramic understanding of God's concern for the whole world.

These are just some preliminary thoughts that show how fertile the book's understanding is for daily faith and living as God's people in God's world. There is ample room for applying the book of Job's teaching about God to a whole range of issues for the benefit of others.

Conclusion

The book of Job is not just a problematic book; it is also a surprising one. While its descriptions of faith and of God might at first seem puzzling, they are actually a central part of the book's abiding value. There are few richer portrayals of God than those in this book, and there is a deeper exploration of faith here compared with almost any other place in the Old Testament. The book's teachings on God and faith are nuggets of gold obscured by years of neglect and fear. There are some tricky hermeneutical issues, but the dividends are priceless. When rightly understood, the book of Job discloses real theological gems. They are worth (re)discovering.

© Lindsay Wilson, 2016

4. READING ECCLESIASTES WITH THE SCHOLARS

Katharine J. Dell

The study of any individual book in the biblical canon is bound to reflect both wider trends in the discipline as a whole as well as a set of individual questions that have built up over the years of scholarly discussion in relation to that particular book. This is certainly the case with Ecclesiastes. The revolution that has taken place in the last few decades in the interpretation of biblical texts – the move towards final-form holistic readings, a prioritization of 'the reader' in the interpretive process, the impact of postmodernism in a wider sense – has had an influence upon interpretation of this one biblical book as well as on our evaluation of method, critical approach, and on our theological evaluation in more general terms. I wish in this paper to show how the wider 'remit' of biblical method and trends in biblical theology, particularly in the area of wisdom theology, have impacted on Ecclesiastes in a way that is peculiar to this book, given its character and uniqueness in the canon.

Contradictions

This is a book long held to be contradictory in its sentiments, from the rabbis up to the present day.[1] A number of statements seem to contradict one another;

---

1. See M. V. Fox, *Qoheleth and His Contradictions*, Bible and Literature Series 18, JSOTSup 71 (Sheffield: Almond Press, 1989).

for example, 2:17, 'So I hated life', versus 9:4, 'But whoever is joined with all the living has hope, for a living dog is better than a dead lion.'[2] Similarly 9:2, 'the same fate comes to all, to the righteous and the wicked, to the good and the evil', seems to contradict 8:12–13, 'I know that it will be well with those who fear God . . . but it will not be well with the wicked.' These kinds of contradictions led scholars to believe that the book might well be composite. However, ironically, the book is also widely regarded as representing the thought of one mind because of its distinctive flavour.

Approaches from different trends of scholarship have over the years been applied to this book, with varying success. The source critics posited redactional stages but also recognized that the bulk of the book was conceived as an essential unity.[3] There was widespread agreement that the end of the book formed an epilogue – hence 12:8–14 or 12:9–14.[4] There are verses where Qoheleth is spoken about in the third person – namely 1:2, 7:27 and 12:8 – that are likely to be editorial. The redaction critics[5] in turn pointed to the same phenomenon: that there was an original 'core' possibly edited with redactions. Indeed, whilst the source critics sought to find the original material by isolating redactions, the redaction critics took the original as read and focused on the additions – thus the overall result is essentially the same.

---

2. All Bible quotes, unless stated otherwise, are from the NRSV.
3. The pioneers of source criticism posited stages of composition beginning with Qoheleth's own work and continuing with various editorial stages by people attempting to neutralize, defend, explain or complement certain features of his thought; e.g. C. Siegfried, *Prediger und Hoheslied*, HAT (Göttingen: Vandenhoeck & Ruprecht, 1898); A. H. McNeile, *An Introduction to Ecclesiastes* (Cambridge: Cambridge University Press, 1904); and G. A. Barton, *Ecclesiastes*, ICC (Edinburgh: T&T Clark, 1912). The presupposition behind this kind of carving up of the text is that the original author must have been consistent, and therefore anything not consistent with the major part of the work must have been added.
4. E.g. G. Sheppard, 'The Epilogue to Qohelet as Theological Commentary', *CBQ* 39 (1977), pp. 182–189.
5. J. L. Crenshaw, *Ecclesiastes*, OTL (London: SCM, 1988) gives a balanced presentation of the redactional options. Also, R. N. Whybray, *Ecclesiastes*, NCB (London: Marshall, Morgan & Scott, 1989). More recently, Thomas Krüger, *Qoheleth*, Hermeneia (Minneapolis: Augsburg Fortress, 2004).

An essential unity?

There is in the modern period a certain unease with these older models of carving up the text. This is because the reconstruction of the different levels is very much hypothesis and scholars argue over the details of each redaction and the number of redactional hands. Given that the book of Ecclesiastes does have an essential integrity of its own in relation to style, language and overall themes, and has done for readers of the past, it seems sensible to try to hold contradictions in tension rather than over-egg the redaction line. The converse problem with taking the text totally in its final form without being aware of the possibility of literary-critical stages is the feeling of overall unease with a contradictory text. This leads even those of a more final-form persuasion to find it hard to get away from at least one redaction, that of the epilogue,[6] especially 12:13: 'The end of the matter; all has been heard. Fear God, and keep his commandments; for that is the whole duty of everyone.' Does this not provide a 'pious' solution that is in contradiction to Qoheleth's usual questioning? Instead of necessarily seeing it as a later addition, Michael Fox[7] has ingeniously suggested that the final-form epilogist 'level' is that of the main author (or frame narrator, as he terms it), with other levels as secondary. Level 1 is the epilogist who is telling his audience about the wisdom of Qoheleth. Level 2a is the reporting 'I' who speaks as an old man looking back on his own experience when younger. Level 2b is the younger Qoheleth, experiencing 'I', who made the investigations described in 1:12 – 2:24. However, even if one phrases it, as Fox does, as the final form being the 'real' text with antecedents, but all ultimately from the same 'pen' (i.e. the older self looking back at the younger self), there is still that same sense of a disjointedness somewhere along the line. Similarly, A. Shead[8] argues in favour of the essential unity of the main text and epilogue. He holds out the possibility that the redactors imitated the style of the original, but argues that there is enough of a preponderance of Qoheleth's favourite words to lend 'a peculiar sense of unity to the work and a feeling of intertextual allusiveness' (p. 75). This moves towards the view that there is no essential divergence of view in the epilogue, and indeed it may form the climax and conclusion of the work. This leads to the modern preference for reading the book as a whole.

---

6. G. H. Wilson, 'The Words of the Wise: The Intent and Significance of Qoheleth 12:9–14', *JBL* 103 (1984), pp. 175–192.
7. M. V. Fox, 'Frame Narrative and Composition in the Book of Qoheleth', *HUCA* 48 (1977), pp. 83–106.
8. A. Shead, 'Ecclesiastes from the Outside In', *RTR* 55 (1996), pp. 24–37.

Why is the sense of one author so strong? The very personal nature of the musings of this author seem to create this impression. The book contains a small amount of narrative (in the Solomonic royal autobiography section), but this is not generally seen as the keynote of the book, except by recent scholar Christianson.[9] The book has the atmosphere of an older man looking back in philosophical mode and with the benefit of hindsight, but with the express purpose of instructing others in what he has learned. One suggestion with historic roots, in that Luther expressed this opinion, is that the book might be seen as a dialogue. Luther suggested that the contradictions might be explained by imagining Solomon in dialogue with political associates.[10] This same idea has resurfaced in recent scholarship in the dialogic reading of T. A. Perry,[11] in which two points of view, K and P, are represented in the book, and in Robert Gordis' idea of 'quotations', whereby the main author uses traditional sentiments as quoted, whether or not he actually inherited the quotations.[12] S. de Jong[13] has, by contrast, found a pattern of alternation between observation and instruction complexes throughout the book. The instruction, he argues, consists mainly of advice, admonitions and imperatives, all of which are in the realm of the possible and the sensible. The observation sections are concerned mainly with the vanity of human labour, and even texts that advocate enjoyment are tempered by the vanity theme. Thus such sections are characterized by either negative or neutral evaluations of wisdom. Like many, de Jong is unable to find a logical ordering of the book; rather he finds some texts unified by keyword association, some linked by repetition, others united by quotation of a traditional saying followed by an opposite reaction, and so on. Alternatively, Qoheleth has been seen to be using the technique of adding interpretation to existing proverbial material, whether quoted or not. However, the evaluation of material as quoted or as the author's own is very much reliant on what the worldview of Qoheleth himself

---

9. E. Christianson, *A Time to Tell: Narrative Strategies in Ecclesiastes*, JSOTSup 280 (Sheffield: Sheffield Academic Press, 1998).
10. See K. J. Dell, *Interpreting Ecclesiastes: Readers Old and New* (Winona Lake: Eisenbrauns, 2013), ch. 1.
11. T. A. Perry, *Dialogues with Kohelet* (University Park: Pennsylvania State University Press, 1993).
12. R. Gordis, 'Quotations in Wisdom Literature', *JQR* New Series 30 (1939), pp. 123–147. Reprinted in R. Gordis (ed.), *Poets, Prophets, Sages* (Bloomington/London: Indiana University Press, 1971), pp. 160–197.
13. S. de Jong, 'A Book of Labour: The Structuring Principles and the Main Theme of the Book of Qoheleth', *JSOT* 54 (1992).

might have been. It is also dependent on which reconstruction of the authorial stages in the book an individual scholar bases his or her arguments upon.

Whether we see the book in terms of a dialogue or simply as an inner struggle to comprehend, citing traditional opinions in order to contradict them, there is an overarching thematic unity and the sense of a voice – the repetitive 'I' that contrasts with the epilogue's third-person description. Yet it is more than just a matter of the contents of the book: the individual nature of it also derives from the claim to authorship made at the start of the book in 1:1 and again in 1:12, and from the 'personal quest' section of 1:12 – 2:24 that has been seen by many as an autobiography. The famous claim that these are the words of Qoheleth (the teacher [cf. 12:9], the assembler, the preacher), the son of David, king in Jerusalem (1:1; 1:12), gives the book a royal authority that has been associated over the centuries with King Solomon. A Solomonic author was taken for granted for many generations of readers of the book; the 'son of David in Jerusalem' was then linked to the quest for pleasure of 1:12 – 2:24, which fitted with the description in 1 Kings 1 – 12 of Solomon's great wealth and power. The link with 'wisdom' and being 'wise' came from these passages as well as from the clear relationship with Proverbs, at the level both of content (the citation of Proverbs) and of authorship, and with Job as well, as another wisdom text. Even at a time when Solomonic authorship is not presupposed and Qoheleth emerges as the author, the adoption of a Solomonic persona in the book is widely acknowledged, the royal autobiography[14] seen as a deliberate technique used to convey his message that, even for someone with all the wealth and power that can be imagined, 'all is vanity and a chasing after wind'.

Date and context(s)

Questions of date follow in the wake of those about authorship. The book has long been regarded as late amongst the Writings of the Old Testament canon – probably third century,[15] but this has been challenged in some quarters. C.-L. Seow has recently argued for a date in the Persian period for the book, specifically between the second half of the fifth and the first half of the fourth

---

14. See discussion in Y.-V. Koh, *Royal Autobiography in the Book of Qoheleth*, BZAW 369 (Berlin/New York: De Gruyter, 2006).

15. See discussion in C. A. Grant, *'Chasing after the Wind?': An Examination of the Social and Historical Background of the Book of Ecclesiastes* (PhD diss., University of Cambridge, 2000).

centuries BCE.[16] He argues this on linguistic grounds, and on the basis of fresh epigraphic finds and the results of archaeological surveys and excavations of Persian-period sites. His analysis is thus essentially a socio-economic one. C. R. Harrison Jr, by contrast, maintains that Qoheleth's thought is to be seen in the context of the sociological milieu of third-century BCE Judea.[17] He finds evidence for social disturbances in cultural and economic life that led to Qoheleth's negative worldview. The book cannot be much later, as it was known to the author of Ben Sira or Ecclesiasticus, who wrote in 180 BCE. It may be more sensible to acknowledge that, like other wisdom books, the precise social location of the author is lost to us. Attempts have been made to discover links with the Hellenistic world,[18] and some sentiments echo Stoicism or Epicurianism, but no one philosophical system seems quite to match the sentiments of this author.

One wonders whether the evidence is really strong enough to place the book in any one socio-economic situation. And yet the quest for further contexts continues into very recent scholarly work. This has led to new theories of Ecclesiastes as an anti-apocalyptic production from the third century. Douglas,[19] following a more literary approach and using the language of genre, sees the use of an anti-apocalyptic genre as part of the use of a hybrid of genres in the book. He cites three passages in particular – 3:10–22; 7:1–10; 9:1–10 – that he sees as polemic against the idea of flaws in the present life that highlight the need for eschatological reward. He argues that apocalyptic seers (rather than sages) might be Qoheleth's opponents. Through his theology of joy, Douglas argues, Qoheleth turns people away from such thoughts towards a restabilization and fresh valuation of their present lives. Perdue,[20] in *The Sword and the Stylus*, with a post-colonial agenda, puts the wisdom literature into the wider historical contexts of succeeding world empires and their rise and fall. In the case of Ecclesiastes, Perdue sees it as sceptical literature from the margins but nonetheless strongly influenced by two major international

---

16. C.-L. Seow, *Ecclesiastes*, AB (New York: Doubleday, 1997).
17. C. R. Harrison Jr, 'Qoheleth among the Sociologists', *BibInt* 5 (1997), pp. 160–180.
18. Hellenistic links are discussed by R. Braun, *Kohelet und die frühhellenistische Popularphilosophie*, BZAW 130 (Berlin: De Gruyter, 1973); and in N. Lohfink's commentary, *Kohelet* (Würzburg: Echter, 1980).
19. J. N. Douglas, *A Polemical Preacher of Job: An Anti-apocalyptic Genre for Qoheleth's Message of Joy* (Eugene: Pickwick, 2014).
20. L. G. Perdue, *The Sword and the Stylus: An Introduction to Wisdom in the Age of Empires* (Grand Rapids: Eerdmans, 2008).

traditions – one from Ptolemaic Egypt and the other from the Hellenistic world. He writes,

> Egyptian sages, from the end of the Persian Empire and the early generations of Ptolemaic rule that blended Egyptian religion and tradition with Greek culture, also betray at times a high degree of doubt about traditional affirmations that were constituent of a conventional and earlier worldview.[21]

He sees Ecclesiastes as a work written in opposition to the conventional wisdom of the Jewish theocracy in the late Persian or Ptolemaic period. He continues,

> The book of Qoheleth and the case that was made for its inclusion in the Jewish canon in the first and second centuries CE present the most developed form of an internal skepticism that gripped the Jewish worldview in Israel and early Judaism. Scholars like Qoheleth seriously contested traditional affirmations in Jewish religious and sapiential circles. In his skeptical views of God, wisdom and human existence, Qoheleth appears to have drawn on similar Greek and Egyptian traditions of wisdom, religious teachings and philosophy vibrant during his time as a teacher. At least his book takes its place in a world in which skepticism was regnant in the cultural climate.[22]

Perdue then sees Ecclesiastes as springing out of a fresh cultural climate that evolves out of power struggles and historical circumstances. It is scepticism that is from the margins and challenges the status quo of Jewish mainstream wisdom, and yet it receives inspiration from cultures that were to go on and dominate the scene for a time; hence it seems that the old colonialism is replaced by a new one, and so the wheel goes on being reinvented.

Another possible context for Qoheleth is that of a businessman in a mercantile setting, business ethics being arguably at the forefront of his concern but put into the wider context of an intellectual debate about meaning in life combined with personal grievances of a profound nature. These reconstructions do not of course rely simply on historical data; in fact they are primarily posited on the grounds of the content of the book. What are Qoheleth's key concerns? Is it all about profit and loss, as Weeks[23] would have us believe, or are we to emphasize other theological concerns above this more pragmatic one? We are brought back to the text and to the thematic concerns of this author.

---

21. Ibid., p. 199.
22. Ibid., pp. 199–200.
23. Stuart Weeks, *Ecclesiastes and Scepticism*, LHBOTS 541 (New York: T&T Clark, 2012).

Pessimist, realist or preacher of joy?

The book of Qoheleth considers a range of theological themes that are profound and existential. Indeed, some have seen it more as a philosophical treatise than a theological work. Furthermore, it may seem to be more humanist than theological, but God appears at key moments in the book, is mentioned forty times and is arguably presupposed throughout. Mention of God is always in relation to the world that God has made and over which he has control. Indeed the author seems to be reflecting on the human condition in a world in which God is undeniably in control, even though many aspects of that control remain a mystery. Whilst humanity, society and the cosmos are Qoheleth's starting points, and hence this could be seen as a theology from below, he discusses the fate of humanity in the hands of God and God's mysterious ways. R. E. Murphy[24] suggested that God is very active in Ecclesiastes. The deity is always giving and doing, he judges righteous and wicked (3:17), he is angry at the violation of religious proprieties (5:6) and he calls the people to account for not enjoying themselves (11:9). However, he is a transcendent God, in his heaven, distant and wholly other for this author. This is an important emphasis in the book which has often been overlooked in the scholarship.

One of the most debated issues to do with Ecclesiastes in recent years is whether Qoheleth is essentially a pessimist or realist, or whether he is in fact, as Whybray termed it, a 'preacher of joy'.[25] The question is raised concerning the tone of the book: was the author an unbridled pessimist or were there more positive aspects of his thought? J. Walsh[26] characterizes the mood of Qoheleth as 'peaceful despair' and there is no denying the sense of the futility of life that comes across in his thought. Whybray and Murphy,[27] on the other hand, speak of joy in the context of this author's thought. In discussing the question of an overall genre of Qoheleth, E. Levine[28] has even suggested that it is intended to be 'serious humour' to teach others to cope with the uncertainties of life.

---

24. R. E. Murphy, 'Qoheleth and Theology?', *BTB* 21 (1991), pp. 30–33. See Mette Bundvad, *Time in the Book of Ecclesiastes* (Oxford: Oxford University Press, 2015), for a fascinating discussion of another neglected theme in this book.
25. R. N. Whybray, 'Qoheleth, Preacher of Joy?', *JSOT* 23 (1982), pp. 87–98.
26. J. T. Walsh, 'Despair as a Theological Virtue in the Spirituality of Ecclesiastes', *BTB* 12 (1982), pp. 46–49.
27. R. E. Murphy, *Ecclesiastes* (Dallas: Word, 1992).
28. E. Levine, 'The Humor in Qoheleth', *ZAW* 109 (1977), pp. 71–83.

This is to draw out one of the greatest contradictions in the book: how can all be vanity if there are frequent exhortations to 'eat, drink and be merry'? How can one so preoccupied with death as the great leveller, one who questions the value of wealth, of work, of relationships, and one who even expresses the sentiment that it might have been better never to have been born, or to have been stillborn, rather than see the oppressions committed by humanity, still call for enjoyment of life on various levels, not just in eating and drinking but also enjoying the wife of your youth and remembering your Creator? The scholars fall into the two camps too, with Crenshaw advocating pessimism or, more recently, irony[29] and, at the opposite end of the spectrum, Lee, more recently than Whybray, advocating joy.

E. P. Lee, in his book *The Vitality of Enjoyment in Qoheleth's Theological Rhetoric*,[30] argues for the importance of 'joy' in the book, but he also puts a fresh emphasis on the 'rhetoric' of the book in relation to the critical method of rhetorical criticism. He is interested then in how the book achieves its rhetorical effect of persuasion. Although he is aware of the contradictions in Ecclesiastes' thought, Lee regards the book as an essential unity with a clear structure and progression of thought within its pages. He engages with Qoheleth as author and finds techniques of multivalence (deliberate multiple levels of meaning), 'miscues' and 'indirection' which challenge false assumptions and deliberately disorientate the reader with pedagogic purpose. Lee's main argument is that readers have been 'persuaded', largely by the repetition of the phrase 'vanity of vanities', into thinking that Ecclesiastes is a pessimistic work. By contrast, Lee wishes to draw out another, alternative 'refrain', the positive commendation to 'eat and drink', as found seven times in the book. His emphasis on this positive phrase, which he sees as in tension with the negative sentiments in the book, leads him to characterize Ecclesiastes as a work of 'faithful realism' rather than of pessimism. Lee also links the 'enjoyment' passages with those that describe religious duty as 'the fear of God', arguing that the divine presence is mediated through God's giving and humanity's taking up of the gift of enjoyment. Lee then is interested in how the book achieves its rhetorical effect in the stress on 'joy' which he finds in eight passages: 2:24–26; 3:12–13, 22; 5:17–19; 7:14; 8:15; 9:7–10; 11:7 – 12:1. He finds 'the use of rhetorical strategies that intentionally exploit contradictions in order to demonstrate that uncertainties and contingencies are an inevitable

---

29. J. L. Crenshaw, *Qoheleth: The Ironic Wink* (Columbia: University of South Carolina Press, 2013).
30. E. P. Lee, *The Vitality of Enjoyment in Qoheleth's Theological Rhetoric*, BZAW 353 (Berlin/New York: De Gruyter, 2005).

reality of human existence',[31] and hence argues for Ecclesiastes as a 'unified and meaningful composition'. The joy passages he sees as having been 'placed strategically within the book and ... crafted to interact with and build upon one another as the author develops his argument from beginning to end'.[32] This is not a hedonistic enjoyment, but one that knows tragedy and is realistic in the face of contradiction; it is about living life to the full 'with a sober recognition of its travails and a grateful acceptance of its possibilities'.[33] It is also about 'doing good' and 'seeing good', and yet all of this is a gift of God. He writes, 'Thus, although the human being is supposed to "do good" the ultimate "doer" is, after all, the deity. The one thing that morals can and ought to "do" in the end, turns out to be due to God's own doing!'[34]

Of course, Lee is taking one side of Qoheleth's argument – the joy side – and playing down its opposite – the vanity, which so many have seen as the key to this book. The sheer volume of use of 'hebel' might lead us to question such theories. Its early appearance (1:2) as a kind of leitmotif of the book might also suggest its importance. The recent work of Pinçon[35] tries to put these two opposite approaches into perspective and argues in favour of the 'enigma' of the relativity of 'bonheur' and 'malheur' (good/bad feeling) that are in tension in the book. He argues that Qoheleth is a two-step work which moves from observation of odd moments of happiness towards a clear exhortation to human beings to enjoy that happiness. He finds a transition section in 6:10 – 7:14, such that the first half of the book mainly concerns the question of the profit of a human life upon earth and the inability of human beings to penetrate life's mysteries, while the second half raises questions as to the future of humankind. Although little can be done about the future, in that no-one knows what it holds, human beings can enjoy occasions for happiness and can fear God. In this way the two sides of disillusionment and yet joy provide the essential enigma of the book.

Is this fluctuation an inner dialogue in the mind of the author? Is this a dialogue with himself or with others? Or is it simply reflective of different moods at different times? Do these opposing sentiments hang together in the thought of this book? We might want to resort to the work of structuralists

---

31. Ibid., p. 9.
32. Ibid.
33. Ibid., p. 10.
34. Ibid., p. 40.
35. B. Pinçon, *L'Énigme du bonheur: Étude sur le sujet du bien dans le livre de Qohélet*, VTSup 119 (Leiden: Brill, 2008).

such as Loader, in *Polar Structures in the Book of Qoheleth*.³⁶ He finds large polar structures that hold together tensions and contradictions in the work. It is the shape of the work itself that throws up the contrasts. Loader goes down the flouting-of-conventions route when he sees the quotation of traditional wisdom forms in the context of overturning traditional wisdom ideas as the overarching polar structure of the book. His polar structures recall structuralist ideas about binary opposition, and yet one wonders whether he has completely got away from ideas of authorship, as he is arguing that the author intended such structures in order to achieve his effect. The modern consensus, then, seems to be that the contradictions make sense after all – that they can be held in tension; but the emphasis scholars choose to place becomes almost a 'readerly' affair rather than a strictly authorially orientated one. This brings us back to readers of Ecclesiastes over the centuries and to an interest in how the book has been read. There seem to be no rights and wrongs when it comes to Qoheleth.

Reading Ecclesiastes

Issues of reader-response find a particularly fruitful home in Ecclesiastes. It was Christian Ginsburg who in 1861 wrote the definitive 'reader-response evaluation' of this book in terms of the history of interpretation.³⁷ He was fascinated by how the rabbis, early Christian interpreters, thinkers of the Reformation and so on 'read this book'. He aired the readings of many individuals – Gregory the Great, Nicholas of Lyra, Martin Luther and Rashbam, to name but a few. Ginsburg's book shows how fascinated our forebears were with this unique treatise. Of course, there was much early discussion amongst the rabbis as to whether this book was suitable for holy writ at all; whether it 'defiled the hands' or not. Once the decision was made to include it – largely because of its authorial unity under Solomon and because of its possible harmonization with the Torah (as demonstrated with painstaking accuracy by the rabbis) – it became a fixed part of the canon from that point.³⁸ This did not,

---

36. J. L. Loader, *Polar Structures in the Book of Qoheleth*, BZAW 152 (Berlin/New York: De Gruyter, 1979).
37. C. D. Ginsburg, *Coheleth or The Book of Ecclesiastes* (London: Longman, Green, Longman and Roberts, 1861), p. 33.
38. See M. Goodman, 'Sacred Scripture and "Defiling the Hands"', *JTS* 41 (1990), pp. 99–107. There was a long discussion amongst the rabbis as to whether Ecclesiastes defiled the hands or not; see discussion in Dell, *Interpreting*, ch. 1.

however, mean that all Christian interpreters liked to engage with it: it appealed to some and not to others. Jerome is famous for his dualistic reading of the text that distinguished between 'things earthly' 'under the sun' and things heavenly.[39] This text was easily read as a disparagement of all human endeavour in favour of an embracing of the divine and as a disparagement of this life in relation to a life to come. Luther found it helpful to read it in a political sense as social commentary rather than theological inspiration. Readings of the past are clearly of interest in modern 'readings', individual texts often being particularly enlightened by certain approaches. This is what advocates of 'despair' and 'joy' are also doing – selecting texts to suit their emphasis. This is true when it comes to modern reader-responses: we may be more aware of what we are doing when we bring a bias to the text, but we still do it anyway! Different readings in fact open up interesting new perspectives:[40] the feminist might linger on chapter 7,[41] whilst the liberation theologian dwells on poverty.[42]

A particularly interesting modern reader-response is found in the work of Christianson, who rereads the book through the lenses of existentialism and the Holocaust.[43] Christianson makes this comparison in order to shed interpretive light on the themes of Ecclesiastes, not for any historical/literary-critical or other reasons. He identifies as key themes of existentialism the role of extreme circumstances, confrontation with absurdity and the individual struggle with or against death or fate. He argues that the Holocaust brought each of these themes 'into sharp and painful relief'.[44] Clearly the Holocaust was an extreme circumstance; Christianson writes, 'The extremities of the experience of Holocaust were a theft of hope, and in existential terms, a theft of freedom to determine and preserve the self.'[45] There are many stories of confrontation with absurdity; one cited by Christianson is a letter from Nazi headquarters suggesting that having lights on in vans carrying Jews to the death camps was

---

39. See Dell, *Interpreting*, ch. 2, for a discussion of the dualistic method and how it was applied to Ecclesiastes.
40. E. S. Christianson, *Ecclesiastes through the Centuries*, BBC (Oxford: Blackwell, 2007); S. Holm-Nielsen, 'On the Interpretation of Qoheleth in Early Christianity', *VT* 24 (1974), p. 76.
41. J. L. Koosed, *(Per)mutations of Qohelet: Reading the Body in the Book*, LHBOTS 429 (London/New York: T&T Clark, 2006).
42. E. Tamez, *When the Horizons Close: Rereading Ecclesiastes* (Maryknoll: Orbis, 2000).
43. Christianson, 'Postscript', in *A Time*.
44. Ibid., p. 262.
45. Ibid., p. 264.

a calming aspect that needed to be changed. The letter was totally serious with no hint of irony, and recommended that lights be put on only at the beginning and end of journeys. The individual struggle against death was also heightened by the knowledge of a common fate within the Jewish community which had the effect of lessening the importance of the social roles of individuals in the light of the great leveller. Christianson goes on to argue for Qoheleth as an existentialist and then to bring these themes together. Christianson sees his taking on of the persona of Solomon as 'absurd' and he argues that Qoheleth shows himself to be an observer of extreme situations in 4:1–3 when he speaks of the tears of the oppressed and non-existence being better than a life of oppression (a sentiment echoed by many a Holocaust sufferer). Qoheleth is a weary observer, worn down by observation of absurdity (e.g. 7:15–18). He describes the results of excess and advocates avoiding it. The very non-systematic nature of his thought and contradictions feeds into this acknowledgment of the absurd. The failure of language – 'All words are wearisome' (1:8) – is another theme echoing the experience of Holocaust survivors who found it impossible to put their dreadful experiences into words. Ecclesiastes has much to say about death, linking up with existential and Holocaust themes. 'Consciousness of human finitude and death is a theme that courses throughout Qoheleth's narrative'[46] – for example, 8:6–9. Another important theme in this context is 'memory' of the past – for example, 2:16, when he talks about the danger of losing the memory of past generations, or 1:11. Christianson links this to the Holocaust when he comments, 'One way survival was managed in the camps was through the determination to remember and be remembered, so that the world would not forget the atrocity of the whole event.' Finally he draws out the theme of hope, against all the odds, that persisted in the Holocaust situation and shines through Qoheleth's narrative at key points (e.g. 5:19–20). Thus Christianson has in a sense adopted two 'readings' – existentialism and the Holocaust angle – and applied them to the text of Ecclesiastes, drawing out themes from the book that we know to be there in a poignant fresh context. This is at the heart of the reader-response technique.

Wider cultural and religious use

Wider cultural use of the Ecclesiastes text is also of interest, such as in art (one thinks in particular of the Dutch *vanitas* movement of the seventeenth

---

46. Ibid., p. 270.

century, with its interest in still life with timepieces, dead animals and human skulls to represent the vanity theme) and music. In a recent article I have explored the way texts from Ecclesiastes have been used as an inspiration for musical expression.[47] Particular themes such as time (Eccl. 3:1–8), the fate of humans and animals (3:9–14) and 'vanity' have been of particular interest to librettists and composers. I wonder how many people realized, as they sang Pete Seeger's song 'Turn, Turn, Turn' in the 1960s, that they were essentially repeating the words of Ecclesiastes 3:1–8 in the AV. Performed by The Byrds, it reached number 1 in the US charts in 1965. The only additions were the words 'Turn, turn, turn', which neatly disguise the citation but also provide an interpretation of the passage by drawing out the repetitive patterns of life; and the last line 'I swear it's not too late'. Occasional lines of the poem are omitted (e.g. 'a time to keep and a time to cast away'), and quite often the order is changed for rhyming reasons (e.g. reap/weep) or in order to put the positive sentiment first. The song is upbeat and positive and loses the world-weary feel of the original text to give a sense of rejoicing at different facets of a rich human life, with the suggestion that what goes around comes around. In the context of the 1960s this song was a celebration of 'counterculture', celebrating human activity freed from social constraints; it was a time freed from 'giving the right impression' or 'doing the right thing' in a narrow social sense. I also found some classical examples – such as Norman Dello Joio's *Meditations of Ecclesiastes* (1956) for string orchestra, which uses the words of the same poem as headings for orchestral music of varying sentiments. So we find *adagio* for 'a time to weep and to mourn', but *spumante* for 'a time to dance and to laugh'.

Postmodernism has opened up awareness of the relativity of all 'readings', so how can we find 'authoritative' readings within church or synagogue? Diversity of interpretation still seems to be the norm; look, for example, at the different uses of the text in the modern church or synagogue. How often does Ecclesiastes come up in the church lectionary? Very rarely. How aware are people of this gem of a book? Yet in Jewish tradition it is read regularly as a festival text, as one of the *Megilloth*, and, with the others, related to the stages of life. Ecclesiastes is the fourth of the five *Megilloth*, the Five Scrolls – with Song of Songs, Ruth and Lamentations before it, and Esther after it. Ecclesiastes is read at Sukkoth and speaks of the autumn of life, when one has gained enough wisdom to know what is truly of value and enduring. Life is evaluated in the

---

47. K. J. Dell, '"A Time to Dance": Music, the Bible and the Book of Ecclesiastes', *ExpTim* 126/3 (2014), pp. 114–121.

context of our common mortality.[48] In both Jewish and Christian tradition, Ecclesiastes 3 is often read at funerals, with its idea that there is a time for everything in life, and with its celebration of life, accompanied by a sense that there is also a time to die. Everything has its time in the natural cycle, birth and death alike.

A wisdom text?

Most treatments of Ecclesiastes (apart from commentaries) will be found in introductions to wisdom literature and this is where it seems to have a natural home. The question of the genre of Ecclesiastes is relevant here and has been the topic of much discussion. Was the author trying to undermine traditional wisdom or did his work represent a fresh direction for wisdom as it developed? M. V. Fox[49] argues that the quest for knowledge is a keynote of Qoheleth's method and in this he has gone beyond the received wisdom of the sages to create knowledge of his own. He does not attack wisdom literature; rather he regards his own thought as wisdom of the same kind as that of his predecessors, tinged, however, with an expression of disappointment at the non-realization of its ideals. As Fox writes, 'He took existing wisdom to himself – not to attack it but to make it his own ... But then he proceeded to extend it boldly by seeking new knowledge in new ways in new frontiers.'[50] Murphy[51] argues a similar case that Qoheleth remains within the boundaries of biblical wisdom. Thus he writes of the author of Ecclesiastes, 'His own wisdom consisted in seeing deeper and further than the traditional wisdom, in purifying it, even to such an extent that it did not appear to be viable. But in style he remained faithful to the tradition of the sages.'[52]

The book in many ways branches out on its own as *sui generis*, and yet it has strong roots in the wisdom literature, particularly, I would argue, in

---

48. I am grateful to Rabbi Rachel Benjamin for these insights.
49. M. V. Fox, *Qoheleth and His Contradictions*, Bible and Literature Series 18, JSOTSup 71 (Sheffield: Almond Press, 1989).
50. Ibid., p. 120.
51. R. E. Murphy, 'The Sage in Ecclesiastes and Qoheleth the Sage', in J. G. Gammie and L. G. Perdue (eds.), *The Sage in Israel and the Ancient Near East* (Winona Lake: Eisenbrauns, 1990).
52. Ibid., p. 271.

Proverbs.[53] Its forms are predominantly from the wisdom tradition and not from other areas of life. For example, 7:1–6 follows the patterns of traditional wisdom sayings, a common wisdom genre found in Proverbs. However, the positive nature of the wisdom in these verses is nullified in verse 6b, when the author makes the adverse verdict that 'this also is vanity'. Verses 7–12, however, continue in traditional wisdom-saying style, the verses culminating in praise of wisdom in verses 11–12. Qoheleth shows by his interpolation in verse 6b that he sees wisdom as a worthless exercise in that humankind gains no achievement by this effort. In this sentiment he is showing a scepticism which is at odds with Proverbs. The author is, then, using a traditional wisdom form – the wisdom saying – and showing its shortcomings by a 'reflection' of his own. He often uses this technique; for example, 8:12–13 is negated by the framework in verses 11 and 14; or he simply contrasts two proverbs, thus throwing up inconsistencies within the wisdom tradition itself (e.g. 4:5–6). Or he may quote a proverb in support of an argument (5:3) or to provide a text or further commentary (e.g. 4:9 is commented on in 4:10–12). Elsewhere Qoheleth narrates a tale to make, for instance, an 'example' story (e.g. 9:13–16). He uses the traditional form of the example story within his own argument which, in content, departs from traditional wisdom. Forms are placed in a new context but the content remains the same.

Much of the content of this book is unorthodox and questions accepted values, although, because of the contradictions, other parts appear to be more traditional. Many preoccupations are the same as in Proverbs – concern with order, knowledge, the meaning of life, the scheme of punishment and reward and God's uncertain role in it, questions about life and death, and the nature and value of the wisdom exercise. In terms of content, we find in Ecclesiastes a sharp questioning of the tradition, with contradiction of thought in a number of areas, and yet one counterbalanced by quotation from the tradition.

In using almost exclusively wisdom forms, the author of Ecclesiastes remains much closer to mainline wisdom than does the author of Job. I have argued in my own work[54] that this book has a less close relation to the book of Job than

---

53. K. J. Dell, 'Ecclesiastes as Mainstream Wisdom (Without Job)', in G. J. Brooke and P. Van Hecke (eds.), *Goochem in Mokum: Papers on Biblical and Related Wisdom Read at the Fifteenth Joint Meeting of the Society for Old Testament Study and the Oudtestamentisch Werkgezelschap, Amsterdam July 2012*, OTS 68 (Leiden: Brill, 2015, forthcoming).

54. K. J. Dell, *The Book of Job as Sceptical Literature*, BZAW 197 (Berlin: De Gruyter, 1991); and *'Get Wisdom, Get Insight': An Introduction to Israel's Wisdom Literature* (London: DLT, 2000).

many have maintained. They may both be 'wisdom in revolt' but they are very different in character: Ecclesiastes moves beyond the feisty challenge of Job towards realistic resignation. It is as if the fight has gone out of this author. Ecclesiastes stands at the end of the biblical wisdom tradition and from that context criticizes it. Therefore, Ecclesiastes, in my view, represents a protesting or sceptical strain which arises closely out of the wisdom exercise even if it is of a deeply questioning kind. Qoheleth's sentiments are anti-wisdom in the sense that they stress the impossibility of being able to know anything with certainty, and yet they confirm the God-given aspect of the wisdom quest. Human wisdom is ephemeral, but God's wisdom endures. Human beings will never fully understand; all they can do is acknowledge the futility of life but trust in God all the same. Confidence in the wisdom quest seems to have been definitively undermined – and yet the use of traditional proverbs juxtaposed with fresh insights suggests that it is not defunct. The author may, then, have belonged to circles of the wise – and this book certainly has a high literary quality – but there is a theological aspect to it that may suggest a broader instructional context: a temple school-type one, perhaps, rather than a more secular, educational one.

Wider questions have been raised recently about the whole nomenclature of 'wisdom'.[55] Should we categorize the book in this way? Would it be preferable to see it as one of the *Megilloth*, or as part of a Solomonic corpus with the Song of Songs, or as simply one of the Writings, standing alone? How we categorize has considerable impact on our interpretation.[56]

For many years – largely in connection with seeing Ecclesiastes as part of 'wisdom literature' which in general (or at least until Ben Sira) has little to do with the history of Israel – the book has been dissociated from the wider Israelite story. However, a recent book by Jennie Barbour[57] has brought us up short in this area. She argues strongly that there are resonances of the wider Israelite story hidden in this book. Her main thesis is that there is a collective memory of the history of the monarchy, presented predominantly in terms of its failure, within the book. She argues that wisdom literature is not 'unhistorical', as many

---

55. S. Weeks, *Introduction to the Wisdom Literature* (London: T&T Clark, 2010).
56. See K. J. Dell, 'Deciding the Boundaries of Wisdom: Applying the Concept of Family Resemblance', in M. R. Sneed (ed.), *Was There a Wisdom Tradition? New Prospects in Israelite Wisdom Studies*, Ancient Israel and Its Literature (Atlanta: SBL, 2015), pp. 145–160.
57. J. Barbour, *The Story of Israel in the Book of Qoheleth* (Oxford: Oxford University Press, 2012).

have argued, and that Ben Sira is not the first to concern himself with historical events and persons within a wisdom context. Rather the shadowy presence of the past is a constant theme of the book, with rich allusion to the narrative of Israel's decline and fall. She argues that Qoheleth himself is a deliberate composite of all the nation's kings, hence the ambiguity in the title. Qoheleth is Solomon as a fiction but also with accretions from his kingly successors, there being echoes of many texts other than just 1 Kings or 2 Chronicles. This thesis leads us to wonder afresh at the nature of this book within the 'canon'.

Intertextuality

There is also recent interest in the book's possible intertexts: Genesis 1 – 11 is frequently cited[58] but there has been little work done beyond that comparison. This has been rectified in a volume edited by myself and Will Kynes[59] which looks first at Ecclesiastes in dialogue with other biblical texts and then at a wider dialogue beyond simply biblical texts. In part 1 Kynes,[60] for example, looks in his essay at the connections between Ecclesiastes 11:9 and Numbers 15:39, a link noted by the rabbis as a potential contradiction and pursued by early translators who made verbal changes to bring the texts into agreement. Kynes looks at the wider context of the allusion by considering the wider story of the spies to which the Numbers text itself alludes and draws attention to an important corrective to the idea that intertextuality is simply about 'source-hunting'. Rather the contextual meeting point should be of key concern, and this leads Kynes to bring in a second intertext with Numbers 15 in Ecclesiastes 5:5. These connections suggest that Numbers 15 and the story of the spies flow as an undercurrent below Qoheleth's turbulent message. Still in Ecclesiastes 5, Bernard Levinson[61] looks at the allusion to Deuteronomy 23:22–24 in

---

58. C. C. Forman, 'Koheleth's Use of Genesis', *JSS* 5 (1960), pp. 256–265. See discussion in the context of intertextuality in K. J. Dell, 'Exploring Intertextual Links between Ecclesiastes and Genesis 1 – 11', in K. Dell and W. Kynes (eds.), *Reading Ecclesiastes Intertextually*, LHBOTS 587 (London: T&T Clark, 2014), pp. 3–14.
59. Dell and Kynes, *Reading*.
60. W. Kynes, 'Follow Your Heart and Do Not Say It Was a Mistake: Qoheleth's Allusions to Numbers 15 and the Story of the Spies', in Dell and Kynes, *Reading*, pp. 15–27.
61. B. Levinson, '"Better That You Should Not Vow Than That You Vow and Not Fulfill": Qoheleth's Use of Textual Allusion and the Transformation of Deuteronomy's Law of Vows', in Dell and Kynes, *Reading*, pp. 28–41.

Ecclesiastes 5:3–4 and argues that the author of Ecclesiastes deliberately reworked that text as a critique and personal ownership of the issue in a wisdom context. In part 2, comparison with the Ancient Near East is made. William Anderson,[62] for example, considers Egyptian texts and the Epic of Gilgamesh, arguing for authorial allusion on the one hand but also echoes that suggest that these texts breathed a shared cultural air. Turning to the Greeks, John Jarick[63] offers a look at Hellenistic cultural parallels through the lens of comedy. He is not arguing for any diachronic link between the thought-worlds, but suggests that Qoheleth's words of pleasure may acquire a comedic tone when read in the light of such parallels, to counteract the usual evaluation of this author as gloomy and pessimistic. The findings of this twenty-three-essay volume start to demonstrate that perhaps this book of Ecclesiastes is not such a unique and lone text after all. Is this text part of a wider phenomenon or still a rather lone exposition? Does it claim to represent Israel's wider story or is it simply an individual musing from a rather world-weary sage? This book has always been elusive and continues to be so; perhaps that is its real character.

© Katharine J. Dell, 2016

---

62. W. Anderson, 'Ecclesiastes in the Intertextual Matrix of Ancient Near Eastern Literature', in Dell and Kynes, *Reading*, pp. 157–176.
63. J. Jarick, 'Ecclesiastes among the Comedians', in Dell and Kynes, *Reading*, pp. 176–188.

5. SEEKING WISDOM IN THE SONG OF SONGS

Rosalind Clarke

Three things are too wonderful for me;
    four I do not understand:
the way of an eagle in the sky,
    the way of a serpent on a rock,
the way of a ship on the high seas,
    and the way of a man with a virgin.[1]
(Prov. 30:18–19)

Thus the book of Proverbs indicates that the subject of the Song of Songs – that is, romantic or sexual love, the way of a man with a virgin – is rightly a matter for wisdom.[2] Indeed the Song of Songs has a long history of connection with wisdom going as far back at least as the LXX when the Song began to be grouped together with the other wisdom books.[3] This history is unsurprising,

---

1. Bible quotes in this chapter, unless stated otherwise, are from the ESV.
2. The proverb is far from an isolated reference to the theme of love. Indeed Gerhard von Rad has noted the prevalence of love as a theme in the wisdom literature: *Wisdom in Israel*, tr. James D. Martin (London: SCM, 1972), p. 166.
3. The Hebrew tradition includes the Song in the Writings and specifically in the small group of books known as the Megilloth. The Greek tradition which underlies the

given the wisdom themes, language, imagery, and recognizable wisdom forms which are present in the Song, even if a wisdom interpretation has frequently been overshadowed by allegorical readings or more recently the so-called literal interpretation.[4] In modern scholarship, the Song has not generally been recognized as a wisdom text, and yet there is wisdom to be found in the Song, for those who will seek it. There is evidence of wisdom in the genre of the Song, in its instruction for women, in its parallels with the personified Woman Wisdom, and in the role of Solomon.

Seeking wisdom in the genre of the Song

The parallels between the Song and other Ancient Near Eastern love poetry have dominated the discussion of its genre since their discovery,[5] and on this basis many scholars now consider it to be a settled matter that the genre of the Song is lyric love poetry.[6] However, there are still some who argue that the Song of Songs is a wisdom book, or at least that, in its canonical form, it exhibits evidence of a wisdom redaction and ought to be read as wisdom literature.

---

order of books in most Christian Bibles puts the Song together with wisdom books. See Lee Martin McDonald and James A. Sanders (eds.), *The Canon Debate* (Peabody: Hendrickson, 2002), pp. 585–590, for extensive evidence of the canon lists from both Eastern and Western church fathers: the important uncial manuscripts and the current Christian canons. In almost every example, the Song is listed together with Proverbs and Ecclesiastes, and frequently as part of a larger wisdom group including Job, Wisdom of Solomon and Sirach.

4. A thorough history of the interpretation of the Song can be found in M. H. Pope, *Song of Songs* (New York: Doubleday, 1977), pp. 89–229; a briefer summary is in Richard S. Hess, *Song of Songs* (Grand Rapids: Baker Academic, 2005), pp. 22–29.

5. See Jerrold S. Cooper, 'New Cuneiform Parallels to the Song of Songs', *JBL* 90 (1971), pp. 157–162, for a summary of the parallels with Egyptian, Arabic, Sumero-Akkadian and other ANE literature.

6. Katharine Dell observes that 'even on a wider definition of the genre of wisdom, which might arguably include works influenced strongly by wisdom forms or ideas, the Song tends to stay off the list. The reason is because "love songs" are a clearly defined genre in their own right and are paralleled by Egyptian love poetry' ('Does the Song of Songs Have Any Connections to Wisdom?', in Anselm C. Hagedorn [ed.], *Perspectives on the Song of Songs*, BZAW [Berlin/New York: De Gruyter, 2005], p. 9).

Brevard Childs argues that the attribution to Solomon in the opening verse of the Song is the key factor in its canonical redaction. For him, the superscription is a clear indication that the Song, as Scripture, is intended to be read as wisdom literature.[7] The attribution links the book with Proverbs and Ecclesiastes, as well as the Wisdom of Solomon, all of which bear Solomon's name and are unambiguously wisdom texts. The form of the superscription does not necessarily imply Solomonic authorship of the book,[8] but invoking Solomon's name may be a deliberate way of connecting the book with the biblical tradition of Solomonic wisdom.[9]

One of the most thorough defenders of the Song as a wisdom text is Michael Sadgrove.[10] He points to the evidence of the didactic refrains addressed to the daughters of Jerusalem throughout the book (2:7; 3:5; 5:8; 8:4), the abstract wisdom teaching about love in the last chapter of the book (8:6–12), and the riddle of the vineyards which begins in 1:6 and concludes in 8:11–12. For Sadgrove, the last aspect forms a frame for the whole book as a wisdom puzzle.[11] Such wisdom elements do not necessarily determine the genre of the whole book,[12] but they certainly lend support to the argument for reading the Song

---

7. Brevard S. Childs, *Introduction to the Old Testament as Scripture* (London: SCM, 1979), p. 574.
8. Dating and authorship of the Song are notoriously difficult to identify with any certainty. The superscription may be translated 'of' or 'for' Solomon, rather than 'by' Solomon, or it may have been a deliberately pseudonymous label added by a later redactor. Evidence of late linguistic features suggests that whatever role Solomon might have played, there was a significantly later redaction. Further, the negative comparison between the lover in the Song and Solomon in Song 8:11–12 is unlikely to have been written by or for Solomon himself.
9. But see Ps. 72 for a similar Solomonic attribution applied to a non-wisdom psalm.
10. M. Sadgrove, 'The Song of Songs as Wisdom Literature', in E. A. Livingstone (ed.), *Studia Biblica 1978: I*, JSOTSup (Sheffield: JSOT, 1979), pp. 245–248.
11. Sadgrove points to the example of Samson's riddle (Judg. 14:12–18) to argue that a wedding was 'a frequent Sitz im Leben for riddles' and thus suggests that the Song as a whole is an 'exploration of the riddle of love' ('Song as Wisdom', p. 247). This claim is overstated, given that he has only one example, and that in unusual circumstances.
12. One scholar who recognizes the wisdom elements in the Song but does not consider them sufficient to transform its genre is N. J. Tromp, 'Wisdom and the Canticle. Ct. 8, 6c–7b: Text, Character, Message and Import', in M. Gilbert (ed.), *La Sagesse de l'Ancien Testament*, BETL 51 (Leuven: Leuven University Press, 1979), p. 6.

as a wisdom text, especially if they are seen to be situated in a wider context of wisdom teaching. Such a context is suggested by the didactic framework running through the book in which the female character instructs a group of women known as the 'daughters of Jerusalem' about the dangers and joys of love (1:4b, 5–6; 2:7; 3:5, 11; 5:1b, 8–16; 6:1–3; 8:4). It is possible to read the whole Song in this framework, with the various scenes and poems being recounted by the woman for the benefit of the women she is instructing. This female instruction has a parallel with the male wisdom teaching in Proverbs 1 – 9, in which a father addresses his son about the dangers and joys of love. The wisdom of the Song is also found in its themes. Love itself is a wisdom theme, as noted above, but so also is the nature imagery which pervades the Song of Songs.[13] Katharine Dell identifies numerous wisdom themes in the Song, including pursuit, waiting, riches and material goods, the tree of life, the bringer of peace, power over death, entrapment, seduction, spices, and female initiation of sexual encounters.[14]

Thus the superscription, the implied setting, the themes, and the inclusion of proverbs, sayings and riddles in the book all suggest that it could be a wisdom text, or, at the very least, a book with strong connections to the wisdom tradition. What then of the commonest reason for rejecting the classification of the Song of Songs as wisdom literature – that is, that it conforms more closely to the expectations of the genre of love poetry? This conclusion is drawn primarily on the basis of the parallels with the other Ancient Near Eastern love poems.[15] Caution needs to be exercised with respect to these parallels, which are not all as persuasive as they first appear.[16] Further, it must be remembered that there are no examples of Ancient Near Eastern love poetry in the extended form we find in the Song, none which contain comparable abstract reflections on the nature of love, none which share its Israelite setting, and, of course, none which

---

13. See Sadgrove, 'Song as Wisdom', p. 247.
14. Dell, 'Does the Song?', p. 20.
15. John B. White, *A Study of the Language of Love in the Song of Songs and Ancient Egyptian Poetry*, SBLDS (Missoula: Scholars Press, 1978); Michael V. Fox, *The Song of Songs and the Ancient Egyptian Love Songs* (Madison: University of Wisconsin Press, 1985).
16. Some of the apparent links between the Song and its contemporary parallels are no more compelling than would be expected between the Song and any other piece of pastoral love poetry, as demonstrated by Hector Patmor in 'The Plain and Literal Sense: On Contemporary Assumptions about the Song of Songs', *VT* 56/2 (2006), pp. 239–250.

have the same context within the Jewish and Christian sacred literature. While the comparative texts are extremely valuable in the identification of the form of many of the poetic units within the book, they lack persuasive parallels with the Song as a whole. The identification of the form of individual units within the Song is not the same as identification of the genre of the whole book: a book may contain stanzas of lyric love poetry without itself being a love poem; it may contain excerpts of nuptial liturgy without being a liturgical text; and indeed it may have wisdom elements without being a wisdom book. If the genre of the Song is identified as love poetry, then it must be acknowledged as the only example of its kind within the limits of that genre. And if the whole book is identified as love poetry, then an explanation must be found for the intrusion of the didactic elements such as instructions to the daughters of Jerusalem and the wisdom elements of chapter 8.

By contrast, if the Song as a whole is identified as a wisdom book with a didactic framework, then the inclusion of the love poetry is easily explained. The woman addresses the daughters of Jerusalem directly throughout, using examples from her own experience in order to add weight to the instruction she is giving. She reports her conversations with her lover, her encounters on the city streets, even the experiences of her wedding night, for the benefit of her students. She invites these other women to celebrate her relationship and aspire to something similar for themselves, and she also warns them about the potential dangers associated with romantic and sexual love. Certainly the Song includes beautiful love poetry, which does have parallels within the other Ancient Near Eastern literature, but the context of those love poems within the Song gives them a further level of meaning. In the context of the Song, and in the context of the canon of Scripture, they bear all the appearance of a wisdom redaction.[17]

Seeking wisdom for women in the Song

The Song of Songs is unique in its focus on teaching by and for women, and this has prompted some scholars to posit a female author of the Song.[18] Kenton Sparks goes so far as to suggest that 'The Song of Songs originated as a wisdom

---

17. See Roland E. Murphy, *The Tree of Life: An Exploration of Biblical Wisdom Literature*, 3rd edn (Grand Rapids: Eerdmans, 1990), p. 106.
18. André LaCocque, *Romance She Wrote* (Harrisburg: Trinity Press International, 1998), and Kenton Sparks, 'The Song of Songs: Wisdom for Young Jewish Women', *CBQ* 70/2 (2008), pp. 277–299, both argue for female authorship.

composition, as a collection of love songs edited to teach young Jewish women propriety in matters of love and sex',[19] although it seems unlikely that the Song ever functioned as a textbook for propriety! Jill Munro agrees that the Song functions as romantic education for women,[20] though she does not go so far as to claim a female wisdom school as its *Sitz im Leben*.

While the authorship of the Song is likely to remain a matter for debate, its internal setting does indicate some kind of female instruction. The woman's role as wisdom teacher may be indicated by her description as the *shulammite* (Song 6:13), an ambiguous identification which may relate to her place of origin,[21] her role in bringing peace (Song 8:10)[22] or her position as a 'female Solomon', that is, a female wisdom teacher.[23] The main problem with reading the woman as a female wisdom teacher instructing a school of women is the complete absence of any evidence that such a school ever existed in Israel. There were certainly 'wise women'[24] and the book of Proverbs refers to a mother's instruction as a source of wisdom (Prov. 1:8). It is possible that some of these women gathered groups of female disciples about them, and that their teaching was passed down through an oral and eventually a written tradition, but this is all speculative. Precisely because of the speculative nature of the female wisdom tradition, Dell suggests the Song might have been used for training young men in wisdom. The content of the Song, she says, 'may well have been relevant in the wisdom context of the training of young men in the ways of the world, notably here in the values of fidelity and mutuality in relation to love between the sexes'.[25] It would certainly be wrong to situate the Song within a wholly feminine wisdom tradition, since the Solomonic attribution in the opening verse of the book brings it firmly into the mainstream – that is, masculine – wisdom tradition. There is wisdom for men to be found in the Song, as we shall see below, but the implied setting within the book is the teaching of the daughters of Jerusalem, and this woman-to-women context should not be overlooked.

---

19. Sparks, 'Wisdom', p. 278.
20. Jill M. Munro, *Spikenard and Saffron: A Study in the Poetic Language of the Song of Songs* (Sheffield: Sheffield Academic Press, 1995), p. 147.
21. By comparison with Abishag the Shunammite (1 Kgs 2:17, 22).
22. As proposed by F. S. Leahy in 'The Song of Solomon in Pastoral Teaching', *EQ* 27 (1955), p. 208.
23. This is Sparks' view ('Wisdom', p. 287).
24. See 2 Sam. 14; 20.
25. Dell, 'Does the Song?', p. 9.

The daughters of Jerusalem appear throughout the Song, as its internal audience. The woman is their teacher, using her own experiences to illustrate her warnings and exhortations. Her repeated instruction in the refrains has all the hallmarks of wisdom as she warns them about the dangers of loving at the wrong time, invoking the created order – in the shape of the gazelles and the does of the field – as the basis of her exhortation (1:7; 3:5). These warnings against loving at the wrong time are supported by the woman's own experiences, particularly in 3:1–5 and 5:2–8. The other refrain, the statement of mutual possession between the lovers (2:16; 6:3; 7:10), provides a strong contrast, celebrating the contentment to be found in the arms of one's lover in the right time and place. The daughters of Jerusalem are thus invited to bear witness to both the joys of love and the pain it can bring. They are urged to celebrate the wedding of the king and the consummation of the marriage, and they are given reasons to admire the woman's beloved and seek him. Such love is worthy of pursuit, at the right time with the right man. The woman in the Song provides a positive role model in her celebration of female sexuality and strength.[26]

The explicit wisdom teaching of Song 8:6–12 consolidates both the warning and the celebration of love. The power of love is as strong as death (8:6), a reminder that it is not to be trifled with. Love is worth more than any possessions (8:7), a reminder that it is worthy of pursuit. The woman's brothers rightly protect her while she is too young for love (8:8–9), but she is the one who chooses to give herself when it is the right time for love (8:10). The parable of the vineyards (8:11–12) is a vivid demonstration of the importance of exclusivity in a romantic and sexual relationship.

The Song's wisdom for women complements that for men in Proverbs 1 – 9. While the male wisdom teacher in Proverbs emphasizes the importance of choosing the right woman, the female wisdom instructor in the Song emphasizes the importance of waiting for the right time and place. Both demonstrate the seductive and dangerous power of love in the wrong circumstances, and both emphasize the importance of fidelity.[27]

---

26. Cheryl Exum points out the unique contribution of the Song of Songs in this regard: 'Without the Song, we could be tempted to conclude from the rest of the Bible that desire in Israel was constructed as male, and as dangerous, something to be repressed or controlled. Because we possess the Song of Songs, we know that a romantic vision of love was available in ancient Israel, a vision that recognized both desire and sexual pleasure as mutual and that viewed positively a woman actively seeking to gratify her desire' (*Song of Songs*, OTL [Louisville: Westminster John Knox, 2005], p. 13).

27. See Prov. 5:15–20 and Song 6:9; 8:11–12.

Seeking Woman Wisdom in the Song

In the Solomonic wisdom books, the two female characters of Woman Wisdom and Female Folly stand out.[28] These women dominate the narrative of Proverbs 1 – 9, and Woman Wisdom also appears in several other places in the wisdom literature.[29] Specific passages in Proverbs and Sirach bear strong verbal and thematic links to the Song, centred on the role of these women.[30] Comparisons of the woman in the Song with both Woman Wisdom and Female Folly demonstrate that she shares characteristics with both women, though ultimately she is shown to be a wise choice for her bridegroom.

Woman Wisdom as she is portrayed in Proverbs has much in common with the woman in the Song: both women, unusually in the Bible, speak at length;[31] both issue invitations;[32] both offer instruction;[33] both take initiative in their relationships;[34] both are utterly desirable;[35] both bring peace.[36] Men are encouraged to pursue Woman Wisdom and make her their bride. The woman in the Song is likewise pursued, though only by one man. The woman in the Song is distinguished from Woman Wisdom in this respect: her relationship is exclusive and mutual, whereas Wisdom seeks many lovers. The woman enjoys and delights in her lover just as he enjoys and delights in her. She gains as many blessings from their relationship as he does. By contrast, Woman Wisdom speaks in condescending terms about the men whom she woos: they are foolish and simple. She bestows blessings upon them, but does not receive any from them.

In Sirach 24, Woman Wisdom is portrayed as a bride who possesses every desirable attribute of beauty and fertility, of fruitfulness and ability to satisfy, of sanctuary and purity. Wisdom describes her growth and fruitfulness in Sirach 24 in terms that are reminiscent of the woman in the

---

28. Occasional brief references are made to women as wives, mothers and adulteresses, but only in generic terms rather than as identifiable individuals (real or metaphorical).
29. Wis. 6:12–23; 7:7 – 8:21; Sir. 4:11–19; 14:20–27; 15:1–8; 24:1 – 25:1.
30. See esp. Prov. 5:15–19; 7:6–23; Sir. 24:16–27.
31. Prov. 1: 22–33; 8:4–36; cf. Song 3:1–5; 5:1–8, 10–16.
32. Prov. 9:5–6; cf. Song 4:16; 7:11–12; 8:1–2.
33. Prov. 1:22, 33; 8:6–11; 9:5–9; cf. Song 2:7; 3:5; 5:8; 8:4.
34. Prov. 1:20–21; 8:1–3; 9:3; cf. Song 3:4; 4:16 – 5:1; 7:13; 8:2–3.
35. Prov. 3:14–15; 8:11, 18–19; cf. Song 2:15; 6:10; 7:2; 8:7.
36. Prov. 3:17; cf. Song 8:10.

Song.³⁷ Her geographical location (in Lebanon, on the heights of Hermon, in En-gedi and in Jericho) is important to her growth (Sir. 24:13–14), just as it is important for the woman in the Song to leave Lebanon and the peaks of Senir and Hermon to come into her fruitful paradise (Song 4:8). Wisdom's perfume is linked to the incense which perfumed the tabernacle (Sir. 24:15), while the woman in the Song is fragranced with frankincense and myrrh (Song 4:14), among other spices. Both women offer their fruits to those who desire them (Sir. 24:19–21; Song 4:16), with eating and drinking the sign of possession (Sir. 24:19–21; Song 4:16 – 5:1). Both women are identified as the garden, and as the water which makes the garden fertile (Sir. 24:30–31; Song 4:12, 15).

In the intertextual reading, the interaction between the texts works in two directions: the reading of Sirach 24 is influenced by Song 4, but so too is the reading of Song 4 influenced by Sirach 24. Just as Woman Wisdom in Sirach 24 portrays herself as a bride, so too the bride in the Song is portrayed as Woman Wisdom, possessing characteristics beyond those of an ordinary woman. She too is located in the land and the sanctuary, abundant with blossoms and fruits, scented with incense. This bride is an Eden-like paradise, being both a garden and the flowing rivers which water it. This bride invites her lover into a sanctuary space, to feast on her fruits. It is as if the woman in the Song performs the role of Woman Wisdom for her husband.

If the woman in the Song has characteristics of Woman Wisdom, she also, however, shares the attributes of Female Folly.³⁸ She is no less a seductress than Female Folly: her lips likewise drip with honey;³⁹ she too goes out looking for a man in the city streets at night;⁴⁰ she invites the man to spend a night with

---

37. See Gerald T. Sheppard, *Wisdom as a Hermeneutical Construct: A Study in the Sapientializing of the Old Testament*, BZAW (Berlin/New York: De Gruyter, 1980), for a detailed intertextual reading of Sir. 24 with the Song. Edmée Kingsmill has also noted that there are twenty-seven Greek words from Sir. 24 found in the LXX of the Song of Songs, with ten of these concentrated in the short section of Song 4:8 – 5:1 (*Song of Songs and the Eros of God: A Study in Biblical Intertextuality*, Oxford Theological Monographs [Oxford: Oxford University Press, 2009], pp. 50–51).

38. Gale Yee argues persuasively that the 'strange woman', the 'adulteress' and 'female folly' should all be identified as part of the same personification in Prov. 1 – 9 ('I Have Perfumed My Bed with Myrrh: The Foreign Woman [*'iššâ zārâ*] in Proverbs 1 – 9', *JSOT* 43 [1989], p. 54).

39. Prov. 5:3; cf. Song 4:11.

40. Prov. 7:6–12; cf. Song 3:1–4; 5:2–7.

her;[41] she too promises that he will be satisfied and delighted with her.[42] The seduction scene in Proverbs 7:1–27 has strong parallels with Song 2:8 – 3:5, such that Martin Paul sees a direct literary dependence between the two.[43] Both passages begin with what Robert O'Connell calls a 'Woman and the Window' scene,[44] which typically contains themes of sexual attraction and threat. In each case the woman leaves her home at night to seek a man in the dangerous city streets. But in Proverbs 7, the woman is the source of danger, whereas in Song 3, she is the one under threat. The superficial similarities of the scene serve to highlight the fundamental difference between the two women. The woman in the Song, despite her seemingly brazen behaviour, does not allow herself to be characterized as the dangerous woman. She is not a villainess, luring innocent, foolish young men to their destruction. She reverses the view through the window and thus transforms the image of a wicked, wanton woman from Proverbs 7 into the beautiful, beloved bride of the Song.

Choosing the right woman is at the very heart of what it means to be wise, as Nancy Tan observes: 'The requirement to choose between these female figures is established . . . even before they are each given an opportunity to speak.'[45] The implied male readers of Proverbs are instructed to choose between Woman Wisdom and Female Folly, two women who in outward appearances appear to have much in common. Both appear desirable, both take initiative, both make their voices heard in public places, and both share these characteristics with the woman in the Song. She comes with no label to indicate whether it would be wise or foolish to choose her. The book provides no instructor to guide the reader other than the woman herself. The wisdom-seeker must study this woman carefully, looking for the clues which would indicate that she is a wise choice, sharing the characteristics of Woman Wisdom herself, or for the signs that she is a wanton woman, seducing the men she tempts into her clutches, as dangerous as Female Folly herself leading men to their death.

---

41. Prov. 7:18–20; cf. Song 7:11–13.
42. Prov. 9:17; cf. Song 7:13; 8:2.
43. Martin Paul, 'Die "Fremde Frau" in Sprichwörter 1 – 9 und die "Geliebte" des Hohenliedes: Ein Beitrag zur Intertextualität', *Biblische Notizen* 106 (2001), pp. 40–46.
44. Robert H. O'Connell, 'Proverbs VII 16–17: A Case of Fatal Deception in a "Woman and the Window" Type-Scene', *VT* 41/2 (1991), pp. 235–241.
45. Nancy Nam Hoon Tan, *The 'Foreignness' of the Foreign Woman in Proverbs 1 – 9: A Study of the Origin and Development of a Biblical Motif*, BZAW (Berlin: De Gruyter, 2008), p. 97.

Whereas the presentation of Woman Wisdom and Female Folly in Proverbs makes them appear easily distinguished, the Song of Songs rejects that sharp dichotomy. It presents only one woman, who shares characteristics with both Woman Wisdom and Female Folly, and often the same characteristics with both. All three women engage in public discourse; all go out into the city streets in search of men; all three issue invitations to enter their home; all offer food and drink; all offer intimacy; all are desirable; all exercise an unusual degree of independence from their menfolk. By embodying aspects of both Woman Wisdom and Female Folly, and especially those aspects which unite Woman Wisdom and Female Folly, the woman in the Song effectively rejects the female dichotomy established in Proverbs 1 – 9.

Real women – women like the woman in the Song – cannot be so easily divided into wives, on the one hand, and whores, on the other. They do not come with labels to identify them as princesses or prostitutes. It is not so easy to be wise in the complicated, grey areas of life as it is in the clear black and white of the opening chapters of Proverbs. In this way, the Song of Songs functions as a true test of wisdom. How should a wise man respond to this woman who takes initiative, who makes her voice heard, who will go out into the public places to seek her lover? Is she a dangerous, foreign woman who will lead a man astray? The answer, in the end, is unequivocally 'no'. Confounding expectation, this woman is a bride to be prized above all things. She is admired not only by her lover but by everyone at the king's court – queens and concubines alike.[46]

Solomon, the wisdom-seeker in the Song

Solomon is referenced throughout the Song, both by name and implication.[47] His role as temple-builder is alluded to in the reference to his curtains in 1:5, and further cultic associations may be implied by the scents and appearance of the temple incense and furnishings (3:6–11). He is the bridegroom in 3:6–11, his harem of wives and concubines appears in 6:8–9, and the parable of the vineyards in 8:11–12 contrasts his promiscuity unfavourably with the exclusivity

---

46. Song 6:9.
47. Dell points out that 'the Solomonic link seems to be more than just an attribution, in that the character of Solomon seems to pervade the Song in a more profound way than is often assumed, since he is implied in every reference to the king' ('Does the Song?', pp. 23–24).

that the woman seeks. Solomon's role as wisdom teacher is absent from the Song, but Solomon is also a wisdom-seeker, most notably in the person of Qohelet, the constructed Solomon of Ecclesiastes, who devotes his life to the pursuit of wisdom (Eccl. 1:13, 17; 2:12; 7:25; 8:16).

The male lover in the Song has one goal: to seek and to find his bride. He seeks her (2:8–9), he loves her (1:2; 7:6) and he calls her his sister (5:1), just as the wisdom-seeker in Proverbs is exhorted to do (Prov. 2:4; 3:13; 4:5–6; 7:4; 8:17). In the cycle of searching, finding and losing in the Song, the man comes leaping over mountains to stand outside his beloved's window and take her away with him (2:8–14); he leads her out of the wilderness and into the lush garden of their love (4:8–16); he makes certain of their love, both in the wedding ceremony and in the consummation of their marriage (3:6–11; 5:1). The single-mindedness of his pursuit matches that of the sage searching for wisdom, and, as indicated previously, the object of his pursuit also has much in common with Woman Wisdom.

This parallel is further strengthened by the allusions to the bridegroom as king. Solomon's kingship is notable in the wisdom books.[48] More significantly, Woman Wisdom portrays herself as a kingmaker (Prov. 8:15; cf. also Wis. 6:20; 8:14; 10:14) who crowns the one who loves her (Prov. 4:9). In the Song, the king is crowned on his wedding day (3:11), thus establishing a link between his marriage and his kingship. In the wisdom literature, to be wise is to become a king, whereas in the Song, to be married is to become a king. But Proverbs 7:4 also describes becoming wise as taking a bride, and thus these two images collude to form a single portrait of the wise king taking Woman Wisdom to be his bride. The Solomonic bridegroom in the Song is the wisdom-seeker, crowned on the occasion of his marriage, the culmination of his search for wisdom.

A straightforward identification of the man in the Song as the historical figure of Solomon is problematic, since Solomon appears in such diverse contexts within the Song. As Barry Webb observes,

> [Solomon] cannot simply be equated with the shepherd figure since in the Song there is an explicit distancing of Solomon's world from the world of the lovers (8:11). But neither can he easily be regarded as an intruder in their world, for this would cast him in the role of a villain and he can hardly be that in a book which is either 'by' him or 'for' him (1:1), and in which he is, if anything, idealized rather than vilified (1:5; 3:11).[49]

---

48. See Prov. 1:1; Eccl. 1:1, 12; Wis. 9:7.
49. B. Webb, 'The Song of Songs: A Love Poem and as Holy Scripture', *RTR* 49 (1990), pp. 92–93.

At one turn Solomon is the great warrior king, coming to claim his bride, and at the next he is the owner of an extensive harem, making him worth less than a shepherd whose woman is his very own. It seems best to view the male lover as a constructed Solomon, in the same way that Qohelet is a constructed version of Solomon in Ecclesiastes, and possibly even in a similar way to the construction of an idealized Solomon in Chronicles. The male character in the Song both embodies the Solomonic ideal (3:6) and is better than the Solomonic reality (8:11–12). The effect of this is to reinforce the image of the man in the Song as the true romantic ideal. He is as good as Solomon in all the ways that Solomon was good, and better than Solomon in all the ways that Solomon failed. He is a wise man, who pursues his bride, enjoys her and is committed to her exclusively. He is a king whose kingdom is at the height of its glory, crowned on the day of his wedding with wisdom and love. The Song's Solomon is an exemplary figure, demonstrating what it means to be a true Israelite in his private life, rather than in the public spheres of politics or religion.

Here, then, is the wisdom of the Song: follow the example of the idealized Solomonic wisdom-seeker, by seeking a wise woman and making her your bride. It is in these activities of seeking and finding that the wisdom-seeker himself becomes wise. Perhaps the parallel descriptions and mirrored speech patterns of the male and female lovers in the Song indicate just this: that by loving wisdom and possessing wisdom, it is possible to take on the characteristics of wisdom and become truly wise.

© Rosalind Clarke, 2016

PART 3:

THEMES

6. IS RUTH ALSO AMONG THE WISE?

Gregory Goswell

The meaning of a literary portion or work is in large measure dependent on its context, and in the case of a biblical book one of the contexts for its interpretation is the other canonical books amongst which it is situated. This phenomenon is an aspect of the biblical 'paratext' (a term coined by Gérard Genette),[1] which includes such features as book titles, book order and internal divisions within books (e.g. paragraphs). These elements provide a frame of reference for the text and exercise a powerful influence on its reception.[2] In other words, an effect

---

1. G. Genette, 'Introduction to the Paratext', *New Literary History* 22 (1991), pp. 261–272; *idem*, 'The Proustian Paratexte', *SubStance: A Review of Theory and Literary Criticism* 19 (1988), pp. 63–77, here 63 ('the marginal or supplementary data around the text'); *idem*, *Paratexts: Thresholds of Interpretation*, tr. J. E. Lewin (Cambridge: Cambridge University Press, 1997).
2. For the 'framing' function of paratext, see Marie Maclean, 'Pretexts and Paratexts: The Art of the Peripheral', *New Literary History* 22 (1991), pp. 273–293; August den Hollander, Ulrich Schmid and Willem Smelik (eds.), *Paratext and Megatext as Channels of Jewish and Christian Traditions: The Textual Markers of Contextualization*, Jewish and Christian Perspectives Series 6 (Leiden: Brill, 2006), p. vii: 'The paratext frames the text and thereby informs perception of the text by the reader'. Cf. Gale L. MacLachlan and Ian Reid, *Framing and Interpretation* (Carlton: Melbourne University Press, 1994), p. 39:

is produced on readers by placing biblical books in a particular sequence.[3] Timothy J. Stone uses the phrase 'compilation consciousness' to refer to the way in which books are associated with neighbouring books in the canon.[4] The paratextual elements embody the evaluations of ancient readers and set up certain expectations for future readers.[5] This discussion focuses on book order, and, in particular, the Proverbs–Ruth sequence found within the Hebrew canonical tradition.

Physical contiguity is regularly understood by readers to indicate that there must be a significant connection between books. This readerly habit forms the basis of the following analysis of the book of Ruth, a book that is put in more than one position by the different interpretive communities that lie behind the various biblical canons; thus, in terms of the history of interpretation, the book of Ruth has been read in more than one context.[6] There is also the possibility that the contemporary reading of biblical books in a prescribed canonical sequence will lead to fresh interpretive insights into their meaning, and that, indeed, is what I am seeking to demonstrate in this chapter which focuses on the book of Ruth in its Hebrew canonical setting.

It is not likely to be the case, however, that different canonical settings will produce wildly different (let alone contradictory) interpretations of the same book; for instance, the prominent role of Ruth herself in the book named after her will be recognized by all readers, whatever canonical position is given to the

---

(*Footnote 2 cont.*) 'But frames are not just borderlines; as we have seen, they also have the potential to carry metamessages about how to interpret what they enclose.'

3. For a recent discussion of this phenomenon, see Ched Spellman, *Toward a Canon-Conscious Reading of the Bible: Exploring the History and Hermeneutics of the Canon*, New Testament Monographs 34 (Sheffield: Sheffield Phoenix, 2014), pp. 108–123; esp. p. 109: 'Where an individual writing is positioned in relation to other writings in a collection (either materially or conceptually) has significant hermeneutical ramifications.'

4. Timothy J. Stone, *The Compilational History of the Megilloth: Canon, Contoured Intertextuality and Meaning in the Writings*, FAT II/59 (Tübingen: Mohr, 2013), p. 12.

5. See Deborah Tannen, 'What Is a Frame? Surface Evidence for Underlying Expectations', in *idem* (ed.), *Framing in Discourse* (Oxford: Oxford University Press, 1993), pp. 14–56, who speaks in terms of 'structures of expectation' (pp. 15, 21).

6. For a brief survey of the alternative canonical positions assigned to Ruth, see Andrea Beyer, *Hoffnung in Bethlehem: Innerbiblische Querbezüge als Deutungshorizonte im Ruthbuch*, BZAW 463 (Berlin: De Gruyter, 2010), pp. 141–145.

book.[7] The book received the title 'Ruth' in both the Greek and Hebrew traditions, despite the fact that the central character is Naomi. The book depicts Naomi's crisis, moving from her emptiness (1:21) to her fullness (4:17). All the other characters – her husband, her sons, her two daughters-in-law, Boaz, even the son whom Ruth bears – stand in relation to Naomi (1:3, 5, 6; 2:1; 4:17). All this tends to focalize the story from Naomi's perspective, but the book is named 'Ruth' for it is the figure of Ruth who captures the reader's interest, since she features in every scene in the book (except the scene at the city gate in 4:1–12, where, however, she is the subject of conversation in that all-male situation). The theme of the book is the manner and method by which Naomi's hopeless condition is reversed, but it is through loyal and active Ruth that the reversal takes place. This makes Ruth the *main* character (the main character need not always be the central character), and so the book is aptly named.

The placing of the book of Ruth between Judges and Samuel (in the Greek canonical tradition) reinforces a reading that gives prominence to the character and actions of Ruth, for women are conspicuous in both books as capable figures or in a heroic pose. Examples include the theologically perceptive Hannah (1 Sam. 2:1–10) and Abigail (1 Sam. 25:23–31), and women specifically described as wise are the 'wise woman' of Tekoa (2 Sam. 14) and that of Abel of Beth-maacah (2 Sam. 20). A listing of women who help rescue others must include Deborah and Jael (Judg. 4 – 5), Michal (1 Sam. 18:20–29), and once again Abigail (1 Sam. 25).[8] What I seek to show is that reading the book of Ruth in the Hebrew canon (in the position following Prov. 31) takes this interpretive move in a certain direction and encourages an appreciation of its heroine as an example of the wisdom ethic that is taught in the book of Proverbs.

---

7. Adele Berlin, *Poetics and Interpretation of Biblical Narrative*, Bible and Literature Series 9 (Sheffield: Almond Press, 1983), pp. 83–110. I acknowledge my dependence on Berlin for the discussion in this paragraph.

8. See Susan Ackerman, *Warrior, Dancer, Seductress, Queen: Women in Judges and Biblical Israel*, Anchor Bible Reference Library (New York: Doubleday, 1998); Lillian R. Klein, *From Deborah to Esther: Sexual Politics in the Hebrew Bible* (Minneapolis: Fortress, 2003), ch. 1: 'Wives and Daughters in the Book of Judges'. Klein looks at Achsah, Deborah, Jephthah's daughter and Manoah's wife, and says: 'all four are resourceful, undertaking actions but deferring to the authority of males' (p. 12); Susan M. Pigott, 'Wives, Witches and Wise Women: Prophetic Heralds of Kingship in 1 and 2 Samuel', *RevExp* 99 (2002), pp. 145–173. I thank John Dekker for alerting me to this material.

The book of Ruth in the Writings

Though the modern Bible reader is accustomed to reading the book of Ruth following Judges (its position in the Greek canon),[9] in the Hebrew canon (Tanak), Ruth is found in the third section of the canon, the *Ketuvim* (Writings). The order of the individual books within the Writings fluctuates in the Jewish tradition,[10] and the book of Ruth is found in more than one position. According to the Babylonian Talmud (*Baba Bathra* 14b), the book of Ruth comes at the beginning of the Writings, presumably because of the early setting of the story, for the events narrated belong to the time of the judges (Ruth 1:1: 'In the days when the judges ruled . . .').[11] In that Talmudic *baraita*,[12] the relevant listing is 'Ruth and Psalms and Job and Proverbs' (coupled together in the way indicated), so that this is a four-book mini-collection, with Ruth (ending with the genealogy of David) positioned as a preface to Psalms, and Psalms–Job–Proverbs forming a tripartite wisdom collection. 'Qoheleth' is the next book in line, unconnected by a conjunction to books either before or after it, though it is strategically placed between books also viewed as Solomonic compositions.[13] Next, we find three *pairs* of books, namely 'Song of Songs and Lamentations' (a genre grouping of songs, romantic and mournful), 'Daniel and Esther' (both court tales wherein the safety of Jews is under threat), and lastly the books 'Ezra(–Nehemiah) and Chronicles' (with their obvious similarities explaining their juxtapositioning).[14]

In some medieval manuscripts Chronicles comes at the beginning of the Writings; however, the sequence that has Chronicles in last position became

---

9. For analysis of the book in this canonical position, see Greg Goswell, 'The Book of Ruth and the House of David', *EQ* 86 (2014), pp. 116–129.
10. A tabulation of eleven alternative orders is provided by C. D. Ginsburg, *Introduction to the Massoretico-Critical Edition of the Hebrew Bible* (London: Trinitarian Bible Society, 1897; repr. New York: Ktav, 1966), p. 7.
11. Rolf Rendtorff, *The Old Testament: An Introduction*, tr. John Bowden (London: SCM, 1985), p. 245. All Bible quotes in this chapter, unless stated otherwise, are from the RSV.
12. Namely, a quotation of earlier rabbinic opinion, originating in the Tannaic period (pre-AD 200).
13. Marvin H. Pope, *Song of Songs*, AB 7C (Garden City: Doubleday, 1977), p. 18.
14. *Pace* Julius Steinberg, *Die Ketuvim: Ihr Aufbau und ihre Botschaft*, BBB 152 (Hamburg: Philo, 2006), pp. 144–151. I do not find Steinberg's explanation of the order in *Baba Bathra* convincing, one reason being that he ignores the way in which books are coupled (often in pairs).

established in the printed editions of the Hebrew Bible: at the beginning is the group of 'three great writings' (Babylonian Talmud, *Ber.* 57b), Psalms, Job and Proverbs, in order of decreasing length. In all the varying sequences for Writings, Psalms, Job and Proverbs are always found together, either in that order or as Psalms–Proverbs–Job. The little group of *Megillot* ('scrolls') that includes Ruth is placed next, and finally Daniel, Ezra–Nehemiah and Chronicles. The order of the five books of the *Megillot* in the Leningrad Codex (B 19^A) (the base text of the scholarly Hebrew Bibles *BHK*^{3}, *BHS* and *BHQ*) and in Sephardic codices appears to be based on the principle of chronology: Ruth, Song of Songs (written by a young Solomon?), Ecclesiastes (by Solomon when he was old?), Lamentations and Esther.[15] It is usually said that these five books are grouped together for liturgical reasons, due to their public reading at the five main festivals, but this rationale has recently been questioned by Stone, who argues that the process was the reverse: namely, it was due to the five-book grouping that Ruth, Song of Songs and Lamentations in particular began to be read at feasts.[16] Certainly, the associations of Ruth with Weeks and Song of Songs with Passover are not strong and could be viewed as contrived. In other Hebrew Bibles (especially those used by Ashkenazic Jews) the order reflects the sequence of the major Jewish festivals in the calendar (assuming the year starts with the month Nisan): Song of Songs (Passover), Ruth (Weeks), Lamentations (Ninth of Ab), Ecclesiastes (Booths) and Esther (Purim).[17] The liturgical use of the *Megillot* explains their placement directly after the Pentateuch in the editions of the Hebrew Bible in the fifteenth and sixteenth centuries,[18] for

---

15. There is, however, some minor variability in the codices; see the tables provided by Michèle Dukan, *La Bible hébraïque: Les codices copiés en Orient et dans la zone séfarade avant 1280*, Bibliologia 22 (Turnhout, Belgium: Brepols, 2006), p. 67; Steinberg, *Die Ketuvim*, pp. 133, 152; Roger Beckwith, *The Old Testament Canon of the New Testament Church and Its Background in Early Judaism* (Grand Rapids: Eerdmans, 1985), pp. 452–464; Peter Brandt, *Endgestalten des Kanons: Das Arrangement der Schriften Israels in der jüdischen und christlichen Bibel*, BBB 131 (Berlin: Philo, 2001), pp. 151–171. The Aleppo Codex appears to have the same order as the Leningrad Codex, but due to damage, leaves are missing after several words in Song 3:11a; see Moshe H. Goshen-Gottstein (ed.), *The Aleppo Codex: Part One: Plates* (Jerusalem: Magnes, 1976).
16. Stone, *Compilational History*, pp. 105–111.
17. L. B. Wolfenson, 'Implications of the Place of the Book of Ruth in Editions, Manuscripts, and Canon of the Old Testament', *HUCA* 1 (1924), pp. 151–178.
18. For details, see Ginsburg, *Introduction*, pp. 3–4; Wolfenson, 'Implications', p. 155, n. 13.

the Pentateuch and the *Megillot* are the only portions read in their entirety in the lectionary of the synagogue.

Ruth read at the feast of Weeks, during the wheat harvest, picks up on the barley and wheat harvests featured in the book (1:22; 2:23; cf. Lev. 23:15–21; Num. 28:26–31).[19] The book of Ruth followed by Song of Songs in the *Megillot*, or preceded by it according to the order of the annual festivals (assuming the year starts with the month Nisan: Song of Songs [Passover], Ruth [Weeks], etc.),[20] emphasizes the love-story aspect of Ruth, most prominent in the public meeting of Boaz and Ruth in chapter 2 and their clandestine meeting in chapter 3. The Ruth narrative, for its part, gives an agrarian setting for the pastoral images of Song of Songs. In the order of books Proverbs, Ruth and Song of Songs (Leningrad Codex), both Ruth and Song of Songs develop the picture of the virtuous and assertive woman pictured in Proverbs 31,[21] and it is worth noting that the female lover is the first and the main speaker in the song.[22] When followed (or preceded) by Song of Songs, the 'romance' aspect of the book of Ruth is highlighted.

Ruth as the first of the *Megillot* follows immediately upon the book of Proverbs (in the Leningrad Codex), presumably because of a link in their subject matter.[23] Proverbs closes with an alphabetical acrostic poem of twenty-two

---

19. David Daube, *The New Testament and Rabbinic Judaism* (London: Athlone Press/ University of London, 1956), pp. 48–49; Jennifer L. Koosed, *Gleaning Ruth: A Biblical Heroine and Her Afterlives* (Columbia: University of South Carolina Press, 2011), pp. 121–126.
20. Wolfenson, 'Implications', p. 157; Johannes B. Bauer, 'Das Buch Ruth in der jüdischen und christlichen Überlieferung', *Bibel und Kirche* 18 (1963), pp. 116–119.
21. Cf. Tremper Longman III, *Song of Songs*, NICOT (Grand Rapids: Eerdmans, 2001), p. 2.
22. See the statistics provided by Athalya Brenner, 'Women Poets and Authors', in idem (ed.), *A Feminist Companion to the Song of Songs* (Sheffield: JSOT Press, 1993), pp. 86–97.
23. As suggested by Edward F. Campbell Jr, *Ruth: A New Translation with Introduction, Notes, and Commentary*, AB 7 (Garden City: Doubleday, 1975), pp. 34, 125; Thomas P. McCreesh, 'Wisdom as Wife: Proverbs 31:10–31', *RB* 92 (1985), pp. 25–46; Robert L. Hubbard Jr, *The Book of Ruth*, NICOT (Grand Rapids: Eerdmans, 1988), p. 216; Frederic W. Bush, *Ruth, Esther*, WBC 9 (Dallas: Word, 1996), pp. 173–174; Yair Zakovitch, *Das Buch Rut: Ein jüdischer Kommentar: Mit einem Geleitwort von Erich Zenger*, Stuttgarter Bibelstudien 177 (Stuttgart: Verlag Katholisches Bibelwerk, 1999), pp. 31–32; Irmtraud Fischer, *Rut*, HTKAT (Freiburg im Breisgau: Herder, 2001), pp. 101–102.

lines, with each verse starting with a successive letter of the Hebrew alphabet. It celebrates the 'worthy woman' (*'ēšet ḥayil*) (31:10–31), with this expression occurring in the opening line (31:10: 'A *good wife* who can find?', my emphasis), and the juxtaposed book of Ruth can be understood as going on to describe just such a woman. The thematic linkage between the books of Proverbs and Ruth is supported by the fact that in Ruth 3:11 Boaz calls Ruth a 'worthy woman' (*'ēšet ḥayil*). The phrase 'worthy woman' occurs only once elsewhere in the Old Testament, namely Proverbs 12:4 ('A *good wife* is the crown of her husband'). The description in Proverbs 31:31 fits the woman Ruth ('and let her works praise her in the gates'), for in Ruth 3:11 Boaz, in praising Ruth, says: 'all my fellow townsmen [lit. 'all the gate of my people'] know that you are a woman of worth', and the people at the gate and the elders who meet there are recorded as praising Ruth (4:11–12). So, also, Proverbs 31:23 applies to Boaz ('Her husband is known in the gates, when he sits among the elders of the land'), for this sounds like an allusion to the scene at the city gate depicted in Ruth 4. The canonical placement next to Proverbs suggests that Ruth the Moabitess is to be viewed as a real-life example of the piety taught in Proverbs and embodied in the exemplary woman of Proverbs 31.

In the face of an earlier over-enthusiastic search for wisdom influences on the narrative portions of the Old Testament, notably in the 'Joseph Story', the 'Succession Narrative' and the book of Esther,[24] J. L. Crenshaw sought to achieve greater methodological stringency,[25] and later scholars have tended to heed his warnings. In the case of both Joseph and Daniel, it is plain that their 'wisdom' (chiefly manifested in their ability to interpret dreams) is not primarily of the ethical variety found in Proverbs.[26] The book of Ruth is not usually considered to be a wisdom work, and I am not arguing that it should

---

24. Gerhard von Rad, 'The Joseph Narrative and Ancient Wisdom', in *The Problem of the Hexateuch and Other Essays* (Edinburgh: Oliver & Boyd, 1965), pp. 292–300; R. N. Whybray, *The Succession Narrative: A Study of 2 Sam. 9 – 20 and 1 Kings 1 and 2*, SBT 2/9 (London: SCM, 1968); S. Talmon, '"Wisdom" in the Book of Esther', *VT* 13 (1963), pp. 419–455.

25. J. L. Crenshaw, 'Method in Determining Wisdom Influence upon "Historical" Literature', *JBL* 88 (1969), pp. 129–142. For a more recent survey, focusing on the Succession Narrative, see Robert P. Gordon, 'A House Divided: Wisdom in Old Testament Narrative Tradition', in John Day, Robert P. Gordon and H. G. M. Williamson (eds.), *Wisdom in Ancient Israel: Essays in Honour of J. A. Emerton* (Cambridge: Cambridge University Press, 1995), pp. 94–105.

26. See Michael V. Fox, 'Wisdom in the Joseph Story', *VT* 51 (2001), pp. 26–41.

be classified in this way. Certainly none of the *dramatis personae* are identified as 'wise' and the story makes no use of what may be viewed as exclusively wisdom terms. On the other hand, the narrative provides in the person of Ruth a paradigm,[27] namely a pattern of behaviour worthy of emulation by readers (e.g. an ethic of hard work [2:7, 17; cf. Prov. 6:6–11; 10:26; 13:14]), and the book of Ruth contains themes that find a place in acknowledged wisdom books (e.g. marriage to a suitable wife, theodicy, providence, the care of the poor and reward).

Similarities and differences

It would appear that thematic considerations are responsible for this positioning of the book of Ruth, though any book is likely to have a number of major themes, such that alternative placements are possible on this basis. There are differences between the portrayal of Ruth and the ideal woman of Proverbs 31 (e.g. their markedly different social status); however, that does not undermine the positing of a connection between the two portraits, but simply confirms that in interpreting the book of Ruth we must not allow the interpretation to be exclusively controlled by Proverbs 31. We should expect a thoughtful consideration of the juxtapositioning of Ruth and Proverbs to throw light on the meaning of Ruth and to enable us to see things that might otherwise have remained unnoticed. On the other hand, this paratextual connection will not exhaust the reading of the book of Ruth.

There are both similarities and differences between the heroine Ruth and the 'good wife' of Proverbs 31.[28] In regard to similarities, both are women of energy and action (e.g. Prov. 31:15, 27; Ruth 2:2, 7, 17); both work to supply the needs of their family and provide food for their household (Prov. 31:15, 21; Ruth 2:18); both show 'kindness' (*ḥesed*) (Prov. 31:26; cf. 31:20; Ruth 3:10); both are praised as superior by their husband and by others (Prov. 31:28–29; Ruth 3:10–11; 4:15); both work hard (Prov. 31:13, 27; Ruth 2:2, 17, 23); and both women are God-fearing (Prov. 31:30; Ruth 1:16; 2:12).

---

27. R. B. Y. Scott, *The Way of Wisdom in the Old Testament* (New York: Macmillan, 1971), pp. 85–87.
28. For similarities and differences, see Samuel T. S. Goh, 'Ruth as a Superior Woman of *ḥayil*? A Comparison between Ruth and the "Capable" Woman in Proverbs 31:10–31', *JSOT* 38 (2014), pp. 487–500. In what follows I acknowledge my dependence on Goh.

As for differences between the two women, these would include their race and class, for the woman of Proverbs 31 is an upper-class Israelite.[29] This is enough to show that neither text has influenced the other, but they are of entirely separate origins. There is nothing to suggest that the author of Proverbs 31 had Ruth in mind, nor is there evidence that the book of Ruth was influenced by the portrait of Proverbs 31. The canonical juxtapositioning of Proverbs and Ruth in the Hebrew canonical tradition is a *post-authorial* phenomenon, with biblical book order reflecting the perceptions and views of ancient readers, who were right, however, to detect the presence of significant thematic connections between these two canonical portions. They were placed side-by-side because they were viewed as belonging together and believed to be mutually enriching, and this prescribed order of reading was intended to be a hermeneutical guide for future generations of readers.

The differences are not to be over-emphasized, for the idealized portrait of Proverbs 31 can be understood to describe what Ruth *became* beyond the time frame of the canonical book that ends with the birth of her first child: she was fully integrated into Israelite society as the wife of a respected local dignitary; she left behind her life of poverty; she became the mother of more than one child (in all likelihood); and she found wider scope for her obvious ability in the management of a large household.[30] In fact, putting the book of Ruth after Proverbs 31 strongly implies that Ruth did go on to achieve all that an Israelite wife and mother could and should do, and so this is one way in which juxtaposing Proverbs and Ruth shapes readerly evaluations.

Reading Ruth alongside Proverbs 31

When the book of Ruth is read with Proverbs as its canonical conversation partner, a number of themes come into prominence: Ruth's worth, her praiseworthy character, her foreign status, theodicy, providence, the practice of kindness, diligence, the use of intelligence and reward. I will explore each of these themes in turn. The book of Ruth read in conjunction with Proverbs 31 serves to highlight the term 'worth' (*ḥayil*), for this is a key descriptor for both women. Certainly the presence of this word in the opening line of the poem

---

29. Leo G. Perdue, *Proverbs*, Interpretation (Louisville: John Knox, 2000), pp. 275, 279.
30. So also Katharine Doob Sakenfeld, *Ruth*, Interpretation (Louisville: John Knox, 1999), p. 62: 'It is easy to imagine, based on what is known of Ruth so far, that as Boaz's wife she would become the epitome of the wife described in Proverbs.'

establishes its thematic importance ('A *good* wife who can find?'). In the case of the book of Ruth, Boaz's declaration of Ruth's 'worth' occurs at a crucial turning point in the plot (3:11),[31] when he commits himself to doing the part of the next of kin (involving marriage to Ruth). This word has a wide semantic range, such that the exact nuance of the epithet applied to Ruth ('woman of worth' [*'ēšet ḥayil*]) may be disputed, but the basic idea is that of *strength*, whether physical strength, competence, efficiency, wealth, social standing, military heroism, moral substance or mental capacity.[32] In Proverbs 31, the mother of Lemuel advises him not to give his strength (*ḥayil*) to women who destroy kings (31:3), whereas in the book that follows, Ruth the 'woman of worth' (*'ēšet ḥayil*) builds up the Israelite kingdom (via her descendant David).[33] In the final poem, the word's initial use in 31:10 and its reuse in 31:29 ('Many women have done *excellently* [*'āśû ḥayil*]') form an *inclusio* around the actual description of the model woman (31:10–29), this being another sign of the importance of this term in Proverbs 31.[34] Lying outside the main body of the poem, 31:30–31 is differentiated as a coda. To designate these two verses a coda is not to deny that they are integral to the poem, but rather identifies them as of special significance. These final verses emphasize the model woman's praiseworthy character (root *hālal* ['to praise'] x2, picking up its use in v. 28). In addition, it is in verse 30 that the key virtue featured in the *motto* of the book of Proverbs ('the fear of the LORD')

---

31. As noted by Stone, *Compilational History*, p. 133.
32. See e.g. R. B. Y. Scott, *Proverbs, Ecclesiastes*, AB 18, 2nd edn (New York: Doubleday, 1985), pp. 185–186 ('a capable wife'); Bruce Waltke, *The Book of Proverbs: Chapters 15–31*, NICOT (Grand Rapids: Eerdmans, 2005), pp. 520–521; Roland E. Murphy, *Proverbs*, WBC 22 (Nashville: Nelson, 1998), p. 243; M. Beth Szlos, 'A Portrait of Power: A Literary-critical Study of the Depiction of the Woman in Proverbs 31:10–31', *USQR* 54 (2000), pp. 97–103 (esp. p. 98: 'how strikingly physical and powerful a depiction it is'); Christine Roy Yoder, 'The Woman of Substance (*'ēšet ḥayil*): A Socioeconomic Reading of Proverbs 31:10–31', *JBL* 122 (2003), pp. 427–447, here p. 427; idem, *Wisdom as a Woman of Substance: A Socioeconomic Reading of Proverbs 1 – 9 and 31:10–31*, BZAW 304 (Berlin: De Gruyter, 2001), pp. 76–77; H. Kosmala, '*gāḇar*', *TDOT* 2:374; H. Eising, '*ḥayil*', *TDOT* 4:350–351; JiSeong Kwon, 'Wisdom Incarnate? Identity and Role of *'ēšet ḥayil* ("the Valiant Woman") in Proverbs 31:10–31', *JESOT* 1 (2012), pp. 167–188, here pp. 171, 173.
33. Goh, 'Superior Woman', pp. 498–499.
34. Murray H. Lichtenstein, 'Chiasm and Symmetry in Proverbs 31', *CBQ* 44 (1982), pp. 202–211, here pp. 205–206, who is followed by McCreesh, 'Wisdom as Wife', p. 32.

(Prov. 1:7; 9:10) is ascribed to the woman, and in verse 31 the poet calls on male readers to 'Give her of the fruit of her hands', namely a share of what she has earned as a reward for her virtuous behaviour.

In the case of the book of Ruth, there is the earlier use of the matching expression for a male in application to Boaz as 'a man of substance' (*'îš gibbôr ḥayil*; Ruth 2:1). This refers to his social standing as one who has an important place in the community and to his material wealth as an owner of fields and servants (2:3–4, 8, 15, 21, 23). A comparable use of this phrase is found in 1 Samuel 9:1 regarding Saul's father Kish, who has asses and servants (cf. 2 Kgs 15:20: 'all the wealthy men' [*kol-gibbôr haḥayil*]). There is, however, sufficient elasticity in the meaning of the term to enable its reapplication to Ruth, who has none of these things (3:11), but whose moral gravitas earns her the equivalent female epithet. In the case of the Moabitess, sojourner and gleaner, the complimentary description of her as a 'woman of worth' cannot refer to social standing, but 'emphasizes the quality of Ruth's person'.[35] It is Ruth's devotion to her mother-in-law and loyalty to the family that causes Boaz to speak of her in such terms (2:11–12; 3:10). His kindly treatment of her in chapter 2 has enabled the reader to come to a recognition of Boaz's own moral worth (for *'îš ḥayil* denoting *moral* worth, see 1 Kgs 1:42). The description of Boaz in 2:1 means that he is in a position of influence and wealth to render assistance to the two widows, Naomi and Ruth, if he is willing to do so, and the account in chapter 2 shows that he exceeds any formal obligation to help them, as recognized by the expressions of gratitude from Ruth (2:10, 13) and Naomi (2:19–20).[36] The fact that Ruth is 'a woman of worth' (using the matching expression for a woman) means that Boaz and Ruth are ideally matched and suited as marriage partners.[37]

In addition, the elders of Bethlehem express the following wish for Boaz's welfare: 'May you prosper [= do mightily (*wa'ăśê ḥayil*)] in Ephrathah and be renowned in Bethlehem' (4:11), an expression that is matched in Proverbs 31:29 ('Many women have done excellently [*'āśû ḥayil*]'). What is in mind is clarified by the continuation of the speech of the Bethlehemite elders in the adjoining verse (4:12), namely the building up of his house through the progeny provided through Ruth. The final praise of Ruth placed on the lips of the women of

---

35. Campbell, *Ruth*, p. 125.
36. Bush, *Ruth*, p. 43.
37. This is also noted by Ellen F. Davis, 'Beginning with Ruth: An Essay on Translating', in Peter S. Hawkins and Lesleigh Cushing Stahlberg (eds.), *Scrolls of Love: Ruth and the Song of Songs* (New York: Fordham University Press, 2006), pp. 9–19, here p. 14.

Bethlehem (4:15) also speaks of her great worth ('[she] is more to you [Naomi] than seven sons'; cf. 1 Sam. 1:8). This is high praise in a culture that placed great value on male progeny and in a story whose plot was initiated by Naomi's loss of husband and sons (1:5), which loss has only now been compensated for by the male descendant provided through Ruth (4:13–17; esp. v. 17b: 'A son has been born to Naomi [through Ruth]').

In praise of Ruth

According to Al Wolters, the genre of the poem in Proverbs 31 is that of hymn, namely a song of praise for a heroic woman ('Song of the Valiant Woman'),[38] but Michael V. Fox is probably right to prefer the category *encomium*, seeing that hymn is a generic category more properly used of the praise of God and Proverbs 31 lacks the usual hymnic Hebrew participles, except for 31:27a (*ṣôpiyyâ*).[39] As noted by Fox, parallels are found in biblical psalms that praise the righteous man who 'fears the LORD' (Pss 112; 128),[40] and extrabiblical examples are Sirach 38:34b – 39:11; 44:1 – 50:24; 1 Maccabees 3:3–9; 14:4–15. In the same way, Ruth is repeatedly praised by other characters in the book named after her (1:8; 2:11; 3:10–11; 4:15), and the association with Proverbs 31 assists the reader to notice this feature in the book of Ruth. The regular praising of Ruth signals that her character and actions (notably her kindness [*ḥesed*] to family and her diligence) are meant to be viewed by readers as exemplary and this anticipates that she will receive her due reward.

Reading the book of Ruth within a wisdom frame

The preponderance of feminine imagery in Proverbs 1 – 9 and 31 suggests to Claudia Camp that these two sections were chosen to frame the book as a

---

38. Al Wolters, 'Proverbs XXXI 10–31 as Heroic Hymn: A Form-Critical Analysis', *VT* 38 (1988), pp. 446–457, here p. 451; *idem*, *The Song of the Valiant Woman: Studies in the Interpretation of Proverbs 31:10–31* (Carlisle: Paternoster, 2001), pp. 1–14.
39. Michael V. Fox, *Proverbs 10 – 31*, AYB 18B (New Haven: Yale University Press, 2009), pp. 902–905.
40. See Tremper Longman III, *Psalms: An Introduction and Commentary*, TOTC 15–16 (Nottingham: Inter-Varsity Press, 2014), pp. 386–389. Longman finds various links between Psalm 112 and Proverbs 31.

whole.⁴¹ Whether Proverbs 31:10–31 is part of an editorial frame around the book is open to dispute, but what cannot be gainsaid is that the poem about 'the good wife' is a fitting end to the book, for the metaphor of *finding* a wife (= Lady Wisdom) forms the subtext of Proverbs 1 – 9. The 'good wife' of Proverbs 31 is the feminine embodiment of the wisdom ethic of Proverbs, but in contrast to Lady Wisdom depicted in Proverbs 1 and 8 – 9, she is a real-life woman and is realistically portrayed.⁴² The poem about the 'good wife' forms a bridge between the teachings of Proverbs and the story of Ruth in which a man finds a suitable wife,⁴³ and the link encourages the reading of Ruth within a wisdom framework.⁴⁴

In the book adjoining Proverbs, Ruth the 'foreigner' becomes a model of proper behaviour and the appropriate wife.⁴⁵ Ruth is repeatedly designated 'the Moabitess' by the narrator and by other characters within the story, so that her outsider status is underlined (1:22; 2:2, 6, 21; 4:5, 10; cf. 1:4: 'These [= the two sons of Naomi] took Moabite wives'). Ruth acknowledges that she is a 'foreigner' (2:10 *nokriyyâ*), and her self-designation is highlighted in her speech to Boaz by means of Hebrew wordplay⁴⁶ when she asks him: 'Why have I found favour in your eyes, that you should take notice of me [*lĕhakkîrēnî*], when I am a foreigner?' In Proverbs, the female foil for Lady Wisdom and the competitor for the young man's affections is pejoratively designated a 'foreign woman' (*nokriyya*) (2:16;

---

41. Claudia V. Camp, *Wisdom and the Feminine in the Book of Proverbs*, Bible and Literature Series 11 (Sheffield: Almond Press, 1985), pp. 187–191; so too R. N. Whybray, *The Composition of the Book of Proverbs*, JSOTSup 168 (Sheffield: Sheffield Academic Press, 1994), pp. 161–162.
42. As emphasized by Bernhard Lang, 'Women's Work, Household and Property in Two Mediterranean Societies: A Comparative Essay on Proverbs XXXI 10–31', *VT* 54 (2004), pp. 188–207; and Yoder, 'Woman of Substance', pp. 75–91.
43. We should not understand the opening line of the poem ('A good wife who can find?') to mean that it is an impossibility (cf. Prov. 20:6b: 'a faithful man who can find?'). Finding a suitable wife is a theme touched on in 18:22 ('He who finds a wife finds a good thing').
44. Cf. Stone, *Compilational History*, p. 16: 'When Ruth is read in conjunction with Proverbs, certain aspects of the book move into the foreground, while others recede into the background.'
45. For Ruth as an ideal wisdom figure, see Beyer, *Hoffnung in Bethlehem*, pp. 219–222.
46. Lisa M. Wolfe, *Ruth, Esther, Song of Songs, and Judith* (Eugene: Cascade, 2011), pp. 10, 35.

5:20; 6:24; 7:5; 23:27),[47] but, in this case, it is probably not an ethnic label (given 2:17: '[she] forgets the covenant of her God [= Yhwh]'),[48] but paints the unchaste wife as a moral 'outsider', that is, one who behaves in ways inconsistent with membership of the covenant community.[49] This woman is an Israelite who acts like an outsider, but, in a variation on the theme, Ruth is an ethnic outsider who acts as a true Israelite (e.g. her Abraham-like oath to leave home and country [1:16–17; 2:11; cf. Gen. 12:1–3]),[50] and she is shown to be a suitable wife for noble Boaz.[51] To have a 'foreigner' as a model of virtue is in line with the *internationalism* of wisdom (cf. the figure of Job) and the acknowledgment in Israelite wisdom circles that figures from other nations can possess wisdom that is compatible with Yahwism (Prov. 30:1; 31:1; 1 Kgs 4:29–34 [Heb. 5:9–14]).

Consistent with wisdom books (esp. Job), Ruth can be read as a theodicy: namely it seeks to justify the mysterious ways of God. Proverbs also makes clear that the events of life often defy human understanding (Prov. 16:1–2, 9; 19:14, 21; 20:24; 21:30–31). The book of Ruth opens with an inexplicable tragedy, for no reason is provided for the deaths of Naomi's husband and two sons (Ruth 1:1–5). Naomi's accusatory statement that 'the Lord has testified against me' (1:21) should not be read as an admission of wrong on her part, as if to say the tragedy was a divine judgment upon her for leaving the land or allowing her

---

47. Carlos Bovell goes so far as to relate Orpah to the 'strange woman' of Proverbs; see 'Symmetry, Ruth and Canon', *JSOT* 28 (2003), pp. 175–191, esp. pp. 183–186.
48. Michael V. Fox, *Proverbs 1 – 9*, AB 18A (New York: Doubleday, 2000), p. 120.
49. Bruce Waltke, *The Book of Proverbs: Chapters 1–15*, NICOT (Grand Rapids: Eerdmans, 2004), pp. 121–122; cf. Christl Maier, *Die 'fremde Frau' in Proverbien 1 – 9: Eine exegetische und sozialgeschichtliche Studie*, OBO 144 (Freiberg, Schweiz: Universitätsverlag, 1995), pp. 97–99, 262, 266 (who notes the parallel with the terminology in Deut. 4:23, 31). Fox argues she is simply someone else's wife and so out of bounds (*Proverbs 1 – 9*, pp. 139–141).
50. Beyer, *Hoffnung in Bethlehem*, pp. 199–203. According to Stone, Ruth is 'in critical dialogue with Proverbs' at this point; see *Compilational History*, p. 136 (p. 139: 'her connection to wisdom's ideals in Proverbs logically brings to the fore her foreign status. Ruth embodies Proverb's ideals and yet is a foreigner').
51. Phyllis Trible, 'A Human Comedy: The Book of Ruth', in Kenneth R. R. Gros Louis with James S. Ackerman (eds.), *Literary Interpretations of Biblical Narratives: Volume II* (Nashville: Abingdon, 1982), pp. 161–190, here p. 168; Neil Glover, 'Your People, My People: An Exploration of Ethnicity in Ruth', *JSOT* 33 (2009), pp. 293–313 (p. 308: 'In Ruth a Moabitess pledges herself to Israel and through various cultural transitions becomes an Israelite').

sons to marry foreigners.⁵² She holds God accountable for the sad events and renames herself 'Mara' (= Bitterness [*mārā'*]), with the explanation that 'Shaddai has dealt very bitterly [*hēmar*] with me' (1:20). This echoes Job, who also lost children, felt himself to be suffering unjustly and swore 'by Shaddai who embittered [*hēmar*] me' (Job 27:2).⁵³ This way of reading Ruth is supported by its relation to Lamentations, a neighbouring book in the *Megillot*, which alludes to destroyed Jerusalem's widow status (1:1: 'How like a widow has she become' [cf. 5:3]), and this forms a parallel to Naomi's situation (e.g. Ruth 1:3, 5). The two books, each in their own way, wrestle with the problem of theodicy,⁵⁴ given their recognition of God's involvement in distressing situations, the decimation of a family on the one hand and of the city of Jerusalem on the other (Ruth 1:20-21; Lam. 2:1-8). The family crisis of Naomi is brought to a happy resolution at the close of the book, when God acts to preserve the familial line (4:13b: 'the LORD gave her [= Ruth] conception, and she bore a son').

The theme of divine providence is prevalent in wisdom literature and is also found in the book of Ruth. Neither overtly miraculous occurrences nor dramatic divine interventions are to be expected in the book of Ruth when read within a wisdom framework. God's direct involvement in events is stated by the narrator of Ruth only once (4:13), though characters within the story repeatedly speak *about* God, so that one of its pervasive themes is the (largely) hidden nature of God's providence (1:6, 9, 16–17, 20–21; 2:4, 12, 20; 3:10, 13; 4:11–12, 14).⁵⁵ More subtly, the apparently *chance* event of Ruth entering the field of Boaz (2:3), together with the arrival of Boaz and of the unnamed close relation on the scene *at just the right time* (2:4; 4:1 [the implication of the *hinnê* clause]),⁵⁶ support a theology of the divine superintendence of events.⁵⁷ We may compare this

---

52. Katharine Doob Sakenfeld, 'Naomi's Cry: Reflections on Ruth 1:20–21', in Brent A. Strawn and Nancy R. Brown (eds.), *A God So Near: Essays on Old Testament Theology in Honor of Patrick D. Miller* (Winona Lake: Eisenbrauns, 2003), pp. 129–143, here p. 136.
53. Amy Kalmanofsky, *Dangerous Sisters of the Hebrew Bible* (Minneapolis: Fortress, 2014), p. 160; Beyer, *Hoffnung in Bethlehem*, pp. 148–151.
54. Noted by Marjo C. A. Korpel, *The Structure of the Book of Ruth*, Pericope: Scripture as Written and Read in Antiquity 2 (Assen: Van Gorcum, 2001), pp. 230–231.
55. See Ronald M. Hals, *The Theology of the Book of Ruth*, Facet Books Biblical Series 23 (Philadelphia: Fortress, 1969).
56. Berlin, *Poetics and Interpretation*, p. 94 ('Just then').
57. Campbell, *Ruth*, pp. 29, 93, 141; Tamara Cohn Eskenazi and Tikva Frymer-Kensky, *Ruth*, JPS Bible Commentary (Philadelphia: JPS, 2001), p. 71.

perspective with the 'string of sayings on divine governance' in Proverbs 15:33 – 16:9.[58] According to Proverbs, even the chance outcome of casting a lot reflects divine control and therefore brings an end to arguments over the right course of action to take (16:33; 18:18).

The 'good wife' of Proverbs 31 speaks wisely and inculcates kindness (31:26: 'the *teaching of kindness* [*ḥesed*] is on her tongue', my emphasis).[59] This may refer to what she instructs her children and household servants, namely to treat the poor with kindness, so that her teaching is consistent with her own humane actions (cf. 31:20: 'She opens her hand to the poor, and reaches out her hands to the needy'). As noted by Fox, this recalls the teaching of Lemuel's mother about the kingly responsibility of caring for the poor (31:6–9; cf. 20:28).[60] It also anticipates the 'kindness' (*ḥesed*) theme in the juxtaposed narrative of Ruth, and Ernst Würthwein goes so far as to claim that Ruth was written as a wisdom composition to illustrate the truth of Proverbs 21:21 ('He who pursues righteousness and *kindness* [*ḥesed*] finds life and righteousness and honour', mg.).[61] Ruth and Boaz practise 'kindness', for their actions for the sake of the welfare of the family go beyond the formal obligations of a daughter-in-law or of the male relative who is not the nearest of kin (2:20; 3:12).[62] Just as Proverbs makes use of antithetical pairs of characters to describe behaviour and its consequences (e.g. wise/foolish, righteous/wicked, lazy/diligent, rich/poor),[63] so also does the book of Ruth. In two situations of choice – whether to go with Naomi or return to Moab (Ruth/Orpah), and whether to redeem the parcel of land (and marry Ruth) or not (Boaz/the unnamed nearer relative) – characters are depicted as coming to opposite decisions,[64] and the choices made have consequences for them: Orpah leaves the story (1:15), the nearer relative remains without a

---

58. Richard J. Clifford, *Proverbs: A Commentary*, OTL (Louisville: Westminster John Knox, 1999), p. 157.
59. With the Hebrew genitive relation (*tôrat ḥesed*) indicating the content of her teaching (= teaching *about* kindness).
60. Fox, *Proverbs 10 – 31*, p. 897. This is one of a number of links between Prov. 31:1–9 and 31:10–31; see Waltke, *Proverbs 15 – 31*, pp. 501–503.
61. *Die fünf Megilloth*, HAT 18, 2nd edn (Tübingen: Mohr, 1969), pp. 5–6.
62. According to Francis I. Andersen, *ḥesed* denotes non-obligatory generous action; see 'Yahweh, the Kind and Sensitive God', in Peter T. O'Brien and David G. Peterson (eds.), *God Who Is Rich in Mercy: Essays Presented to Dr D. B. Knox* (Homebush West, NSW: Lancer Books, 1986), pp. 41–88, here pp. 59–60.
63. Clifford, *Proverbs*, p. 22.
64. Bush, *Ruth*, p. 42.

name (4:1: 'Mr So-and-So' [pĕlōnî 'almōnî]),⁶⁵ and Boaz marries Ruth and she gives birth to a son (4:13).

Both Proverbs and the book of Ruth contain the theme of diligence and commend the use of intelligence and resourcefulness to overcome difficulties. Like Ruth the gleaner (ch. 2), the woman of Proverbs 31 labours with her hands (31:13) and is hard-working (31:15, 18–19, 27). Reflecting this work ethic, Proverbs places side-by-side for comparison the industry of the ant and its consequences (6:6–8) and the sluggard's indolence and its consequences (6:9–11; cf. 24:30–34).⁶⁶ In the night scene at the threshing floor, Ruth departs from the script given to her by Naomi (3:4b: 'he will tell you what to do'),⁶⁷ for instead of waiting for instructions from Boaz, she takes the initiative and instructs *him* what to do,⁶⁸ proposing marriage as the best solution for the family's problems (3:9), and Boaz sees the good sense and propriety of what she calls on him to do.

Lastly, the theme of recompense or reward plays an important role in both books. Actions have consequences, and the receiving of reward or punishment is integrally related to how people behave.⁶⁹ While it is not always explicit in Proverbs that God upholds the act–consequence nexus, in a number of passages God is said to be active in retribution (e.g. 5:21–23; 23:10–11; 24:11–12; 29:26).⁷⁰

---

65. For an attempt to discern the reasons for Mr So-and-So's refusal, see Peter H. W. Lau, *Identity and Ethics in the Book of Ruth: A Social Identity Approach*, BZAW 416 (Berlin: De Gruyter, 2011), pp. 74–80.
66. Fox, *Proverbs 1 – 9*, p. 218.
67. As noted, for example, by Hubbard, *The Book of Ruth*, p. 212; Danna Nolan Fewell and David Miller Gunn, *Compromising Redemption: Relating Characters in the Book of Ruth*, Literary Currents in Biblical Interpretation (Louisville: Westminster John Knox, 1990), pp. 52–53.
68. Samuel L. Adams, *Social and Economic Life in Second Temple Judea* (Louisville: Westminster John Knox, 2014), p. 57.
69. For this paragraph, I acknowledge my dependence on Fox, *Proverbs 1 – 9*, pp. 91–92.
70. Lennart Boström, *The God of the Sages: The Portrayal of God in the Book of Proverbs*, ConBOT 29 (Stockholm: Almqvist & Wiksell, 1990), pp. 90–140, esp. pp. 101, 136; Katharine J. Dell, *The Book of Proverbs in Social and Theological Context* (Cambridge: Cambridge University Press, 2006), pp. 90–124. For the same issue in prophetic texts, see Patrick D. Miller Jr, *Sin and Judgment in the Prophets: A Stylistic and Theological Analysis*, SBLMS 27 (Chico: Scholars Press, 1982), pp. 121–139.

There is an element of intrinsic retribution (e.g. 26:27), but it is not wooden or mechanical (e.g. the requirement to care for the poor, who presumably are destitute through no fault of their own [21:13; 22:22; 28:27]).[71] Turning to the book of Ruth, we find that Naomi and Boaz both express the wish that God might reward Ruth for her actions on behalf of the family (1:8–9; 2:11–12). Naomi makes mention of a correspondence between Ruth's loyal action and the response hoped for from God ('May the LORD deal kindly with you, as you have dealt [kindly] with the dead and with me').[72] For his part, Boaz specifically expresses the hope that God will recompense Ruth for what she has done ('May the LORD repay your deed' [translation mine]). In Naomi's mind the reward needs to take the form of Ruth finding 'a home' (*měnûḥâ*), and for Boaz, the hope is that Ruth will find shelter under God's 'wings' (*kānāp*). They place upon God the obligation of rewarding Ruth, but, as it happens, each has an essential part to play in the process of reward, as indicated by the reuse of significant terms when Naomi sends Ruth to the threshing floor (3:1: 'Should I not seek *a home* for you?' [*mānôaḥ*]), and when Ruth calls on Boaz to marry her (3:9: 'Spread your *skirt* [*kānāp*] over your maidservant'). The implication is that Naomi and Boaz are instruments through which God ensures that Ruth receives her just deserts, but the subtle handling of this theme in the book of Ruth is consistent with the way in which the book of Proverbs depicts God's involvement in retributive justice.

Conclusions

What we have found is that the placement of Ruth after Proverbs 31 in the Hebrew canonical tradition reflects a perception by ancient readers that there are significant connections between the two texts. The similarities and differences between the passages are such that the link must be viewed as post-compositional. This canonical positioning encourages the reading of the book of Ruth within a wisdom frame, with Ruth modelling key aspects of the wisdom ethic of Proverbs. The outcome is that certain features of the

---

71. Raymond C. Van Leeuwen, 'Wealth and Poverty: System and Contradiction in Proverbs', *HS* 33 (1992), pp. 25–36.
72. Hubbard, *The Book of Ruth*, p. 104: 'Here emerges a key theological assumption of the book: the intimate link between human action and divine action. In this case, human kindness has earned the possibility (even likelihood) of a God-given reward.'

narrative of Ruth are given greater prominence than might otherwise be the case. Nine themes in particular are highlighted: Ruth's moral worth, her praiseworthy character, her foreign status, the issue of theodicy, divine providence, the practice of kindness, diligence, the use of intelligence and recompense.

© Gregory Goswell, 2016

7. RETRIBUTION AND WISDOM LITERATURE

Lennart Boström

Introduction

The idea of retribution is an issue of interest in Old Testament theology since it relates to the understanding of God's activity in the world. It is closely connected to the idea of justice as well as revenge and reward for different kinds of actions. It might be argued that even if the term 'retribution' is not frequently employed in modern societies, it is in the mindset of most people in different cultures around the world, not least since it constitutes a basis for legal systems. David Clines argues that the doctrine of retribution is in one way or another shared by most human beings.[1]

Definition

A broad and general definition of retribution would be that it is a belief in a correspondence between people's actions and the consequences of those actions for the people themselves. The definition of retribution is often conceived in negative terms, but needs to be understood with both negative and positive

---

1. D. J. A. Clines, *Job 1 – 20*, WBC 17 (Dallas: Word, 1989), p. xxxix.

connotations. The term 'retribution principle' indicates that there is a norm that decides which actions will bring good or bad consequences for the acting person. In a collective sense it can be applied to groups of people or nations, while in an individual sense it has to do with the single person. There can be differences in how close the correspondence between action and consequence is envisioned. Walton gives the following definition: 'The "retribution principle" is the conviction that the righteous will prosper and the wicked will suffer, both in proportion to their respective righteousness and wickedness.'[2] That there is some kind of proportionality between actions and consequences is usually assumed, especially in a legal context. In other texts the correspondence between a person's actions and the consequences may be less precise, as in proverbial sayings.

Retribution in the Old Testament

Belief in the retributive justice of the Lord has traditionally been regarded as a fundamental idea in the Old Testament. In 1955 Klaus Koch wrote his epoch-making article 'Is There a Doctrine of Retribution in the Old Testament?' and questioned that divine retribution is vital to the Israelite understanding of reality.[3] Koch's article is full of important insights, but his view of retribution is unnecessarily restricted, which also influences his arguments. According to him, retribution by definition involves a judicial process in which a higher authority, according to a previously established norm, imposes upon a person either reward or punishment as a separate act subsequent to the action. With examples from the book of Proverbs and other parts of the Old Testament, Koch argues that the Old Testament worldview is not characterized by retribution. Instead he comes to the conclusion that the Israelites had an understanding of actions as having built-in consequences. In this he comes close to K. Fahlgren's idea of a 'synthetic view of life'.[4] Fahlgren analysed different words

---

2. J. H. Walton, 'Retribution', in Tremper Longman III and Peter Enns (eds.), *Dictionary of the Old Testament: Wisdom, Poetry and Writings* (Downers Grove: InterVarsity Press; Nottingham: Inter-Varsity Press, 2008), p. 647.
3. Abbreviated version in English in J. L. Crenshaw (ed.), *Theodicy in the Old Testament* (Philadelphia: Fortress, 1983), pp. 57–87. Original: K. Koch, 'Gibt es ein Vergeltungsdogma im Alten Testament?', *ZTK* 52 (1955), pp. 1–42.
4. K. Fahlgren, 'Die Gegensätze von *s^edakā* im Alten Testament', in K. Koch (ed.), *Um das Prinzip der Vergeltung in Religion und Recht des Alten Testaments*, Wege der Forschung 125 (Darmstadt: Wissenschaftliche Buchgesellschaft, 1972), pp. 87–129. Original 1932.

for sin and evil in the Old Testament and noted that they are used to signify both actions and the consequences of those actions. This led him to the conclusion that originally sin and punishment were inseparable in the mind of the Israelite.

Koch's view has to do with the understanding of God's involvement in the world. In his view the consequences of actions come from within the actions themselves and God's role becomes somewhat unclear. God does not actively reward or punish. Instead he functions like a '"midwife who assists at a birth" *facilitating the completion of something which previous human action has already set in motion*'.[5]

However, it is difficult to get away from the notion that the Old Testament regards God as actively involved in the management of the world and justice. In the Psalter the Israelites express firm belief as well as disappointment in God's way of upholding retribution and justice. Psalms of lament do not refer to some impersonal force built into actions, but rather the conviction that the Lord is responsible for the injustice experienced.

> Hear the voice of my supplication,
>   as I cry to you for help,
> as I lift up my hands
>   towards your most holy sanctuary.
>
> Do not drag me away with the wicked,
>   with those who are workers of evil,
> who speak peace with their neighbours,
>   while mischief is in their hearts.
> Repay them according to their work,
>   and according to the evil of their deeds;
> repay them according to the work of their hands;
>   render them their due reward.
> (Ps. 28:2–4)[6]

This is an individual lament that turns to the Lord expecting him to do something. The psalmist expects the Lord to execute justice, to 'give to the workers of evil' in accordance with their deeds and to bring back upon them what they deserve. This repayment is not something that happens by itself. The description of the situation is designed to put pressure upon God who 'ought

---

5. Koch, 'Retribution', p. 61.

6. All Bible quotes in this chapter, unless stated otherwise, are from the NRSV.

to do something'. Interestingly, in psalms like this the expectation is that it makes a difference if people voice their prayers. If they did not, evil might prevail. Thus it seems that justice is upheld through human prayer and God's response. This idea of God as the active upholder of justice seems to be the dominating view behind many of the Israelite psalms.

This idea of God's active involvement is also evident in legal texts. In the blessings and curses of Deuteronomy 28 the idea is expressed collectively for the nation. If they obey the commandments there will be abundant blessings for them as a nation, but if they do not live according to the law the Lord will send all kinds of calamities upon them, eventually dispersing them all over the world. This understanding forms the basis for the Deuteronomistic history. Even when God's activity is hardly mentioned, as in the Succession Narrative (2 Sam. 9 – 1 Kgs 2), the implication is that God directs Israel's history and upholds the retribution principle and justice.[7]

Roland E. Murphy admits that the phrasing of many sayings in the book of Proverbs could promote a view like Koch's, but he puts it in a larger perspective:

> It is certainly true that the *verbal expression* allows one to infer a correspondence, even a mechanical correspondence, between a good/bad action and its good/bad results. But along with such statements is the view that directly connects good and bad results with the Lord who rewards and punishes. This is not found only in the wisdom literature but throughout the Bible.[8]

We would argue that the concept of retribution pervades the Old Testament as a whole and is closely related to belief in an active God who was seen as responsible for an order in which faithfulness and goodness are rewarded while evil instead gets its punishment.

Retribution in the book of Proverbs

In the book of Proverbs the idea of retribution seems unproblematic, at least in the general sense that people's fates are described as related to their character

---

7. See G. von Rad, *Old Testament Theology, Volume I* (New York: Harper & Row, 1962), pp. 311–317, for a description of the secular stance of the Succession Narrative.
8. R. E. Murphy, *The Tree of Life: An Exploration of Biblical Wisdom Literature*, 2nd edn (Grand Rapids: Eerdmans, 1990), p. 117.

and how they live their lives. Characteristic of the book of Proverbs is that retribution is applied almost totally to the life of the individual. Disaster is asserted for the wicked person while prosperity and well-being are pronounced for the good and righteous person. The assertion of this is not problematized; there is almost no indication that the retribution principle does not always apply.[9] The absence of problematization can probably be explained as being due to genre. Brevity is characteristic for both the short proverbial sentences of chapter 10 and onwards and the longer instructions in chapters 1–9.[10] In genres like these there is no room for discussion or fine nuances. The world is painted black and white and everything is simplified into two simple alternatives for people to choose from. The good alternative is for individuals characterized as wise, righteous, good, or in similar terms. The bad alternative is for those who are fools, wicked, evil or similar. The result of the choice between the two alternatives is expressed in rather general terms. Choosing the right alternative leads to a long life, happiness and goodness, while the wrong alternative leads to disaster as expressed in different ways. The negative alternative tends to be referred to in the passive sense without any agent even implied, as, for example, when Lady Wisdom finishes her speech in the first chapter:

> For waywardness kills the simple,
>   and the complacency of fools destroys them;
> but those who listen to me will be secure
>   and will live at ease, without dread of disaster.
> (Prov. 1:32–33)

---

9. C. G. Bartholomew ('The Theology of Ecclesiastes', in Mark J. Boda, Tremper Longman III and Cristian G. Rata [eds.], *The Words of the Wise Are Like Goads: Engaging Qohelet in the 21st Century* [Winona Lake: Eisenbrauns, 2013], p. 376) follows Gladson in seeing that 'retributive paradox' is present in the book of Proverbs, which means that there is no radical break between the views on retribution in Proverbs and Ecclesiastes. In our view, however, there are few passages in Proverbs that indicate disbelief in the retribution principle. The righteous person may fall seven times but will in contrast to the wicked rise again (24:16). Prov. 24:11 indicates an awareness of injustice in legal matters, but the point is that God repays each person according to what he or she has or has not done.
10. For an attempt at a standardization of genres in wisdom, see P. J. Nel, 'The Genres of Biblical Wisdom Literature', *Journal of Northwest Semitic Languages* (1981), pp. 129–142.

A reading of the book of Proverbs shows that the terminology 'act–consequence' is not adequate since the specific actions are seldom specified. Even when a specific act is specified, the outcome tends to be general and common to other types of behaviour too. A better terminology would be 'character–consequence' since it is rather the attitudes and resulting lifestyles that are in focus.[11] The aim of the book of Proverbs is to guide its readers towards making the right choices of lifestyle, underlining the importance of choice not mainly for society but for the individuals themselves.

'Secular' proverbs

The main bulk, around 90%, of the book of Proverbs does not mention God at all. While some chapters refer to God several times, there are five chapters in the different parts of the book that do not mention God at all. That does not necessarily indicate that those parts that do not mention God were secular or chronologically early. To a large extent this absence of God-references may also be considered a matter of genre. The usage of instructions and short, pithy sentences had a clear objective: to teach young men the traditional and advisable way to a good life. God was naturally part of this tradition, but wisdom deals with many aspects of everyday life where it may not be necessary to mention God explicitly.

The favourite pair in the description of different characters in the book of Proverbs is wise/fool. 'Wise', *ḥākām*, occurs as an adjective forty-seven times, most of the time in contrast to 'fool', *kĕsîl*[12] or *'ĕwîl*.[13] The wise person is characterized as one who is careful with words, cautious, respects his or her parents and loves knowledge, while the opposite is said about the fool. There is no close connection in these passages between God's activity and the wise person or the fool. It is stated, 'Do not be wise in your own eyes; fear the LORD' (3:7), but in most cases the passages do not explicitly say anything about the relationship between God and the wise person. The interest is rather in the relationship between the wise person and other people, as well as in the different ways of describing the positive features of the wise person's character in contrast to that of the fool:

---

11. See C. G. Bartholomew and R. P. O'Dowd (*Old Testament Wisdom Literature: A Theological Introduction* [Downers Grove: InterVarsity Press; Nottingham: Apollos, 2011], pp. 270–275), who also find this vocabulary more appropriate.
12. Prov. 10:4; 13:20; 14:16, 24; 15:2, 7, 20; 21:20; 26:5, 12.
13. Prov. 10:8, 14; 11:29; 12:15; 14:3; 17:28; 29:9.

> The wise will inherit honour,
>> but stubborn fools, disgrace.
>
> (Prov. 3:35)

> The wise of heart will heed commandments,
>> but a babbling fool will come to ruin.
>
> (Prov. 10:8)

These sayings are representative. The consequences are as usual stated in general terms without any agent specified. The wise person will be honoured and the fool will fall, but how that will come about is not specified. The main purpose is guiding young men to choose wisdom and stay away from behaviour described as foolishness.

Another popular theme in Proverbs is that of diligence versus laziness. Diligence is a way of life that is naturally promoted because it results in production. Here it could be relevant to talk about actions with built-in consequences! For the man who does not work his fields the outcome is obvious. With irony and vivid metaphors the sluggard is admonished to stay in bed. No work will bring no income, and poverty will inevitably be the result.

> Go to the ant, you lazybones;
>> consider its ways, and be wise.
>
> Without having any chief
>> or officer or ruler,
>
> it prepares its food in summer,
>> and gathers its sustenance in harvest.
>
> How long will you lie there, O lazybones?
>> When will you rise from your sleep?
>
> A little sleep, a little slumber,
>> a little folding of the hands to rest,
>
> and poverty will come upon you like a robber,
>> and want, like an armed warrior.
>
> (Prov. 6:6–11)

The observation that can be made from this survey of the 'secular' proverbs is that they are general in both the description of the different groups of people and the result of their lifestyles. The outcome will be radically different for people characterized as wise, righteous and diligent compared with those described as fools, wicked and lazy. Nevertheless, the way in which these different outcomes will come about is left open. The primary interest was to encourage young men to choose the alternative in life characterized by wisdom and similar criteria.

God-sayings in Proverbs

It has been common in the history of research to consider speeches and sentences in the book of Proverbs that mention God as of later origin.[14] This seems to be an idea that is too modern and not adequate for ancient civilizations like Israel in Old Testament times. Leo Perdue states it this way:

> It is doubtful that early wisdom was secular and then only later was baptized into Yahwistic faith by religious scribes, who developed more acutely their theological expertise. Religious imagination about God is a part of the wisdom tradition from its earliest beginnings.[15]

This idea of an originally 'secular' wisdom tradition that later in history was theologized is also contradicted by resemblance with similar texts from the Ancient Near East. The text that has been widely used in comparison with the book of Proverbs is the Egyptian *Instruction of Amenemopet*. This text is assigned to the Ramesside period and thereby predates any possible date for the book of Proverbs. It seems to have been a popular text representing a shift in emphasis towards a more religious attitude than that found in earlier Egyptian instructions.[16] So even if one can observe a certain development towards a more theological stance in wisdom-like literature in Egypt, this is earlier in history than the book of Proverbs. There seems to be no need to argue for a later date for the theological strains of the book of Proverbs.[17]

---

14. W. McKane's commentary is an example of this separating and ascribing the theological material to a later date. McKane classifies the sentences in the book of Proverbs into three categories, with the sentences in the third group considered to be from a later stage in history and 'identified by the presence of God-language or by other items of vocabulary expressive of a moralism which derives from Yahwistic piety' (*Proverbs: A New Approach*, OTL [London: SCM, 1970], p. 11).
15. L. G. Perdue, *Wisdom and Creation: The Theology of Wisdom Literature* (Nashville: Abingdon, 1994), p. 56.
16. See M. Lichtheim, *Ancient Egyptian Literature, Vol. 2: The New Kingdom* (Berkeley: University of California Press, 1976), p. 146; J. L. Crenshaw, *Old Testament Wisdom: An Introduction* (Louisville: Westminster John Knox, 1998), pp. 212–213.
17. For a discussion on non-theological and theological speeches and sayings in the book of Proverbs, see L. Boström, *The God of the Sages: The Portrayal of God in the Book of Proverbs*, ConBOT 29 (Stockholm: Almqvist & Wiksell, 1990), pp. 33–45.

When God is referred to in the book of Proverbs it may be as an admonition to put trust in him or to emphasize the value of fear of God in a person's character. God is the sole creator, with wisdom present at his side (Prov. 8:22–31), and the wise person is aware that God knows everything that happens in the human world and acts accordingly.

> For human ways are under the eyes of the LORD,
>   and he examines all their paths.
> The iniquities of the wicked ensnare them,
>   and they are caught in the toils of their sin.
> They die for lack of discipline,
>   and because of their great folly they are lost.
> (Prov. 5:21–23)

Interestingly, though there is reference here to the Lord's eyes, implying that he watches human paths, the consequences for the wicked are still stated in impersonal terms. It is their iniquities that will ensnare them, and they will be caught in the toils of their sin. Still the context of the preceding verse indicates that all this is related to God's awareness and that the outcome for sinners has in some way to do with God's activity. Waltke, commenting on these verses, writes concerning the relationship between God's activity and other factors: 'As elsewhere in Proverbs, no distinction is made, nor is any tension felt by the sage, between the Lord who upholds the moral order and the moral order of act–consequence itself.'[18]

The relationship between a person's character and God's activity appears in a peculiar way in chapter 19:

> One's own folly leads to ruin,
>   yet the heart rages against the LORD.
> (Prov. 19:3)

In this passage the person's rage is turned against the Lord, most likely reflecting a general belief that God is the cause of misfortune, though, seen from another perspective, the cause is the person's own folly. As usual, the folly is not specified. The person committing folly is described as of the opinion that God is the agent of the misfortune. This is the reason for the person's rage against the Lord. The

---

18. B. Waltke, *The Book of Proverbs: Chapters 1 – 15*, NICOT (Grand Rapids: Eerdmans, 2004), p. 324.

saying points out the possible tension between what is considered to be God's activity and other factors operating. The fool blames God, but the saying points to human folly as the cause of the misfortune. The latter could be used as an argument for the sages' belief in actions with built-in consequences.

Another of the favourite pairs in the book of Proverbs is righteous/wicked. The term 'righteous', *ṣaddîq*, occurs sixty-six times and is almost consistently contrasted with 'wicked', *rāšā*. Many of the passages about the pair deal with the consequences for both groups. The righteous will not go hungry, their desires will be granted, they will be established for ever, they will be delivered from trouble, stand firm, and so on. The righteous person may fall, even seven times, but rises again (24:16). A few sayings also refer to the social aspect. When the wicked rise, people hide (28:28),[19] but when the righteous are in authority, the people rejoice (29:2).

The fate of the wicked stands in contrast to that of the righteous. While the righteous are delivered from trouble, the wicked get into trouble (11:8). Since the mouths of the wicked conceal violence and their counsels are treacherous they will come to ruin, suffering want, trouble and calamity. The following saying is representative for both groups:

> The desire of the righteous ends only in good;
> > the expectation of the wicked in wrath.
>
> (Prov. 11:23)

Even though the word-pair righteous/wicked may appear more religiously coloured in the Old Testament than the word-pair wise/fool, there are only four cases where God is mentioned in connection with the righteous. These passages express the closeness between righteous people and the Lord and also the assurance that God actively assists the righteous.

> The LORD does not let the righteous go hungry,
> > but he thwarts the craving of the wicked.
>
> (Prov. 10:3)

Nothing is specified about how God will act, but these kinds of sentences function like promises. The message is that the Lord is in power and will arrange circumstances so that the righteous and the wicked receive retribution according to their characters.

---

19. See also 11:10; 29:16 for similar statements.

Almost simultaneously with Koch's article in the 1950s, Hartmut Gese published an interesting study on wisdom in which he argued for similar views to those of Koch and claimed that in both Egypt and in Israel there was belief in an order that closely linked acts and consequences. Gese states: 'We can almost speak in a scientific way about how consequence follows from deed.'[20] But Gese goes on to explain that this strong connection between act and consequence is based on observation and that the actual forces that are at work in this order for both Israelites and Egyptians were considered as beyond access and understanding.[21]

Gese has another interesting observation that has to do with God's activity in the world. He observes that there are a number of sentences that do not fit into this concept of order. He labels those sayings as 'special cases' and in contrast to the traditional understanding.[22] These sayings indicate a belief in what can be termed God's mysterious ways of acting out his will. The order and correspondence between human activity and what actually happens is broken, since God acts independently and in sovereign ways.

> The plans of the mind belong to mortals,
>   but the answer of the tongue is from the LORD.
> (Prov. 16:1)

> The human mind plans the way,
>   but the LORD directs the steps.
> (Prov. 16:9)

Gese argues that what is expressed here is not only a lack of human understanding in the way the order works. To him these 'special cases' represent a more fundamental shattering of wisdom thinking and another kind of determinism than the one otherwise dominating in both Egyptian and Israelite wisdom texts.[23] God is sovereign and not limited to laws of causality.

---

20. My own translation of 'Wir können fast von einer naturgesetzlichen Weise sprechen, in der sich die Folge aus der Tat ergibt', from H. Gese, *Lehre und Wirklichkeit in der alten Weisheit: Studien zu den Sprüchen Salomos und zu dem Buche Hiob* (Tübingen: Mohr, 1958), p. 35.
21. Gese, *Lehre*, pp. 34–35.
22. Gese's term for these 'special cases' is 'Sondergut'.
23. Gese, *Lehre*, p. 46.

Conclusions about retribution in the book of Proverbs

Both the longer instructions and the short sentences in the book of Proverbs leave much unstated. An attempt to understand the way the texts were received inevitably involves a certain degree of speculation and generalization. The texts that we have at our disposal indicate what can be termed 'double causality' or even 'multiple causality'. What happens in the world could be derived from different factors; both God's and human activity, as well as forces of nature and also what can be regarded as natural consequences, could be seen as the causes of human fortune. And it seems that these explanations of phenomena were not mutually exclusive.

We have argued that genre is of importance. The purpose of both the instructions and short sentences was not to clarify in any exact way what caused different consequences in life for people. Instead there seems to be an intentional openness in the texts whereby the sages deliberately left open the question of how the consequences would be brought about. The objective of the teachings was to encourage people to make the right choices and choose a lifestyle of wisdom and righteousness. A strong argument for the right choice was to emphasize the contrasting outcomes for the individuals themselves. How these outcomes would be realized was of less importance.

Even if it is true that the book of Proverbs shows little interest in specifying how the consequences of different characters and lifestyles will come about, a few conclusions can be made from the observations above.

1. The overruling idea seems to have been belief in God as the sovereign Creator and the one who is able to uphold justice in the world. Even if the number of God-sayings in the instructions and sentences is relatively small, the same idea of God seems to permeate the book of Proverbs as other parts of the Old Testament. Regardless of the possible prehistory of individual passages, the material in the book has been adapted and included in the Hebrew Bible. When God is referred to, it is *Yhwh* as God-designation that is overwhelmingly dominant in the book of Proverbs. Factors like these indicate that the book shares the overall theology and worldview of other parts of the Old Testament. As noted above, when God is referred to, there is an emphasis upon trust in him and his sovereign control. God is referred to as active in relation to human and retributive activity, but it seems probable that the sages also counted on other factors as instruments for God's retributive justice.

There are a few sayings where God is explicitly described as the agent of reward or punishment, as in Proverbs 15:25, where it is stated that the Lord tears down the house of the proud and maintains the boundaries of the widow. These passages are, however, not in a majority among the God-sayings, where the outcome is usually phrased in a more general way.

2. In some passages the social aspect of reward–punishment is indicated. Wisdom and foolishness will in any social setting bring consequences from other people. People characterized as wise or foolish will experience different responses from family, friends and neighbours.[24] The man who commits adultery can expect a reaction from the deceived husband who in his fury will take revenge. The result can be both bodily harm and disgrace in the community (6:32–35). Those who share their grain in times of need will experience blessing in contrast to those who hold it back (11:26). Blessing here is to be understood primarily as response from society, which is indicated by the contrasting first part of the sentence stating that the people will curse the one who holds back grain.

3. A third aspect of how reward–punishment can take place was noted by the word-pair lazy/diligent. Here it is relevant to talk about acts with built-in consequences. Diligence is promoted and promised rich rewards, with no exceptions (10:4; 13:4). For the lazy there is no need to ascribe the consequences to either God or society. Those who do not plough in the autumn will find their fields without produce at harvest time (20:4). The consequence is just the natural outcome of doing nothing or too little. The same reasoning applies to drunkards or gluttons: their poverty comes as a natural consequence of their lifestyle (23:20).

These different aspects of retribution are not mutually exclusive in Proverbs; instead they complement each other. The social aspects and the natural causes are not opposed to belief in God's retributive activity. In other Old Testament texts too there is a reciprocity between what is described as God's action and what is caused by human powers or nature. When the Assyrians invade Judah it is described as God's punishing activity, but it is also made clear that the Assyrians act by their own initiative (Isa. 10:5–19). Double or multiple causality seems to permeate retributive thinking in Proverbs. The important point in both the instructions and the sentences is the emphasis that retribution will inevitably happen and that any wise person should live his or her life in accordance with that belief.

Retribution in Job

The book of Job is in genre similar to the complaint psalms of the Psalter. This makes the book more realistic and a contrast to the simplistic teachings of the

---

24. For an interesting view of the social aspect of retribution, see C.-A. Keller, 'Zum sogenannten Vergeltungsglauben im Proverbienbuch', in H. Donner, R. Hanhart and R. Smend (eds.), *Beiträge zur alttestamentlichen Theologie: Festschrift für Walter Zimmerli zum 70. Geburtstag* (Göttingen: Vandenhoeck & Ruprecht, 1977), pp. 223–238.

book of Proverbs. The fact that the most upright person on earth experiences all possible misfortune is simple evidence that the application of the retribution principle cannot be applied rigidly. Job's friends appear as firm believers in the retribution principle but the shocking words of the epilogue state that they have spoken incorrectly about God!

David Clines notes that belief in the moral order is foundational to the book of Job and characteristic for all parties, including Job himself – up to the point when his life is shattered.[25] Moshe Greenberg reasons similarly: 'The speeches of Job reveal the collapse of his former outlook. For the first time in his life, he has become aware of the prevalence of disorder in the government of the world.'[26] The doctrine now represented only by his friends – that suffering is the result of sin – is as logical as mathematics. In maths you can turn figures around: two plus two is four, which means that four minus two is two. This makes it possible for the friends to conclude that Job's sudden reversal of fortune and extreme suffering must have a cause – and the logic says that it is his sin. Eliphaz starts out by cautiously suggesting this, but when Job does not give in he ends up making stark accusations. He accuses Job of cruelty against the poor and needy and of denying help to widows and the fatherless. Habel states: 'The bill of particulars [22:6–9] cited against Job are typical sins of "one with a strong arm" who takes advantage of the underprivileged to maintain his position of power.'[27] The conclusion is logical in the mind of Eliphaz:

Therefore snares are around you,
    and sudden terror overwhelms you . . .
(Job 22:10)

It seems inevitable to assume that the characterization of Job's friends' arguments is a critique of the retribution principle. Job's friends represent the ideas of traditional wisdom while Job is depicted as the truly wise and God-fearing person. God himself, in the introduction to the book, refers twice to Job as blameless and upright (1:8; 2:3), saying that there is none like him on the earth. With this as a background the irony of the plot becomes obvious, especially as Job's friends become more and more harsh in their accusations.

---

25. Clines, *Job 1 – 20*, p. xxxix.
26. M. Greenberg, 'Reflections on Job's Theology', in I. Kalimi (ed.), *Jewish Bible Theology: Perspectives and Case Studies* (Winona Lake: Eisenbrauns, 2012), p. 224.
27. N. Habel, *The Book of Job: A Commentary*, OTL (Philadelphia: Westminster, 1985), p. 335.

God's words in the epilogue constitute the final blow to a legalistic application of the retribution principle in the Old Testament. It is not only that the logic of Job's friends is wrong; shockingly, to the readers of the book, they have not spoken what is right about the Lord. And this is in contrast to Job, whom the Lord refers to as 'my servant' who has spoken what is right about God (42:7–8). This is astonishing, especially bearing in mind that Job has just been rebuked by the Lord: 'Will you condemn me that you may be justified?' (40:8b). The question relates to the issue that is crucial through the book: whether the innocent, suffering Job will curse God or not. And Job certainly comes close to doing this several times, especially if 9:24 is read as a reference to the Lord:

> The earth is given into the hand of someone wicked;
> he covers the faces of its judges –
> if it is not he, who then is it?[28]

Job here appears as a disillusioned believer in the same retribution principle his friends stand up for. His worldview has until recently been basically the same as that of his friends: that what happens in the world derives from God and is fair and just for each individual. And in a remarkable way the humble Job in the book becomes the rebellious Job. Instead of relying on faith in God as the upholder of justice in the world, Job now claims that God acts as a criminal.

The matter is highly theological and seems to be addressing both God's way of ruling the world and his upholding of the retribution principle. Retribution, which was so unchallenged in the book of Proverbs, is here seriously disputed!

The introduction and the God speeches in the book of Job introduce another aspect of the retribution principle: that there is more to a person's fate than is caused by God and humanity. In the introduction an unknown adversary comes before the Lord together with the sons of God. Most interpreters agree that though the Hebrew word *śatan* is used here, this is not the devil of later Jewish and Christian theology. The adversary's relationship to the Lord, to the sons of God and to Job and mankind can be debated, but of interest is his influence. His speech is antagonistic and he acts like an adversary not only to Job, but also to the Lord. Though he appears as God's subordinate, he boldly challenges God's way of ruling the world, but gets permission to function as the active agent in ruining Job's life (1:9–12; 2:4–6). Clines argues that the tension between

---

28. My own translation, translating 'wicked' in the singular, following T. Mettinger, *Namnet och Närvaron: Gudsnamn och Gudsbild i Böckernas Bok* (Örebro: Libris, 1987), p. 175. (English translation: *In Search of God*, 2006.)

the Lord and the heavenly adversary 'can be simply accepted as a datum of the narrative, or it can be probed theologically for its hidden resonances'.[29] The role of the adversary has deeper implications than are necessary for the narratological structure. The opposition between the adversary and both God and humanity indicates that here is an early beginning to the belief in evil powers that develops in late Old Testament times and the intertestamental era.[30]

The arguments of Job and his friends indicate no kind of dualism. Neither Job nor his friends suggest any forces other than God and Job himself that could have influenced Job's fate. Job refuses to admit flaws that would suffice to explain his disaster. Instead he arrives at the logical conclusion that it must be God who is capricious or evil. His friends defend God's justice and logically state that Job must have committed serious transgressions. The readers of the book of Job, however, have additional information, not only from the introduction. The divine speeches at the end of the book describe God's awesome world created for mankind, but without ever explicitly referring to human beings. Again, the speeches hint at the possibility that other factors play a role in the world of people. In the first speech God speaks among other things about the sea that is restrained by him and only by him. The depiction here is 'an unmistakable allusion to the common Semitic myth of a struggle of the deity with the sea at creation'.[31] Here the Lord sets limits for chaos by blocking the doors of the sea.[32] The personification of the sea seems to convey the idea that there are evil forces in the world and that the Lord upholds order and stability by restraining them.

In the second speech the terrible monsters of Behemoth and Leviathan are described. The point of the vivid descriptions seems to be that these terrifying monsters threaten mankind and can be controlled only by the Lord. Scholars generally agree about an Ancient Near Eastern mythological background for Leviathan and other monsters. Lipinski points out that in Israel the polytheistic elements of original myths about these monsters were removed and they were referred to as part of God's creation.[33] This means that no real dualism is

---

29. Clines, *Job 1 – 20*, p. 22.
30. The question whether the Old Testament is monistic or not is not settled. Concerning interpreting passages that state Yahweh as the single cause of all that happens in the world, W. Brueggemann, *Theology of the Old Testament: Testimony, Dispute, Advocacy* (Minneapolis: Fortress, 1997), pp. 354–355, argues that the intention of these passages is not to claim monism but to assert Yahweh's sovereignty.
31. D. J. A. Clines, *Job 38 – 42*, WBC 18B (Nashville: Nelson, 2011), p. 1101.
32. The same idea occurs in Ps. 104:9; Prov. 8:29, Jer. 5:22.
33. E. Lipinski, 'liwyatan', in *TDOT* 8 (Grand Rapids: Eerdmans, 1995), p. 509.

implied here. Nevertheless, both the challenging adversary in the introduction and the threatening powers in the divine speeches indicate that there are forces in God's creation that in a profound way threaten the world, even though they are subordinate to the Lord. The presentation of such a worldview affects people's perception of reality and also has implications for belief in justice and retribution. The simple fact that there might be factors other than divine and human activity behind what happens to people changes the settings of life and fate and opens up further alternatives.

In the narrative setting of the book, Job knows nothing of the heavenly drama that functions as the introduction. He cannot do anything but in humble response to the divine speeches withdraw his charges against God. Habel states:

> Job is left to deduce both his innocence and the answer to his questions through the theophanic appearance and enigmatic answers of Yahweh. Job may be ignorant of the higher wisdom principle which governs God's design, but he has gained sufficient understanding to know that pursuing litigation is futile. He knows, at least, that the design of God is not governed by a necessary law of reward and retribution. God's wisdom is of a higher order – and remains a mystery.[34]

For the readers of the book, including the introduction, it may be possible to go one step further and to argue that the book of Job implies a worldview, also hinted at elsewhere in the Old Testament, in which the retribution principle not only relates to God and to man, but also is affected by the influence of evil powers in the world.

The final blow to the retribution principle in the book of Job is in the epilogue, when Job is acquitted and his three friends are instead condemned for not having spoken what is right about the Lord. Job, called 'my servant Job', has to pray for his friends in order that they will be able to receive forgiveness (42:7–8). The rebellious Job was rebuked for his challenging of God's justice, but in the end he comes out as the winner of the debate with his friends!

Retribution in Ecclesiastes

The book of Ecclesiastes is ambivalent about belief in retribution. 'Belief in retribution assumes that the universe makes sense. Qoheleth, the speaking

---

34. Habel, *Job*, p. 579.

voice in the book of Ecclesiastes, questions whether there is any evidence of that.'[35] At times the book expresses the belief that God will bring both the righteous and the wicked to judgment, but it also observes righteous people who perish while wicked people live long lives. The recurring idea, however, is that it makes no big difference, because life is limited and in the end the same fate awaits everyone, regardless of how life has been lived. In his quest for meaning in life, Qohelet arrives at the disillusioned conclusion:

> For there is no enduring remembrance of the wise or of fools, seeing that in the days to come all will have been long forgotten. How can the wise die just like fools?
> (Eccl. 2:16)

This is far from the optimistic view of the book of Proverbs that rather states that the memory of the righteous is a blessing while the name of the wicked rots (Prov. 10:7).[36]

Robert Gordis states that it is the sceptical outlook that is basic to Qohelet which is related to his position among the well-to-do classes of society. Gordis' definition of sceptic is 'one who refuses to be convinced without proof'.[37] It is careful observation that leads Qohelet to question the retribution principle. On the one hand Qohelet says to himself that God will judge the righteous and the wicked (3:17; 8:12b–13), but on the other hand this view is contradicted by his observation of righteous people who perish though righteous, while evil people live long lives (7:15; 8:14).

Qohelet has an interesting explanation for why the retribution principle does not give the appropriate results: there is too much time between evil deeds and their sentence.

> Because sentence against an evil deed is not executed speedily, the human heart is fully set to do evil.
> (Eccl. 8:11)

The dominating system of the Old Testament that tightly relates, on the one hand, man's character and acts and, on the other hand, the consequences is here

---

35. D. Penchansky, 'Retribution', in *NIDB* 4 (Nashville: Abingdon, 2009), p. 782.
36. Cf. Ps. 112:6.
37. R. Gordis, *Koheleth – The Man and His World: A Study of Ecclesiastes*, 3rd edn (New York: Schocken, 1968), p. 128.

criticized. The critique is hardly against slow and corrupt human legislation, but rather against God and his way of upholding the universe. It is in line with Qohelet's repeated conclusion that man is not able to fathom what happens under the sun.

Michael Fox comments upon Qohelet's dilemma concerning the inconsistency and delay in judgment upon evil:

> Whereas earlier commentators found Koheleth's skeptic assertions difficult to accept at face value (and sometimes attributed them to a student or a fool), modern interpreters find it hard to credit him with his expressions of faith. Yet Koheleth's problem is precisely that he holds both to what he observes and to what he believes (in his words, what he says he 'knows'). This is a dilemma shared by many believers. They cannot deny the injustice of the Holocaust, to take the extreme case, but they choose not to abandon faith in God's justice. Koheleth 'knows' the doctrine of retribution and nowhere denies it. At the same time, he *also* knows there are cases that violate the rule.[38]

The book of Ecclesiastes ends, however, traditionally. The disillusion, doubts and critique concerning the adequacy of the retribution principle that mark the book are corrected in the end by the concluding admonition to fear God and keep the commandments, for God will bring all into judgment, whether good or evil (12:13–14). Most commentators are united in considering this pious and traditional statement as some kind of corrective to this book that deals with several deep philosophical issues of human existence, among them the idea of divine retribution.

Conclusions

It can hardly be argued that belief in retribution is a central issue in the wisdom literature of the Old Testament. The book of Proverbs expresses a firm belief in justice at a personal level. The wise, righteous and good person will be rewarded, while the foolish, wicked and evil person will be sentenced. The timetable and details of how this justice will be executed is, however, in most cases left open and unspecified. Ultimately the belief in the retribution principle is built upon belief in a God who is active in the world and upholds justice in relation to both good and evil.

---

38. M. V. Fox, *Ecclesiastes*, JPS Bible Commentary (Philadelphia: JPS, 2004), p. 59.

The books of Job and Ecclesiastes, as well as certain other Old Testament texts, indicate that the world is more complicated than can be laid down as a law of retribution. The book of Job challenges the retribution principle by severe critique of its representatives, Job's friends. Even if the book gives no answer to the matter of innocent suffering, the introduction and the divine speeches indicate that human life is also affected by evil powers in the world. The presence of evil in the world also influences the fate of the individual and thereby what is commonly understood as retributive justice. All that happens in the world is not caused by God!

The book of Ecclesiastes ends up by traditionally promoting the retribution principle, but throughout the book it is criticized, mainly through observations that it does not apply in all cases and that in the long run it makes no difference since all people die and are forgotten.

The wisdom literature of the Old Testament shows that belief in divine retribution is fundamental, though not unproblematic. Wisdom literature's belief in retribution is in line with the rest of the Old Testament. The difference is that in the wisdom literature the matter is individualized, which also makes it more open to critique.

Belief in retributive justice continued to be a matter of discussion and belief, as can be evidenced by both Jewish sources and the New Testament. A saying about Rabbi Hillel quoted in the Talmud illustrates that at least for some a rigid retribution principle seems to have been fundamental in Judaism around the start of the Common Era:

> He also saw a skull floating on the face of the water. He said to it: Because thou didst drown [others] they drowned thee, and the end of those that drowned thee [will be that] they will be drowned.
> (b. Aboth II. 6)

An episode from the New Testament is another example from the same era that also points towards a dogmatic belief in retribution:

> As he walked along, [Jesus] saw a man blind from birth. His disciples asked him, 'Rabbi, who sinned, this man or his parents, that he was born blind?'
> (John 9:1–2)

If everything that happens needs to be derived from a person's character or acts, how can a man be born blind? Jesus answers that in this particular case there is another purpose, but he gives no clear answer to the larger issue, and the applicability of the retribution principle continues to be an open question.

Jerry Allen Gladson underlines and regrets this dogmatizing tendency in his doctoral dissertation on retributive paradoxes in wisdom, with a note concerning the thinking about retribution in the post-Old Testament era:

> It is significant to note that the later traditional expressions of wisdom seem to preserve less of the retributive tension, or they respond to it more directly, than do the earlier proverbial collections. There is more of a tendency to spiritualize, or theologize, life's enigmas, than previously. There is, in short, less of a proclivity toward empirical openness and, hence, a movement away from retributive conflict in the literature.[39]

© Lennart Boström, 2016

---

39. J. A. Gladson, *Retributive Paradoxes in Proverbs 10 – 29* (unpublished diss., Vanderbilt University; Ann Arbor: University Microfilms International, no. 7909275, 1978), p. 354.

8. WORRYING ABOUT THE WISE: WISDOM IN OLD TESTAMENT NARRATIVE

David G. Firth

In Shakespeare's *Merchant of Venice*, Morocco observes to Portia that 'all that glisters is not gold'.[1] In the play, the phrase appears as a proverb, and it has (with the change of 'glisters' to 'glitters') continued to function as such in English today, essentially warning that things are not always what they seem. It is the classic proverb for pointing out that things which seem too good to be true almost certainly are. Put simply, reality might be rather different from what is claimed. The purpose of this paper is to show that this disjunction between what is claimed and what is delivered is a key element of the Old Testament's narrative traditions in which the introduction of someone as 'wise' (using *ḥkm* or a synonym) tends to indicate that one so described is either not wise or that his or her wisdom is not consistent with the patterns of which the Old Testament approves.

For the purposes of this paper, 'narrative traditions' is restricted to Joshua–Kings, Chronicles, Ezra–Nehemiah and Esther. Narrative occurs more widely in the Old Testament than this, with wisdom themes particularly notable in the Joseph story,[2] but this narrower range of literature can be understood as responding to wisdom's presentation in the Pentateuch and so as an appropriate set of

---

1. William Shakespeare, *The Merchant of Venice*, Act II, Scene 7.
2. See Lindsay Wilson, *Joseph Wise and Otherwise: The Intersection of Wisdom and Covenant in Genesis 37 – 50* (Milton Keynes: Paternoster, 2004).

texts to read together. Of course this definition cuts across standard canonical and scholarly organizations of these texts,[3] mixing the Former Prophets with the Writings, or the Deuteronomistic History with the Chronistic texts, but this makes their shared perspectives on this that much more interesting.

Other canonical patterns of wisdom

This critical perspective is a surprise if we approach wisdom in these traditions through the Old Testament's wisdom texts. Proverbs is notable for how it encourages its readers to see wisdom as something to be sought (e.g. Prov. 2), something prized which is to be passed on (e.g. Prov. 4:1–9). Even Qoheleth, not usually noted for cheering thoughts, sees wisdom as something positive (e.g. Eccl. 7:19) that can achieve unexpected things (Eccl. 9:15), even if he also acknowledges its limits (e.g. 7:23–29). Certainly the book's frame narrator views wisdom positively, even if it can be uncomfortable (Eccl. 12:11). Although Job has a more problematic view of wisdom, chapter 28 is representative of the view found in Proverbs that wisdom is something positive to be sought.

It is, however, less surprising if we approach this motif from other parts of the Old Testament, where both the Pentateuch and the Prophets are frequently ambivalent about wisdom. The book of Isaiah, for example, has very little that is positive to say about the wise.[4] Sometimes, as in 5:21, it is expressly stated

---

3. One classical arrangement of the canon (following LXX and represented in English Bibles) labels these the 'historical books' (e.g. Robert B. Chisholm Jr, *Interpreting the Historical Books: An Exegetical Handbook* [Grand Rapids: Kregel Academic, 2006], covers the same range of texts as here). Any label we give is problematic in that 'narrative' occurs more widely than in them, whilst calling them 'historical' tends to encourage reading them in terms of the 'facts' of Israel's past rather than as a word from God which addresses us today. On the hermeneutical problems, see Iain Provan, 'Hearing the Historical Books', in Craig G. Bartholomew and David J. H. Beldman (eds.), *Hearing the Old Testament: Listening for God's Address* (Grand Rapids: Eerdmans, 2012), pp. 254–258.
4. For a helpful treatment of this theme, see Lindsay Wilson, 'Wisdom in Isaiah', in David G. Firth and H. G. M. Williamson (eds.), *Interpreting Isaiah: Issues and Approaches* (Nottingham: Apollos, 2009), pp. 145–167. Wilson shows that the book's interest in wisdom transcends the occurrence of key terminology, though where the key terms (such as *ḥkm* and its derivatives) do occur, they mostly fall into his treatment of 'True and False Wisdom' (pp. 156–157).

that the concern is with those who regard themselves as wise (with the clear implication that they are not), though elsewhere (such as 3:3 or 29:14) the wise are specifically singled out for judgment. This does not mean the book rejects wisdom. That which comes from Yahweh is clearly affirmed, most obviously in the designation of Yahweh himself as wise (Isa. 31:2; cf. 10:13). Yahweh is the source of Israel's true wisdom, the one who brings justice to Zion (Isa. 33:5–6), in contrast with the conditions Israel's leaders have brought about. This is why the wisdom of the messianic figure in 11:1–9 comes from an endowment of Yahweh's Spirit. For the book of Isaiah, human claims of wisdom are suspect, though wisdom itself is not rejected, as can be seen in the wisdom tropes it uses.

The Pentateuch is likewise ambivalent. Setting aside Joseph as something of a special case (his wisdom is recognized even by Pharaoh as being divine [Gen. 41:38–39][5]), we can observe that it too criticizes humanly initiated wisdom. So Pharaoh's counsellors are described as his 'wise' men (Gen. 41:8; Exod. 7:11), though the text does not accept the validity of their wisdom, either because they cannot interpret a dream or because, through their replication of Yahweh's acts, they set Egypt against Yahweh. Likewise, Pharaoh decides to 'act wisely' in dealing with the growing Israelite population (Exod. 1:14), but is then duped by the midwives (Exod. 1:15–17). The label 'wise' thus has considerable irony here.

However, Egyptian wisdom is the exception within the Pentateuch, which instead focuses its treatment of positive expressions of wisdom in three broad fields. First, it treats artisanship as an expression of wisdom in the case of Bezalel and Oholiab, the two craftsmen responsible for the construction of the tabernacle. As with Joseph, there is a close association between these artisans and the Spirit of God (Exod. 31:3; 35:31), though they are placed within a larger group of artisans who contribute to this work (Exod. 28:3; 31:3). Second, it notes that wisdom can be recognized in those who respond appropriately to what God is doing. This wisdom might be seen in individuals who see the need to contribute to the construction of the tabernacle (Exod. 35:26) or in a community which responds appropriately to God's initiatives and gift of *Torah*

---

5. Pharaoh's observation that the *rûaḥ 'ĕlōhîm* dwells within Joseph is ambiguous. As a polytheist, for Pharaoh it means 'a spirit of the gods', but for Israelites the more specific meaning 'Spirit of God' is possible. See further, David G. Firth, 'The Spirit and Leadership: Testimony, Empowerment and Purpose', in David G. Firth and Paul D. Wegner (eds.), *Presence, Power and Promise: The Role of the Spirit of God in the Old Testament* (Nottingham: Apollos, 2011), pp. 261–263.

(Deut. 4:6).[6] Finally, particularly in Deuteronomy, wisdom is seen in leaders who practise and enable justice (Deut. 1:13–15).[7] Although Moses embodies this most completely in Deuteronomy, it is Joshua who is described as being full of the 'spirit of wisdom' (Deut. 34:9).[8] Although this final group's wisdom is never said to be from God, it is so consistent with God's purposes that it too should be seen as an appropriate response to what God has done.

Moving to the narrative literature

The patterns from the Prophets and Pentateuch are informative for reading the narrative books. Both allow for the existence of true and false wisdom, with the former either something given directly by God or expressed in consistency with God's revelation, while the latter is humanly initiated. Put that way, it would seem that the nature of any wisdom should be easily recognized. In practice, however, the criteria for distinguishing between true and false wisdom are much harder to apply. How does one know, short of a divine oracle, that some claimed wisdom is actually from God? The wisdom in the Latter Prophets resolves this problem through its inclusion in a book which is understood as a word from God, validating its perceptions on wisdom. Although the Pentateuch rejects the wisdom of Pharaoh's counsellors, the fact that they are associated with Egyptian polytheism and reject the claims of Yahweh again makes it easier to see this as false wisdom. By contrast, association with God's Spirit or Moses as Yahweh's servant makes it clear that such wisdom is acceptable. Yet very little claimed wisdom can pass this test. Artisanship, as an expression of wisdom, can point

---

6. Though note the counter-example here in Deut. 32:6 (cf. 32:29), where a nation which does not practise Yahweh's judgment is unwise. Daniel I. Block, *How I Love Your Torah, O LORD: Studies in the Book of Deuteronomy* (Eugene: Cascade, 2011), p. 172, points to the importance of this statement for the chapter, seeing it (along with v. 5) as the thesis statement of the whole song.
7. Though the counter-example of the danger of a bribe to the wise in Deut. 16:19 should also be noted.
8. Although Exodus connects such wisdom to God's Spirit, it is unlikely that this is the intent here since Deuteronomy never refers to God's Spirit – indeed, apart from this passage, *rûaḥ* occurs only in 2:30, where it is clearly an anthropological term. However, Jack. R. Lundbom, *Deuteronomy: A Commentary* (Grand Rapids: Eerdmans, 2013), p. 947, leaves open the possibility of such a connection by linking this passage to Exod. 28:3.

to a record of achievement, but otherwise recognizing those who are truly wise is quite difficult. It is certainly possible for someone to claim the title of 'wise' (or an equivalent), but is it true wisdom?

Hence, although the wisdom literature encourages readers to seek wisdom, both the Latter Prophets and the Pentateuch recognize that all wisdom is not equal, and some wisdom is to be rejected. This does not require us to establish a conflict between the wisdom literature and other parts of the canon, but it does raise the practical question of how true wisdom is to be recognized. It is the Old Testament's narrative literature which particularly wrestles with this problem. Although there is a minor precedent here in the treatment of Pharaoh's counsellors, the narrative literature does not (for the most part[9]) deal with polytheists whose wisdom is more easily seen as false, but rather with Israelites who one might hope would express true wisdom – but frequently do not. Artisanship is still accepted without challenge, but claims of others to wisdom are shown to be much more questionable. What is particularly notable in this respect is that no figure for whom wisdom is claimed is ever expressly said to embody false wisdom. Rather, by adopting external focalization in which the narrator refrains from omniscient expressions,[10] these texts consistently ask readers to identify true wisdom through what is done rather than through what is claimed. Wisdom is validated by actions rather than claims.

Wisdom in the Former Prophets

Because the Old Testament's narrative traditions come in diverse forms it will be helpful to explore them through three main groups. We can divide them for the most part by the Hebrew canonical traditions, and so consider the Former Prophets from the second division of the canon, and then the Chronistic works from the Writings. Finally, we can consider Esther, also from the Writings, but placed in a special collection by its inclusion in the Megilloth.

Joshua

Joshua stands out from the rest of the Former Prophets in that it makes neither overt reference to wisdom nor any significant use of wisdom forms.[11] Joshua himself applies the sort of rhetorical skills we also see in Deuteronomy in his

---

9. The exceptions all occur in the book of Esther.
10. Gérard Genette, *Narrative Discourse: An Essay in Method* (Ithaca: Cornell University Press, 1980), pp. 189–194.
11. Given that the Pentateuch often associates wisdom with God's Spirit, it is notable that Joshua makes no reference to the Spirit either.

three closing speeches (Josh. 22:1–8; 23:1–16; 24:1–28), and one could make the case that using such rhetoric is employing wisdom. Likewise, the association of *Torah* and wisdom in Psalms could be seen as having an analogue in Yahweh's directive to Joshua in 1:8. However, doing so in a book which at no point makes any explicit connections to wisdom traditions is perhaps trying too hard to make wisdom connections. Likewise, although Deuteronomy 34:9 has noted Joshua's 'spirit of wisdom', the wisdom employed in the book is the wisdom of obedience to *Torah*. This is something Proverbs also encourages (e.g. Prov. 29:18), but these connections with wisdom operate at a fairly general level, and since Deuteronomy 32:6 regards disobedience as foolishness it seems better to accept that the primary connections in Joshua are with the Pentateuch, especially Deuteronomy.

Judges

Judges, likewise, makes little in the way of direct reference to wisdom, though it does have some striking examples of wisdom forms. The one explicit reference to wisdom occurs in the Song of Deborah in Judges 5, which imagines Sisera's mother looking through the window and wondering why he is so long returning, and her counsellors (*ḥakmôt śārôteyhā*[12]) responding (with the mother's agreement) that it is probably because of the amount of plunder, including women,[13] which delays them. That these Canaanite women view others here as little more than reproductive parts to be claimed by their men, considering rape as a benefit which accrues to a victorious army, is an irony[14] which Webb regards as being as telling a critique of Canaanite life as the earlier vignette about Adoni-Bezek (Judg. 1:4–7).[15] From an Israelite perspective – and this is a polemic which imagines Canaanite perspectives rather than reporting them – there can be no clearer evidence of the failure of such wisdom. It is clearly associated with

---

12. The form of MT here is extremely difficult. See Barnabas Lindars, *Judges 1 – 5: A New Translation and Commentary* (Edinburgh: T&T Clark, 1995), pp. 283–284, for a convenient summary; or, more fully, Ze'eb Weisman, 'שרותיה (Jud V 59)', *VT* 26 (1976), pp. 116–120.
13. Verse 30 refers simply to 'a womb or two' and so further dehumanizes these women.
14. Danna Nolan Fewell and David M. Gunn, 'Controlling Perspectives: Women, Men, and the Authority of Violence in Judges 4 – 5', *JAAR* 58/3 (1990), p. 408, believe that within the overall structure of Judges 4 – 5 this effectively becomes the means by which they approve of their own upcoming rape. However, as rape is never approved, this seems to over-read the text.
15. Barry G. Webb, *The Book of Judges* (Grand Rapids: Eerdmans, 2012), p. 217.

Canaanite life and practice, and is therefore as ineffectual as any of the advice given by Pharaoh's counsellors. Sisera's mother's counsellors might merit the label 'wise' but seen from the perspective of *Torah* they do not have true wisdom. Indeed, that they completely misrepresent the situation after the battle shows how limited their understanding is. Wisdom can be claimed, but its misrepresentation of reality shows that it is flawed.

Although this one reference to wisdom in Judges is thus highly critical, the book still makes significant use of wisdom forms. In particular, we can note the interpretation of the dream about Gideon (Judg. 7:13–14), the proverb quoted to Gideon (8:21), Jotham's fable (9:7–15) and Samson's riddle and its answer (14:10–20). We will note an ambiguous attitude to wisdom in these, though the key point remains that only wisdom that acknowledges Yahweh's authority is valid. Nevertheless, even those who do not know Yahweh may employ wisdom which points to his sovereignty, though without realizing this reality.

This becomes especially apparent in the scene in Judges 7:13–14, where Gideon hears two Midianite soldiers discussing a dream about a barley loaf striking the Midianite camp. Once the first has recounted the dream, the second interprets it as evidence that God has given their camp into Gideon's power. Dream interpretation is a standard motif in portrayals of the wise, particularly Joseph[16] and Daniel.[17] Although not particularly significant, it does occur in the generally recognized wisdom literature.[18] This dream, however, does not require a great deal of wisdom to interpret. As Webb notes, it is 'the projection of a strange, inexplicable dread that has come upon the enemy'.[19] Indeed, given that the preceding narrative has been careful to set up the Midianite position as being massively stronger than that of Israel, it might also be an example of fear contrary to wisdom. However, its contribution to the narrative is that it is the first time that Israel can be seen to have the advantage, a possibility which the narrative has hitherto suggested is improbable.[20] So, although at one level the dream's interpretation is an example of wisdom, its place within the narrative shows that it is anything but, putting it on the same level as the supposed wisdom of the ladies advising Sisera's mother.

---

16. Gen. 40:5–19; 41:14–36.
17. Dan. 2:24–45; 4:19–27.
18. E.g. Job 4:12–21 (though the validity of Eliphaz's interpretation is questioned by its place in the book).
19. Webb, *Book of Judges*, p. 245.
20. See Bernon Lee, 'Fragmentation of Reader Focus in the Preamble to Battle in Judges 6.1 – 7.14', *JSOT* 97 (2002), pp. 83–85.

The problem of foreign wisdom is also evident in the proverb cited by Zebah and Zalmunna to Gideon in Judges 8:21. Gideon has captured these Midianite leaders and confronted them over an otherwise unnarrated event when they killed Gideon's brothers and for which Gideon seeks revenge. Gideon claims Yahweh's support for his actions through his oath in 8:19, but given his earlier violence it is more likely that here we see violence spinning out of control.[21] Gideon initially directs his son Jether to kill them, perhaps to humiliate them. Jether, though, is afraid to act, so Gideon is goaded by them through their proverb, 'a man is measured by his strength' (*kā'îš gᵉbûrātô*). A key test of true wisdom is the ability to apply the right perspective to a situation – something Job's friends signally fail to do – and on that score Zebah and Zalmunna's final belligerent use of proverbial language shows that, though they use a wisdom form, as foreigners who do not submit to Yahweh they are not themselves wise.

Foreign wisdom is not an issue in Jotham's fable, although by personifying trees it draws on an established Ancient Near Eastern genre in which trees are used to describe a contest of some sort.[22] Rather, the question is the legitimacy of Abimelech's claiming of kingship at Shechem through the hiring of mercenaries and murder of Gideon's other sons (Judg. 9:1–6). Jotham therefore deploys an established wisdom trope (the fable) which he mixes with another standard wisdom trope, the three–four pattern,[23] something he continues in his application speech in 9:16–20.[24] In the fable, three trees decline kingship while the fourth accepts it, while in the application the three conditional clauses of 9:16–19 establish the issue, including a digression in 9:17–18, before the contrasting fourth point in verse 20. Within the narrative, it may initially seem that Jotham has been unsuccessful. After all, neither Abimelech nor the Shechemites pay him much attention; but this would be to assume that biblical narrators need to comment directly. Rather, as Oeste has observed, their failure to heed

---

21. Hence Robert B. Chisholm Jr, *A Commentary on Judges and Ruth* (Grand Rapids: Kregel Academic, 2013), p. 290: 'It appears that Gideon was more committed to personal vengeance than the Lord's cause.' Similarly, A. J. Culp, *Puzzling Portraits: Seeing the Old Testament's Confusing Characters as Ethical Models* (Eugene: Wipf & Stock, 2013), p. 110.
22. See Silviu Tatu, 'Jotham's Fable and the *Crux Interpretum* in Judges IX', *VT* 61 (2006), pp. 108–110. Cf. 2 Kgs 14:9.
23. E.g. Prov. 30:18–21.
24. Gordon K. Oeste, *Legitimacy, Illegitimacy, and the Right to Rule: Windows on Abimelech's Rise and Demise in Judges 9* (London: T&T Clark, 2009), pp. 137–145.

Jotham's charge is a further demonstration of how they have failed to act uprightly.[25] Although Jotham is not called 'wise' his wisdom is validated by the wider narrative. Abimelech demonstrates that he is not a valid king by his failure to act justly even though he claims the position; Jotham is shown to be wise by the truth of what he says, even though he never claims to be wise.

A more complex example is found in Samson's riddle in Judges 14:14-19, something set as a test for the guests at his unsuccessful wedding at Timnah. Although the riddle (*ḥîdâ*) is not especially prominent in the acknowledged wisdom literature, it is one of the words for wisdom listed in Proverbs 1:6, a term which features in the Queen of Sheba's visit to Solomon in determining his wisdom (1 Kgs 10:1; 2 Chr. 9:1) and also an important wisdom term in Psalms 49:4 (MT 49:5) and 78:2. The exact form and meaning of the riddle is much disputed, and although its solution may depend on some form of folk etymology[26] it is also quite probable that the narrative in which it is embedded is designed to obscure as much as reveal.[27] Its key function here, as with the Queen of Sheba, is to challenge those being tested by it.[28] As with Jotham, it may initially seem as if Samson's riddle fails to be difficult enough to challenge the wedding guests, but of course they resolve it only through the weeping entreaties of Samson's wife. Samson is shown to be more able than the guests in spite of them answering the riddle. But does this make Samson wise? The answer is almost certainly not, because the narrator has already noted that Samson's wedding was actually something Yahweh had initiated to act against the Philistines (Judg. 14:4). Samson's wisdom succeeds almost in spite of himself because Yahweh would achieve something that Samson never intended.

Judges thus demonstrates a complex attitude towards wisdom, but faithfulness to Yahweh's purposes remains at the core of the book's perspective. It takes a critical view of foreign wisdom, though if foreigners recognize Yahweh's actions they may display true wisdom. Yet all wisdom must ultimately be subservient to Yahweh's purposes, so that even apparently effective displays of wisdom may be subverted to his greater purpose.

---

25. Oeste, *Legitimacy*, p. 145.
26. See J. R. Porter, 'Samson's Riddle', *JTS* New Series 13 (1962), pp. 106-109.
27. Jeremy Schipper, 'Narrative Obscurity of Samson's חידה in Judges 14:14 and 18', *JSOT* 27 (2003), pp. 339-353. It is likely that the Samson narrative grew in stages (see esp. Hartmut Gese, 'Die ältere Simsonüberlieferung [Richter 14-15]', *ZTK* 82 [1985], pp. 264-265), but our concern is with the finished text.
28. Philip J. Nel, 'The Riddle of Samson (Judg 14:14-18)', *Bib* 66 (1985), p. 540.

Samuel

Where Joshua and Judges ask us to feed on scraps when exploring wisdom motifs, there is a significant shift in Samuel where, especially once David's court is established, wisdom becomes especially prominent.[29] In spite of those who claim that the so-called Succession Narrative[30] is essentially a sapiential text, it is a reduction of the larger narrative to make this the primary focus. Wisdom is certainly prominent, and we can accordingly find many parallels with Proverbs, but it is more likely that this is because a well-written narrative ought to reflect real issues, as also does wisdom. As such, although Whybray especially points to many parallels between these chapters and Proverbs,[31] the connections are general rather than directly with the emerging wisdom literature. However, where weight does need to be paid to Whybray's work is in his observation that the so-called Succession Narrative emphasizes the place of wisdom in a way that is quite distinct from the rest of the traditions about David, though not as absolutely as he suggests.

We can illustrate this by noting the paucity of wisdom motifs prior to 2 Samuel 9 – 20. Save for one important block, wisdom elements barely feature in 1 Samuel 1 to 2 Samuel 8, though those that do appear are important and are themselves also clustered. In particular, we can note the prevalence of wisdom themes in 1 Samuel 24 – 26,[32] even though none appear directly in the preceding chapters of 1 Samuel. These are pivotal chapters in the story of David's move to the throne because David here must learn that violence cannot be the means by which to claim the throne. More particularly, it is in these chapters that Saul first acknowledges that David will succeed him (1 Sam. 24:21). Although Jonathan has previously acknowledged that David will be king and claimed that

---

29. Wisdom within David's court is explored by R. N. Whybray, *The Succession Narrative: A Study of 2 Sam. 9 – 20 and 1 Kings 1 and 2* (London: SCM), pp. 56–95; and J. A. Loader, 'Jedidiah or: Amadeus. Thoughts on the Succession Narrative and Wisdom', *OTWSA* 27/28 (1984/5), pp. 167–201.
30. I have argued elsewhere that it is better to think of the relevant chapters as a court history of David rather than as a succession narrative (see David G. Firth, *1 and 2 Samuel: A Kingdom Comes* [Sheffield: Sheffield Phoenix, 2013], pp. 46–47), but this does not affect the reading of these chapters on this point.
31. Whybray, *Succession Narrative*, pp. 71–95.
32. Chapters 24 and 26 are often seen as doublets (see Ralph W. Klein, *1 Samuel* [Waco: Word, 1983], pp. 236–237, for parallels). But Robert P. Gordon, 'David's Rise and Saul's Demise: Narrative Analogy in 1 Sam 24 – 26', *TynB* 31 (1980), pp. 37–64, shows that we need to read each as a discrete contributor to the larger narrative.

Saul understands this (1 Sam. 23:17), Saul's acknowledgment is a vital change, even if his subsequent actions do not follow through on this. The fundamental point is that when the validity of David's coming reign is recognized we see a sudden increase in wisdom forms, showing how David can be a wise king (in contrast to Saul), and these passages provide a key backdrop to the later wisdom references.

In these chapters wisdom is shown either by David or by those who model to him appropriate actions for a king. David remains a flawed character, but through wisdom he can achieve key developments. In 1 Samuel 24:13 (MT 24:14) this is evidenced by his citation of a proverb to support his claim that he is not seeking to harm Saul. This is reinforced by a series of rhetorical questions, each of which introduces a trope that recurs later in Samuel,[33] but which themselves model wisdom by forcing Saul to conclude that David means him no harm. David's wisdom here is effective because it leads to Saul accepting David's testimony. By the time we reach chapter 26 Saul seems to have forgotten this, and so again is challenged by David's use of wisdom in his resumption of the image of Saul hunting a single flea like someone hunting a partridge in the mountains. Reference to the flea connects this speech to the previous encounter (though also differentiating it), whilst comparison with the partridge represents a standard mode of wisdom that offers insight into an experience through observation. The analogy here depends on the fact that when partridges were chased they tended to run on the ground until they were worn out and thus easy to catch.[34] The effectiveness of David's wisdom here is immediately recognized. Saul confesses to having sinned against David – indeed he has acted foolishly (1 Sam. 26:21) – and he also blesses David (26:25). David's wisdom has enabled both to continue, and without violence.

These accounts, however, pivot around David's encounter with Abigail in 1 Samuel 25, and wisdom motifs are particularly prevalent here.[35] The most obvious mode for this is the play Abigail makes on her husband Nabal's name in verse 25. It is unlikely that his parents would have named him 'Fool', and since other derivations of the name are possible it is likely that we have a

---

33. David resumes the motif of the flea in 1 Sam. 26:20, whilst Mephibosheth will tell David that he is a dead dog in 2 Sam. 9:8.
34. Though David also puns on the bird's name, in Hebrew *qōrē'*, reflecting earlier use of the verb *qr'* in v. 14.
35. Waldemar Janzen, *Old Testament Ethics: A Paridigmatic Approach* (Louisville: Westminster John Knox, 1994), pp. 14–15, makes this story his lead example of a 'wisdom paradigm' for ethics, though the reasons for this are not clearly laid out.

nickname which is easily distorted.[36] Nevertheless, it is this connection that Abigail makes when asserting that 'folly' ($n^ebālâ$) is what characterizes him,[37] though in fact there is a range of ways in which the narrative as a whole demonstrates that Nabal is the archetypal churl of the wisdom tradition.[38] Although the narrative never describes Abigail as wise, she embodies key characteristics of wisdom. Although it is possible that this is simply a function of a realistic portrait, it is the concentration of such motifs that make this relevant here. Hence in Abigail's initial speech to David she invokes wisdom motifs by her characterization of Nabal, whilst David's initial speech to Abigail characterizes her in wisdom terms, blessing her because she is a woman of discretion ($ṭa'am$). Proverbs 11:22 warns against a beautiful woman who lacks discretion, so Abigail is approved within the wisdom tradition because she is both beautiful and discreet. These two allusions allow us to see how the rest of her answer also fits the wisdom ideal, demonstrating the value of a soft answer which turns away wrath, the opposite of what Nabal achieved through his harsh response (Prov. 15:1). She shows David that he does not need to employ violence, something that shapes his subsequent dealings with Saul. Abigail thus embodies the characteristics that the wisdom tradition encourages, and seeing the placement of her story between the two accounts of David not killing Saul is vital for understanding wisdom's potential.

It is against this background that we need to note the wisdom themes in 2 Samuel 9 – 20. These have been largely absent since their cluster in 1 Samuel 24 – 26 but are especially prominent here. The range of texts means that we cannot survey them in depth, but for our purposes it is sufficient to note that, whereas Abigail's wisdom is shown by actions rather than labelling, it is much more likely in these chapters that anyone who is associated with the court will not be truly wise even when called 'wise'. Although wisdom motifs can be seen earlier,[39] they

---

36. David G. Firth, *1 & 2 Samuel* (Nottingham: Apollos, 2009), pp. 264, 267.
37. When Saul confesses to folly in 1 Sam. 26:21 he uses the root *skl*, but these terms are synonyms.
38. See Jon D. Levenson, '1 Samuel 25 as Literature and as History', *CBQ* 40 (1978), pp. 13–17. Although Levenson recognizes wisdom elements in the characterization of Abigail (pp. 17–20), he focuses on her relationship to the ideal wife of Prov. 31. Although she does as much as anyone in the Old Testament to match this – and of course concludes the chapter as David's wife – Levenson does not make the more explicit verbal connection.
39. See e.g. Carol Fontaine, 'The Bearing of Wisdom on the Shape of 2 Samuel 11 – 12 and 1 Kings 3', *JSOT* 34 (1986), pp. 61–77.

become explicit in the story of Amnon's rape of Tamar. Amnon's friend[40] Jonadab is explicitly described as 'very wise' (*ḥākām m^e'ōd*)[41] and he immediately applies his wisdom to the question of resolving Amnon's sexual frustration concerning his sister by concocting a plan where Amnon can be alone with her. It is a plan which is clearly contrary to anything of which the Old Testament approves. That it is the antithesis of wisdom is made clear by Tamar's description of what Amnon desires as *n^ebālâ*, something disgraceful and foolish, and also the term Abigail used of Nabal. Jonadab may be called 'wise', but his actions show that while he is politically astute, he is not truly wise.

This reference provides a frame for exploring the 'wise woman' from Tekoa whom Joab employs to convince David to restore Absalom to the court in 2 Samuel 14, employing a strategy that draws on 2 Samuel 12:1–15a. Although the woman is called 'wise' there is a lack of overt wisdom motifs in her presentation, and she is in many ways a reverse of Abigail.[42] The one exception is in the comparison she makes to water spilled on the ground (v. 14),[43] though the implication she draws from it is unfortunately vague. So is she truly wise? In fact, this remains ambiguous, perhaps in part because her actions unwittingly contribute to Yahweh's punishment of David. She does manage to convince David to bring Absalom back, so her 'wisdom' at that level is vindicated, as also is the fact that she negotiates a fine line in almost accusing David but without doing so directly. However, unlike Abigail, whose wisdom limited violence, the Tekoite woman's wisdom will contribute to its increase. Her wisdom achieves its immediate goal, but her willingness to work for Joab suggests that her wisdom is not to be trusted. By contrast, the portrayal of the wise woman of Abel (2 Sam. 20:16–22), who negotiates with Joab for her town's survival, is more positive. She shows considerable authority when summoning Joab, but also situates herself in the wisdom tradition by opening her discussion with an ancient proverb (v. 18).[44] The

---

40. It is possible that a royal 'friend' is a counsellor; Hushai is called David's 'friend' (2 Sam. 15:37). But this term occurs so widely across the OT that it is difficult to claim anything distinctive concerning it within the wisdom traditions.
41. 2 Sam. 13:3. Many modern translations (e.g. NRSV) use 'very crafty' in order to hint at the negative connotations of his actions, thus hiding the more neutral terminology with which he is introduced.
42. Firth, *1 & 2 Samuel*, pp. 443–444.
43. For which there is some similarity with Prov. 17:14.
44. The text here is unclear, with many preferring LXX. But Robert P. Gordon, 'The Variable Wisdom of Abel: The MT and Versions at 2 Samuel xx 18–19', *VT* 43 (1993), pp. 215–226, has shown that MT may be retained.

challenge she faces is to reduce violence by challenging Joab, her reference to the 'heritage of Yahweh' (v. 19) perhaps indicating that Joab's actions against the city contradict Deuteronomy 20:10. Faced with the town's destruction and many deaths, she negotiates with the townsfolk to execute Sheba, the wisdom of which is emphasized in verse 22. She is like Abigail in many ways, and her wisdom also reduces violence. Indeed, within Samuel it becomes clear that Abigail is the paradigmatic wise woman, and only to the extent that they replicate her can either of these women be truly wise; that is, true wisdom is once again seen by what it does, not by what it claims.[45]

This mode of assessing wisdom, though with one important development, is also evident in the portrayal of Ahithopel and Hushai in 2 Samuel 15 – 17. Neither is called 'wise' but both are counsellors. Ahithopel's advice is noted for its quality (2 Sam. 16:23), which is why David prayed that it be turned to foolishness[46] (2 Sam. 15:31). Although we do not know it at the time, it is David's encounter with Hushai immediately after this that enables his prayer to be answered.[47] In fact, Ahithopel's position will be undermined by a combination of David's native cunning in sending Hushai back to Jerusalem and then by Hushai's ability to convince Absalom that good advice is in fact bad. That he does this is related not to his own wisdom but rather to Yahweh's determination that Ahithopel's good advice be defeated (2 Sam. 17:14).[48] Ahithopel's wisdom would apparently have been confirmed if this was a normal military matter, but where necessary Yahweh overcomes wisdom. Wisdom may be validated through

---

45. For a more positive reading of these women, see Claudia V. Camp, 'The Wise Women of 2 Samuel: A Role Model for Women in Early Israel?', *CBQ* 43 (1981), pp. 14–29.
46. The verb used here, *skl*, echoes Saul's confession in 1 Sam. 26:21. Elsewhere in Samuel it is used only by Samuel to describe Saul's sacrifice (1 Sam. 13:13) and by David to describe his census (2 Sam. 24:10).
47. Although it is not emphasized within Samuel, that Hushai is an 'Archite' suggests he is descended from a Canaanite group that remained after Israel's entry (Josh. 16:2). If so, it is part of the remarkably positive treatment of surviving Canaanites within Samuel (note Araunah the Jebusite in 2 Sam. 24:18–24 or the Gibeonites in 2 Sam. 21:1–14). A wise Canaanite is the means by which Israel's king is delivered by Yahweh.
48. Song-Mi Park, 'The Frustration of Wisdom: Wisdom, Counsel, and Divine Will in 2 Samuel 17:1–23', *JBL* 128 (2009), p. 455, argues that it was the semblance of wisdom used by Hushai which convinced Absalom. There is merit in this, but the text's perspective is clear: it was Yahweh who intervened.

what it achieves, but where wisdom contradicts Yahweh's purposes it can be thwarted, something consistent with the perspective on wisdom affirmed by texts such as Proverbs 19:21.

Samuel thus displays a complex approach to wisdom, offering nuances that go beyond Judges. It is consistent with Judges in being suspicious of those who are called 'wise' unless their actions are consistent with Yahweh's purposes, whilst also recognizing that wisdom is often demonstrated in those who would not be recognized as wise. It also, however, demonstrates that human wisdom is subject to Yahweh's purposes, albeit purposes that are shaped by prayer, which is more effective than wisdom.

Kings
The wisdom themes which were prominent in Samuel's latter chapters find their natural climax in Solomon's reign, a narrative where wisdom is central. Since this has been widely studied only a few brief comments are offered here. What is less often recognized is how marginal wisdom is in Kings after Rehoboam's rejection of counsel (1 Kgs 12:8). Although wisdom motifs occasionally occur (such as Jehoash's tree fable (2 Kgs 14:9–10), it is notable that the key terms do not occur outside 1 Kings 1 – 11.[49] It is as if, after displaying Solomon's wisdom and ultimate failure, Kings sets aside wisdom, returning to the theme of *Torah*, with David, not Solomon, as the model monarch throughout. Kings goes to considerable lengths to show the extent and effectiveness of Solomon's wisdom (1 Kgs 3:28; 5:9–14, 26 [4:29–34; 5:12, EVV]; 10:4–8, 23–24), but it is notable that the account of his reign is bounded by two references which present it in a much less positive light. So in 1 Kings 2:6 David advised him to act in accord with his wisdom in dealing with Joab, the clear implication being that he should find a pretext for his execution, something Solomon subsequently achieved (1 Kgs 2:28–34). Solomon was already recognized as wise before his famous dream in 1 Kings 3:2–15 when he requested wisdom, though not in a positive way. Likewise, although his reign's closing summary mentions his wisdom (1 Kgs 11:41), the fact of his oppressive behaviour in 1 Kings 11 again questions his wisdom. This is perhaps because his request had been for an

---

49. This is frequently treated as two main blocks of text, with 1 Kings 1 – 2 completing the so-called Succession Narrative, and then 1 Kings 3 – 11 telling of Solomon's reign. But Gillian Keys, *The Wages of Sin: A Reappraisal of the 'Succession Narrative'* (Sheffield: Sheffield Academic Press, 1996), pp. 54–70, has demonstrated that 1 Kings 1 – 2 do not belong with 2 Samuel 9 – 20. If so, it is better to treat 1 Kings 1 – 11 as a single unit, even if chapters 1–2 are a subsection.

'obedient heart to judge' Yahweh's people (1 Kgs 3:9, AT), whereas by the time of the Queen of Sheba's visit it is clear that wisdom was associated with the court's wealth, not justice (1 Kgs 10:1–10). Indeed, the only wisdom to emerge unscathed from these chapters is that of the Canaanite artisan Hiram who oversaw the temple's construction, something rooted in a close parallel with Bezalel and Oholiab, the chief artisans in the tabernacle's construction whose wisdom is also stressed.[50] Wisdom is known by output rather than by social location, and the more closely wisdom is associated with the royal court's wealth and power, the more suspect it is.

Conclusion
The books of the Former Prophets have distinctive views of wisdom and it is important not to flatten them into a single approach; nevertheless, a broadly consistent approach still gradually emerges. Those labelled as 'wise' are typically associated with a royal court and all such wisdom, whether Israelite or not, is suspect. This may be because it promotes attitudes associated with Canaanite worship or because Israel's court no longer promotes justice. However, it is notable that throughout these texts anyone who is labelled as 'wise' almost never practises true wisdom. These texts suspect claims of wisdom except for artisanship, and this in turn follows patterns rooted in the exodus. In spite of this, wisdom is consistently appreciated when it is applied constructively and promotes faithful obedience to Yahweh. The ultimate measure of wisdom, however, is never simply that it is claimed. If wisdom is meant to be grounded in real-life experiences then the only way of truly discerning its presence is to see its fruit in justice and dependence on Yahweh.

Wisdom in the Chronistic texts and Esther
Chronicles and Ezra
The Chronistic texts have relatively little interest in wisdom, reflecting their focus on temple worship. All references to Solomon's wisdom in 2 Chronicles 1 – 9 have a direct parallel in 1 Kings, so the only additional reference is to the artisans associated with building the temple (1 Chr. 22:15; 28:21; 2 Chr. 2:7, 13–14). Since Chronicles recounts neither Solomon's dubious actions in establishing himself on the throne nor his later apostasy, one could conclude that references to his wisdom are more positive. However, establishing this

---

50. Exod. 31:1–6; 36:1–2. Their 'wisdom' is placed in the context of other artisans who also give their skills to the construction (Exod. 31:6; 35:26–35).

on the basis of what is not said is a risky process, and in any case we have to remember that the Chronicler writes for a different audience from that of Kings.[51] The more telling evidence is that Chronicles elsewhere makes very little use of wisdom forms. This suggests that even the retribution theme in the book cannot be rooted solely in the wisdom tradition but must instead be seen as drawing on a range of elements from elsewhere in the Old Testament.[52]

The only direct mention of wisdom in Ezra–Nehemiah occurs in Ezra 7:25, and even references to wisdom patterns are sparse. Unfortunately, interpretation of this verse is widely disputed,[53] though for our purposes the chief concern is the possible linkage of wisdom and law. In this chapter the Aramaic *dat* can be equated with *tôrâ*,[54] though of course the Aramaic more commonly refers to Persian law.[55] Since 7:25 seems to develop the concepts associated with law mentioned in 7:14, save for the addition of the reference to wisdom, it is quite possible that the 'wisdom' Ezra is to apply is simply the law. However, as will emerge in the subsequent chapters, the issues Ezra will face are not strictly those mentioned in the law, though his responses to them are rooted in the law.[56] The interrelationship of law and hermeneutics seems to be the particular area of wisdom meant here, and Ezra's training as a scribe would mean he was well equipped for this,[57] even if there remained ambivalence over how he did this.[58]

---

51. See Raymond B. Dillard, *2 Chronicles* (Waco: Word, 1987), p. 75.
52. See ibid., pp. 76–81.
53. See H. G. M. Williamson, *Ezra–Nehemiah* (Waco: Word, 1985), pp. 103–105, for a helpful summary.
54. Rolf Rendtorff, 'Esra und das "Gesetz"', *ZAW* 96 (1984), p. 166.
55. Sebastian Grätz, 'Gottesgesetz und Königsgesetz: Esr 7 und die Autorisierung der Tora', *ZTK* 106 (2009), p. 10.
56. See Csilla Saysell, 'Deuteronomy in the Intermarriage Crises in Ezra–Nehemiah', in David G. Firth and Philip S. Johnston (eds.), *Interpreting Deuteronomy: Issues and Approaches* (Nottingham: Apollos, 2012), pp. 197–208.
57. Cf. Gerda de Villiers, '"Die pen is magtiger as die swaard": Oor skrifgeletterdheid, skrifgeleerdes en Israel se Tweede Tempeltydperk', *HTS Teologiese Studies/ Theological Studies* 69/1, Art. #1987, <http://dx.doi.org/10.4102/hts.v69i1.1987>, p. 6.
58. See the conclusions of Thomas Bänziger, *'Jauchen und Weinen': Ambivalente Restauration in Jehud. Theologische Konzepte der Wierderherstellung in Esra–Nehemia* (Zurich: TVZ, 2014), pp. 281–288.

Esther

By contrast, Esther is replete with wisdom references,[59] though we cannot explore them here because of the complex issues of intertextuality they raise. Rather, we can note that there are two explicit references to wisdom, and that both of these conform to the pattern we have noted in the Former Prophets, though with an intriguing link to Ezra. In 1:13 the king consults his 'wise men' after Vashti's refusal to present herself at his banquet (1:10–12). These men had the specific task of advising the king because they were well versed in law (*dat*). Although this clearly refers to Persian law it echoes the description of Ezra noted above, except that, whereas Ezra attempts to apply the law to a complex situation, it is clear that these advisors make no such attempt. Instead, in a scene that approaches farce, they avoid the question of law, although they are still wise enough to realize that doing so resolves the issue of dealing with a capricious monarch. However, in proposing a decree that formalizes Vashti's removal they succeed in revealing her disobedience to the king, the very thing they have declared to be troubling. Their lack of true wisdom is patent.

A similar situation applies to Haman's advisors, also called his 'wise men' in 6:13. Haman has returned from honouring Mordecai and reported what happened to him when he went to ask for Mordecai's execution, applying their advice from 5:14. Haman had mentioned to them that Mordecai was Jewish (5:13), but they now feign surprise at this, observing only that if Mordecai is Jewish then Haman's fall is certain. Again, there is an ironic level at which they are truly wise because their observation is correct, but in reality they are fools, as indeed are all the Persian authorities within the book. Esther may recognize the reality of true wisdom, but it makes clear that it is not found in Persian structures, and so draws on the portrayal of the so-called wise in the Former Prophets to point to the existence of something better.

Conclusion

Israel's narrative traditions are therefore well aware of the importance of wisdom, though the different contexts into which these texts were written means

---

59. See the classic study of Shemaryahu Talmon, 'Wisdom in Esther', *VT* 13 (1963), pp. 419–455; and also the critique of Robert Gordis, 'Religion, Wisdom and History in the Book of Esther: A New Solution to an Ancient Crux', *JBL* 100 (1981), pp. 359–388. On the limitations of tying the characters too closely to wisdom, see Kevin M. McGeough, 'Esther the Hero: Going beyond "Wisdom" in Heroic Narratives', *CBQ* 70 (2008), pp. 44–65.

that they draw on those traditions to different extents. What is striking, though, is that although there are distinctive elements in each of them that refuse to be flattened into a univocal perspective, certain themes emerge with consistency. The most important of these is that the true test of wisdom is whether or not its application promotes justice and faithfulness to Yahweh. These texts are well aware that the royal court (especially) was a place where those who claimed to have wisdom would be found, but they are all concerned to show that simply because the court claimed wisdom it did not mean that it was present, whether or not the court was Israelite. These texts never acknowledge wisdom in non-Israelite courts, though they are doubtless aware that these were wisdom centres. Indeed, the best examples of wisdom are found in people like Abigail, someone who is never said to be wise, because they live and embody the claims of wisdom. Many could claim it, but too often they would demonstrate that all that glisters is not gold.

© David G. Firth, 2016

9. WISDOM AND BIBLICAL THEOLOGY

Christopher B. Ansberry

The wisdom literature's place within and contribution to biblical theology has a chequered past. Once considered a full-blooded member of the canonical household, a corpus consonant with the theological vision of Israel's covenant and prophetic traditions, recent works have perpetuated the sentiment of the late nineteenth and early twentieth century and ostracized the wisdom literature in biblical-theological reflection, characterizing it as an 'errant child', an 'alien body' and even 'an orphan in the biblical household'.[1] On this account, wisdom resides within a canonical twilight zone, where she mingles with pagan sources of wisdom and peddles an anthropocentric vision of life that is destructive for the witness of the church.[2] She refuses to play by the rules and cooperate with

---

1. R. E. Clements, 'Wisdom and Old Testament Theology', in J. Day et al. (eds.), *Wisdom in Ancient Israel: Essays in Honour of J. A. Emerton* (Cambridge: Cambridge University Press, 1995), p. 271; H. Gese, *Lehre und Wirklichkeit in der alten Weisheit* (Tübingen: Mohr, 1958), p. 2; James L. Crenshaw, 'Prolegomenon', in J. L. Crenshaw (ed.), *Studies in Ancient Israelite Wisdom* (New York: Ktav, 1976), p. 1.
2. See G. Ernest Wright, *God Who Acts: Biblical Theology as Recital*, SBT 8 (London: SCM, 1952), p. 104; H.-D. Preuss, 'Alttestamentliche Weisheit in christlicher Theologie?', in C. Brekelmans (ed.), *Questions disputées d'Ancien Testament: Méthode et*

salvation-historical approaches to biblical theology. Her affinities with Ancient Near Eastern wisdom literature suggest that she fraternizes with the wrong crowd. And her resemblance to more 'secular' forms of wisdom intimates that her contribution to the life and witness of the church is minimal. No wonder many consider the wisdom literature as peripheral to the theological witness of the canon, as a 'minority report in the Old Testament' and a second-class citizen in formulations of biblical theology.[3]

Admittedly, the wisdom literature possesses some distinctive characteristics. Its distinctive posture, modes of discourse and emphases, however, do not mean that the corpus is cut from a different cloth. The wisdom literature fits within and contributes to biblical theology; it operates under an 'integrated system of assumptions' that form and inform other corpora in the canon.[4] It approaches and assesses reality in a manner comparable to other portions of Scripture.[5] And the anthropocentric and theocentric dimensions of the wisdom literature complement and nuance significant theological concepts that pervade Christian Scripture. These concepts include creation, anthropology and ethics. In view of its concern with the created order, the wisdom literature provides a framework within which to understand the world in general and the theological value of the ordinary in particular. The anthropology of the wisdom literature mirrors and enhances conceptions of humanity elsewhere in the canon. And the moral vision of the wisdom literature is comparable to covenant, prophetic and New Testament ethics. This essay will reflect on these concepts and their related themes in order to assess the contribution of the wisdom literature to biblical theology.

---

théologie, BETL 33 (Leuven: Leuven University Press, 1974), pp. 165–181; C. Westermann, 'Weisheit und praktische Theologie', *Pastoraltheologie* 79 (1990), p. 515.

3. John Goldingay, 'The "Salvation History" Perspective and the "Wisdom" Perspective within the Context of Biblical Theology', *EQ* 51 (1979), p. 200.

4. See Michael V. Fox, 'The Epistemology of the Book of Proverbs', *JBL* 126 (2007), pp. 669–684, esp. pp. 676–684.

5. See Roland E. Murphy, 'Wisdom: Theses and Hypotheses', in W. A. Brueggemann et al. (eds.), *Israelite Wisdom: Theological and Literary Essays in Honor of Samuel Terrien* (Missoula: Scholars Press, 1978), p. 39; Craig G. Bartholomew, *Reading Ecclesiastes: Old Testament Exegesis and Hermeneutical Theory*, AnaBib 139 (Rome: Editrice Pontificio Istituto Biblico, 1998), p. 259; Raymond C. Van Leeuwen, 'Liminality and Worldview in Proverbs 1 – 9', *Semeia* 50 (1990), p. 111.

Wisdom, worldview and biblical theology

As noted above, the wisdom literature evinces a conspicuous interest in creation. Creation provides the overarching horizon of wisdom's worldview; it is the arena of human activity as well as the classroom in which wisdom, patterns of conduct and particular consequences are revealed. While this concern with creation presents certain difficulties in situating the wisdom literature in a biblical theology, the corpora's attention to creation may be more of an asset than a liability.

The cosmic vantage point of the wisdom literature captures something of the order, symmetry, goodness, beauty and wonder of the created world. The structure embedded in the cosmos, manifested through its recurrent patterns and discernible through human observation, provided the sages with a window into the structure of the socio-moral world. To be specific, the cosmic order shaped the sages' vision of the moral order, social life and human flourishing. The intimate relationship between the cosmic and moral order of the universe suggests that Israel's wisdom literature is not necessarily at odds with the moral order envisioned by Israel's covenant and prophetic traditions. Each discloses and orients the community to God's moral order. And each is concerned with life and human flourishing. The wisdom literature's cosmic vantage point, however, provided a wide-angle lens through which to view the order of life and moral norms. This vantage point and concern with order is fundamental to the wisdom literature's worldview. And it is characteristic of Ancient Near Eastern wisdom literature.

The concept of a cosmic order instituted by the deity for the organization of human life and the management of human affairs served as the basic premise of Egyptian and Mesopotamian wisdom traditions. Whereas Egyptian wisdom literature associated this primordial order with the concept of Maat ('truth, justice'),[6] Mesopotamian literature attributed this divine order to the institution and regulation of *me*s.[7] In both cultural contexts, these concepts of order provided the veritable foundation of ethics, religion and civilization. They

---

6. See H. H. Schmid, *Gerechtigkeit als Weltordnung: Hintergrund und Geschichte des alttestamentlichen Gerechtigkeitsbegriffs*, BHT 40 (Tübingen: Mohr, 1968), pp. 46–61; Erik Hornung, *Conceptions of God in Ancient Egypt: The One and the Many*, tr. J. Baines (Ithaca: Cornell University Press, 1982), pp. 213–216.
7. See 'Inanna and Enki', tr. G. Farber, in W. W. Hallo (ed.), *The Context of Scripture* (Leiden: Brill, 2003), 1.161:522–526; Samuel N. Kramer, *The Sumerians: Their History, Culture, and Character* (Chicago: University of Chicago Press, 1971), pp. 115–116.

forged the framework within which to understand the cultural values delineated in Ancient Near Eastern wisdom texts and the way in which conformity to these values contributed to the maintenance of the cosmic and social order. And they defined the responsibilities of both the king and the royal establishment, each of which was entrusted with the actualization and preservation of cosmic and social order.[8]

While Israelite wisdom literature does not express the concept of cosmic order through a specific term,[9] its belief in a cosmic and moral order inscribed by Yahweh in the very structure of creation is clear. This belief is expressed through several well-known texts, two of which deserve specific comment. The first is Proverbs 3:19–20. As a hymnic colophon to the beatitudinal poem in 3:13–18, this quatrain reflects on Yahweh's comprehensive creation and artistic design of the cosmos by means of wisdom, understanding and knowledge. Wisdom and understanding are portrayed as the tools or powers employed by the divine architect to construct a sure, enduring cosmos (3:19), while knowledge serves as the instrument through which Yahweh exercises his providential care for and preservation of the created order (3:20). Together with its parallel terms, wisdom is presented as the instrument of Yahweh's cosmic handiwork, the skill by which creation is fashioned and sustained according to a stable and discernible design. To acquire wisdom, therefore, is to acquire knowledge of this design and the ability to live in accord with the cosmic order.

This implication is elaborated upon in the second text: Proverbs 8:1–36. This extended poem unpacks 3:19–20, devoting specific attention to Wisdom's involvement in the social order and her presence at the construction of the cosmic order. Wisdom's involvement in the social order is described through her possession and distribution of the faculties of statecraft (8:12–16). Just as Wisdom served as the instrument through which Yahweh fashioned the cosmos

---

8. For discussion, see L. Kalugila, *The Wise King: Studies in Royal Wisdom as Divine Revelation in the Old Testament and Its Environment*, ConBOT 15 (Lund: CWK Gleerup, 1980), pp. 39–56; W. G. Lambert, 'Kingship in Ancient Mesopotamia', in *King and Messiah in Israel and the Ancient Near East: Proceedings of the Oxford Old Testament Seminar*, JSOTSup 270 (Sheffield: Sheffield Academic Press, 1998), pp. 54–70.

9. While some follow H. H. Schmid and argue that the Hebrew root *ṣdq* ('justice') corresponds with the Ancient Near Eastern concept of 'order', this connotation is not always foregrounded in the use of the root. The root may convey this shade of meaning, but it is difficult to demonstrate that it originally designated the concept of cosmic order. See John Barton, *Ethics in Ancient Israel* (Oxford: Oxford University Press, 2014), p. 100.

(3:19), so also Wisdom is the instrument through which leaders establish and maintain a just, ordered society. Her role in the cosmological realm corresponds with her role in the social world. This notion is reinforced by Wisdom's birth in the primordial past and her presence at the construction of the cosmos (8:21–31). Wisdom's eyewitness account of Yahweh's formation and ordering of the cosmos intimates that she possesses a unique knowledge of the basic structures, patterns and components of reality (8:22–29). This knowledge of the fundamental patterns of the cosmos provides her with the resources to endow leaders and individuals with the skills necessary to live in concert with the cosmic order and to flourish in accord with Yahweh's design. Together with Proverbs 3:19–20, Proverbs 8 illuminates the intimate relationship among the fundamental pillars of the wisdom literature's worldview, namely, creation, order and wisdom.

In addition to these texts from Proverbs, creation and the concept of order play a significant role in Job and Ecclesiastes. Creation serves as the panoramic backdrop of the elusive search for wisdom in Job 28; its wild yet wise order is the focus of the divine speeches in Job 38 – 41; and its structure and rhythms are captured by the poems in Ecclesiastes 1:4–11 and 3:1–8. Similar to Proverbs, these texts associate creation with the concepts of wisdom and order. However, these connections are drawn in distinctive ways and for discrete purposes. The cosmic search for wisdom's residence in Job 28 reveals the limits of human power and ingenuity. The untameable yet wonderful order projected in the divine speeches deconstructs Job's myopic perspective; it situates the sufferer within a cosmic community where the foundations, fringes and creatures of the created order are governed by Yahweh's wisdom, power and providential care. And the patterns in the natural world as well as the seasons of human life observed by Qoheleth may reveal the rhythm and rhyme of the created order. For Qoheleth, however, this rhythm and rhyme does not appear to have any reason.

Whether the order of creation is affirmed or questioned, it remains a fundamental component of the wisdom literature's worldview. This concern with creation and cosmic order not only provides a wide-angle lens through which to view life; it also serves as a paradigm for the ordering of human life. The cosmic order shapes one's conception of and life within the social order. Put differently, the structure embedded in the cosmos structures one's vision of and vocation within the socio-moral order. The way in which the components of wisdom's worldview inform one's perception of life and order various cultural activities is captured by the canonical construal of Proverbs 3:19–20.

As noted above, Proverbs 3:19–20 affirms that the cosmos reflects Yahweh's wisdom; but it does more than this. The poetic description of Yahweh's construction of the cosmic house also provides a metaphorical counterpart to humanity's construction of a terrestrial house. Just as Yahweh founded the earth 'by wisdom' (*běḥokmâ*, 3:19b[10]), established the heavens 'by understanding' (*bitbûnâ*, 3:19d) and filled particular realms 'by his knowledge' (*běda'tô*, 3:20a), so also a human home is built 'by wisdom' (*běḥokmâ*, 24:3a), established 'by understanding' (*bitbûnâ*, 24:3b) and filled with precious materials 'by knowledge' (*běda'at*, 24:4a). The content and sequence of the prepositional phrases in Proverbs 24:3–4 mirror the content and sequence of phrases in 3:19–20 (cf. Jer. 10:12; 51:15), suggesting that the principles of human house building, cultural formation and social provisioning are inextricably linked to Yahweh's design, construction and maintenance of the cosmos.[11] The tools employed by Yahweh in the establishment and provisioning of the cosmos are the tools employed by humans in the establishment and provisioning of a home. The divine house builder provides a paradigm for human house building.[12]

This conclusion is reinforced by the accounts concerning the construction of the tabernacle and temple. As microcosmic representations of the universe, the tabernacle and temple not only reflect the created world; they are also constructed in the same manner as the cosmos. Similar to Proverbs 3:19–20 and 24:3–4, Exodus 31:3 indicates that Yahweh filled the human builder, Bezalel, 'with wisdom' (*běḥokmâ*), 'with understanding' (*bitbûnâ*) and 'with knowledge' (*běda'at*) to construct parts of the tabernacle. And 1 Kings 7:14 declares that God filled Hiram 'with wisdom' (*'et-haḥokmâ*), 'with understanding' (*'et-hattěbûnâ*) 'and with knowledge' (*wě'et-hadda'at*) to construct elements of the temple. While the latter text lacks the preposition *bêt*, the sequence of terms is the same as in Proverbs 3:19–20, Proverbs 24:3–4 and Exodus 31:3 (cf. Exod. 35:31, 35; 36:1). Just as human house building mirrors the work of the divine builder, so also the construction of the tabernacle and temple mirrors Yahweh's construction of the cosmos. Each builder uses the same tools or instruments; and each text presents these instruments in stereotypical order. The striking similarities among these texts indicate that human wisdom in general and human building in particular are rooted in divine wisdom manifested in the construction, ordering

---

10. All Bible quotes in this chapter, unless stated otherwise, are the author's own translation.
11. See Raymond C. Van Leeuwen, 'Cosmos, Temple, House: Building and Wisdom in Mesopotamia and Israel', in R. J. Clifford (ed.), *Wisdom Literature in Mesopotamia and Israel*, SBLSymS 36 (Atlanta: SBL, 2007), p. 81.
12. Van Leeuwen, 'Cosmos, Temple, House', p. 81.

and filling of the cosmos.¹³ One who acquires wisdom, then, reflects God's wisdom, imitates his creation order and manifests his provision for the cosmos through one's life, work and care for others.

The orderly world projected by the wisdom literature provides a paradigm for understanding, actualizing and imitating the divine order in the different dimensions of social life. The cosmic order shapes one's vision of life and being-in-the-world. And the cosmic order shapes the vision and mission of the church. Perhaps this is why Paul prays that God would grant members of early Christian communities 'wisdom', 'understanding' and 'knowledge' to comprehend the cosmic scope of Christ's redemption and animate their cruciform lives (Eph. 1:17; 3:10; Phil. 1:9; Col. 1:9–10, 28; 2:2–3; 3:16; Phlm. 6).¹⁴ The wisdom literature's cosmic vantage point and concern with Yahweh's created order is valuable, for it offers an alternative to understanding the moral order apart from the salvation-historical mode dominant elsewhere in Scripture.¹⁵ Together with Genesis 1, several prophetic oracles (Hos. 2:21–22; Isa. 40:25–26; Jer. 10:12; 33:25–26; 51:15), many psalms (Pss 19:1–4; 33:4–9; 65:5–13; 74:12–17; 89:5–18; 104; 136:4–9) and the witness of the New Testament (Acts 14:15–17; 17:24; Rom. 1:20), the wisdom literature perceives creation as a structured unity and an important medium of Yahweh's revelation.¹⁶ Irrespective of the provenance of Israel's creation theology, the wisdom literature's theology of creation is neither subordinate to nor at odds with salvation history; rather it complements Israel's theology of history, offering a different perspective on one's relationship to God and place in the world. Its wide-angle lens hearkens back to the pristine condition of the primordial order, points forward to the cosmic restoration at the end, and provides a theological framework through which to understand life in God's good and orderly world in the interim. The wisdom literature's worldview prevents one from restricting God's presence within the world and relationship to humanity strictly in terms of the *magnalia dei*; its vision of creation serves as the overarching horizon of biblical theology and the framework within which to understand human history. And its worldview offers a robust

---

13. Ibid., p. 89.
14. See Craig G. Bartholomew and Ryan P. O'Dowd, *Old Testament Wisdom Literature: A Theological Introduction* (Downers Grove: IVP Academic; Nottingham: Apollos, 2011), pp. 250–251.
15. Roland E. Murphy, *The Tree of Life: An Exploration of Biblical Wisdom Literature*, 3rd edn (Grand Rapids: Eerdmans, 2002), p. 126.
16. See Rolf P. Knierim, *The Task of Old Testament Theology: Substance, Method, and Cases* (Grand Rapids: Eerdmans, 1995), p. 187.

theological perspective on the ordinary in general and on the place, purpose and vocation of God's people in this world in particular.[17]

Wisdom, anthropology and biblical theology

The wisdom literature, however, is concerned with much more than cosmology and the inculcation of a particular Yahwistic worldview. The wisdom literature's vision of the cosmos contributes to its agenda of education for character formation. Cosmology shapes character. Put differently, one's character reflects one's cosmology. The dance between cosmology and anthropology within the wisdom literature is delicate. Both are integral to the world projected in these documents. And both are necessary for formulating a comprehensive view of the wise life within the world. The methodological danger is that one will play second fiddle to the other; that cosmology or anthropology will be subsumed under the other to the extent that the discrete tunes of one are muffled or even silenced by its counterpart.[18] Nonetheless, this danger should not detract from the theological pay-off of the dialectic. The intimate relationship between cosmology and anthropology, creation and character, reflects the intimate relationship between revelation and reason, God's world and human worship. Like other documents in the canon, the wisdom literature refuses to separate the sacred from the secular; it promotes an inclusive view of life that recognizes the goodness and order of the created world as well as the theological significance of mundane, human activities within the world. As humans live within the world, they partake in creation, and, by implication, live in relation to Yahweh. The delicate relationship between cosmology and anthropology in the wisdom literature situates all human conduct in the presence of the Creator. In this context, God is concerned with all of life, and all of life is concerned with God. And in this context, humans are invited to collaborate with creation, to live wisely in relation to God, others and the creatures, and to

---

17. Ibid., p. 224.
18. For an emphasis on the cosmology, see e.g. Gese, *Lehre und Wirklichkeit*; Schmid, *Gerechtigkeit als Weltordnung*. For an emphasis on anthropology, see e.g. Walther Zimmerli, 'Concerning the Structure of Old Testament Wisdom', tr. B. W. Kovacs, in J. L. Crenshaw (ed.), *Studies in Ancient Israelite Wisdom* (New York: Ktav, 1976), pp. 175–207; Walter Brueggemann, *In Man We Trust* (Atlanta: John Knox, 1972). For an attempt to balance the dialectic, see Leo G. Perdue, *Wisdom and Creation: The Theology of Wisdom Literature* (Nashville: Abingdon, 1994).

participate in the expansion of the kingdom as they anticipate the dawn of the new creation.

Actualizing the wisdom literature's worldview and living in accord with the grain of the created order, however, necessitates a certain type of character. The common cast of character types within the wisdom literature evinces its concern with the formation and cultivation of normative character. These character types typify what is desirable and undesirable; they project distinctive moral worldviews; and they embody either wisdom and virtue or folly and vice. In so doing, they serve as models for how one should and should not think, feel and act. And these models, to borrow from Athanasius' theological approach to the Psalter, create an ethical pattern on which readers may form their character.[19] By outlining the fundamental traits of normative character through various 'characterizations of character',[20] the wisdom literature attempts to shape the disposition, desires and worldview of the reader by providing a vision of life rooted in the fear of Yahweh, marked by the possession of virtuous attitudes and manifested through the performance of virtuous actions. In this respect, the wisdom literature's portrayal of various literary characters is not merely descriptive; it is also transformative. These characters are presented to form one's desires, sharpen one's thinking, pinpoint one's vices, cultivate virtue and offer a wise perspective on life so that one might flourish in relation to God, self and others.

This pedagogical vision operates within the context of the wisdom literature's worldview; its vision of the formation of character in accord with moral order is intimately related to Yahweh's design of the cosmic order. And this pedagogical vision assumes a particular anthropology.[21] To be specific, it assumes a particular understanding of the moral self.[22] In the light of the characterization

---

19. Athanasius, *The Life of Antony and the Letter to Marcellinus*, tr. R. C. Gregg, Classics of Western Spirituality (London: SPCK, 1980), p. 108, para. 10.
20. William P. Brown, *Character in Crisis: A Fresh Approach to the Wisdom Literature of the Old Testament* (Grand Rapids: Eerdmans, 1996), p. 19.
21. This corresponds with the axiom expressed by James K. A. Smith, viz., 'behind every pedagogy is a philosophical anthropology'. See James K. A. Smith, *Desiring the Kingdom: Worship, Worldview, and Cultural Formation* (Grand Rapids: Baker Academic, 2009), p. 27.
22. For discussion of the moral self in the Hebrew Bible, see Jacqueline E. Lapsley, *Can These Bones Live? The Problem of the Moral Self in the Book of Ezekiel*, BZAW 301 (Berlin: De Gruyter, 2000); Carol A. Newsom, 'Models of the Moral Self: Hebrew Bible and Second Temple Judaism', *JBL* 131 (2012), pp. 5–25.

of and co-referential relationship between the wise/righteous and the fool/wicked, it appears Proverbs operates under the assumption that humans possess an innate ability to choose wisdom and act in accord with the moral order. This ability, however, 'exists in potential only';[23] it must be shaped, aligned and directed by external instruction and correction. The wise/righteous possess the receptive posture necessary to accept instruction and acquire wisdom. The principal addressee of Proverbs, the 'uncommitted' (*petî*), possesses the potential to form this posture, for this personage is neither wise nor foolish, neither righteous nor wicked, but malleable and capable of acquiring wisdom.[24] The foolish/wicked, on the other hand, do not possess this receptive posture: they reject instruction, despise correction, follow their distorted perceptions and do what is right in their own eyes. In so doing, they fail to live in accord with the moral order Yahweh has woven into the fabric of the cosmos. Put another way, by spurning the divine order of the cosmos, they fail to live within proper boundaries. They project an alternative moral worldview, a vision of life oriented towards a particular *telos*: death.

This concern with boundaries links creation with character, one's worldview with one's way, and provides a backdrop for exploring another dimension of the wisdom literature's conception of the human condition and the moral self, namely, humanity's limitations. While Proverbs assumes that certain characters possess the capacity to think, to choose and to act in accordance with wisdom and the divine will, many sayings acknowledge that humans and human wisdom are finite and limited (16:1–2, 9; 19:21; 20:24; 21:30; 27:1; 30:2–4). This acknowledgment of mortal limits is attributed to inevitable contingencies as well as to the omnipotence, omniscience and inscrutability of the divine. And the reality of human limits is the focus of attention in Job and Ecclesiastes. As intimated above, the wisdom hymn in Job 28 indicates that, despite their power and ingenuity, humans are unable to find wisdom, for their capacities are limited. The barrage of rhetorical questions as well as the wild and wondrous world projected in the divine speeches force Job to recognize this reality (Job 38:1 – 41:34). In fact, Job acknowledges these limits in his climactic confession (Job

---

23. Anne W. Stewart, *Poetic Ethics in Proverbs: Wisdom Literature and the Shaping of the Moral Self* (Cambridge: Cambridge University Press, forthcoming); T. Frydrych, *Living Under the Sun: Examination of Proverbs and Qoheleth*, VTSup 90 (Leiden: Brill, 2002), p. 134.

24. See Michael V. Fox, *Proverbs 1 – 9: A New Translation with Introduction and Commentary*, AB 18A (New York: Doubleday, 2000), pp. 42–43; Bruce K. Waltke, *The Book of Proverbs: Chapters 1–15*, NICOT (Grand Rapids: Eerdmans, 2004), pp. 111–112.

42:2–6); he concedes that he overreached or transgressed particular intellectual boundaries: he declared things he did not understand, things too wonderful, which he did not know (Job 42:3). This acknowledgment of creatureliness and the limitations inherent in human nature shapes the document's theological anthropology and its conception of the human condition.[25]

The same is true of Ecclesiastes. Qoheleth's recognition of fundamental frustration in every human endeavour is inextricably linked to his anthropology in general and his conception of human limitations in particular.[26] Qoheleth observes that human memory is short-sighted and faulty (Eccl. 1:9–11; 6:10). Human activity is transient (Eccl. 2:18–19). Human life is ephemeral (Eccl. 1:4; 7:15); all humans are frail and wicked (Eccl. 3:18; 7:20, 29). Human power and planning are deficient (Eccl. 3:14; 8:8; 9:11–12); human wisdom is finite (Eccl. 7:14, 23–24; 8:17; 11:5); and the human appetite is insatiable (Eccl. 4:8; 5:10; 6:7). Together with his reflections on human finitude and limitations, Qoheleth observes that the world in which humans live is broken. The weak are crushed by the powerful (Eccl. 4:1; 5:8; 8:9); the oppressed live without a comforter (Eccl. 4:1); the worker is left with neither colleague nor companion (Eccl. 4:7–8); and the wise ruler governs without faithful followers (Eccl. 4:13–16). The wicked are a walking advertisement for evil (Eccl. 8:11). And the social as well as the economic structures within the world are unjust and oppressive (Eccl. 3:16; 4:13–16; 5:8–9; 8:9).[27] In view of these observations, it is not surprising that Qoheleth restricts the verdict *hebel* to human activities and aspirations. Qoheleth accentuates the severe limitations placed upon humans. These limitations, combined with the consequences associated with being situated in a crooked world, shape Qoheleth's conception of the human condition and the moral self.

It is important to note, however, that Qoheleth's fundamental problem is not human limits per se; the problem is that humans refuse to acknowledge their creatureliness and live within these limits. That is, humans fail to accept

---

25. For discussion of the way in which the book of Job uses images from nature to envision the world, the human condition and the moral self, see Brian R. Doak, *Consider Leviathan: Narratives of Nature and the Self in Job* (Minneapolis: Fortress, 2014).
26. See Stephan de Jong, 'God in the Book of Qohelet: A Reappraisal of Qohelet's Place in Old Testament Theology', *VT* 47 (1997), pp. 154–167; Mark R. Sneed, *The Politics of Pessimism in Ecclesiastes: A Social-Science Perspective*, SBL Ancient Israel and Its Literature (Atlanta: SBL, 2012), p. 162.
27. See Frydrych, *Living Under the Sun*, pp. 163–164.

their lot and embrace life's limited possibilities within God's inscrutable design.[28] They overreach; they transgress the boundaries appropriate to creaturehood.[29] They place inappropriate expectations on the profit of human activities. They invest in things that cannot yield the supposed gain. They consume things that are not built to bring definitive satisfaction. Ecclesiastes gives particular attention to the nature and limits of human beings and human activities in a broken world. In so doing, the document seeks to recalibrate the expectations of humans by identifying the boundaries of human ability and the space within which humans should live.[30]

These general observations intimate that the wisdom literature does not paint a monochromatic portrait of the moral self. The individual documents acknowledge, embrace and hold in tension human potential and human limits, the acquisition and the elusiveness of wisdom, human planning and divine providence, and perception of the world's order and the mystery of its design. If nothing else, the wisdom literature's sketch of the moral self creates space within which to recognize the power and potential of human wisdom and ability within the context of the Creator–creature distinction. Humans may be limited creatures, but they also possess the sensory and rational capacities to discover and understand the divine order. This may be the reason for Paul's contention that humans have no excuse, because God's attributes, power and nature are ingrained in the cosmic order (Rom. 1:20). While Paul emphasizes the negative dimensions of the human condition through humanity's suppression and distortion of the truths revealed in the created order, the wisdom literature, so it seems, presents a more positive evaluation of the human condition and the moral self. It recognizes human limits and the innate sinfulness of humanity; but it also assumes human potential. The created order illuminates the texture of the moral order. This order and its obligations, however, are not just read off creation. A deeper understanding of this order and its implications for the order of one's life is dependent upon an epistemological prerequisite: the fear of Yahweh.

The fear of Yahweh/God represents the 'motto' or epistemological prerequisite for the acquisition of wisdom and virtue in the wisdom literature. The

---

28. See Michael V. Fox, *A Time to Tear Down and A Time to Build Up: A Rereading of Ecclesiastes* (Grand Rapids: Eerdmans, 1999; repr. Eugene: Wipf & Stock, 2010), p. 11.
29. Mark E. Biddle, *Missing the Mark: Sin and Its Consequences in Biblical Theology* (Nashville: Abingdon, 2005), p. 33.
30. Sneed, *Politics of Pessimism*, pp. 162, 240–252.

concept is employed in the discrete corpora of the Old Testament to refer to the complex emotions associated with fear in relation to Yahweh/God – dread, trembling, awe and wonder (Exod. 20:19–21; 2 Sam. 6:6–11; Hab. 3:2; Ps. 22:23). This range of emotions is encapsulated in the wisdom literature's use of the expression. And this spectrum of emotions serves as a window into the multifaceted nature of the attitude or posture this prerequisite forms within Yahweh fearers. The fear of Yahweh is much more than an intellectual virtue that provides a distillation of Israelite epistemology.[31] It is the fundamental requirement for the formation of one's character in accord with wisdom. That is, the fear of Yahweh is a disposition that is developed and nurtured in intimate relationship with Yahweh and through knowledge of his will. It is an intellectual posture that recognizes humanity's responsibilities, limitations and place within the cosmos under Yahweh's gracious governance (Prov. 9:10; cf. 30:1–6; Eccl. 3:14; 5:7). It is an attitude characterized by a love of what is beautiful or good and a hatred of what is evil (Prov. 8:13; 16:6; Job 1:1, 8; 2:3; 28:28). And it is a trait that motivates the moral life and manifests itself through concrete activities performed through wisdom, in accordance with the will of Yahweh, and for the sake of the other as well as for the created world (Prov. 31:10–31; Eccl. 12:13; cf. Deut. 10:12–16). Put simply, it is the wisdom literature's expression for faith.[32] This form of faith serves as the seedbed within which wisdom and virtue may develop and flourish. From this theological and epistemological frame of reference, the wisdom literature contends that a fearful faith does not hinder knowledge; rather it liberates knowledge, for it places knowledge in proper relationship, in proper perspective and within proper boundaries.[33]

This motto contributes to an understanding of wisdom epistemology. While many, if not most, of Qoheleth's observations reveal the limits and insufficiency of an autonomous epistemology,[34] the general witness of the wisdom literature intimates that its epistemology is far from empirical. It is rooted in particular assumptions. That is, wisdom epistemology is grounded in particular theological convictions. Although certain texts within the wisdom literature are cast in

---

31. Gerhard von Rad, *Wisdom in Israel*, tr. J. D. Martin (Harrisburg: Trinity Press International, 1972), p. 67.
32. Daniel J. Treier, *Proverbs and Ecclesiastes*, Brazos Theological Commentary on the Bible (Grand Rapids: Brazos Press, 2011), p. 12.
33. See von Rad, *Wisdom in Israel*, p. 68.
34. See Craig G. Bartholomew, *Ecclesiastes*, BCOTWP (Grand Rapids: Baker Academic, 2009), pp. 56–59 *et passim*.

autobiographical form and appear to be based on personal or sensory experience, the perceptions or discoveries delineated in these passages are not empirical observations; rather they are 'statements of faith' shaped in accordance with specific ethical, theological and cultural assumptions.[35] The purported observation or experience serves as the rhetorical and imaginative medium through which an axiomatic belief is taught.[36] Put differently, the personal experiences or autobiographical observations within the wisdom literature do not produce knowledge; rather these observations and experiences reinforce the sage's values and assumptions.[37] They are pedagogical, not epistemological.[38] Far from offering wisdom and practical advice through mere observation or sensory experience, the materials in the wisdom literature communicate fundamental assumptions, truths and values under the guise of observation and experience. These assumptions and truths underlie Proverbs' evaluation of certain character types and actions. They serve as the basis of the Joban poet's portrait of the righteous (Job 31:1–40), which includes expressions and ethical concepts redolent of Israel's covenant, prophetic and psalmic traditions.[39] And these assumptions and truths are reflected in a few of Qoheleth's shocking 'I know' statements (Eccl. 3:12, 14; 8:12; cf. 11:9). The sages did not approach the created world as blank slates, as autonomous observers. They viewed life and the created world through certain fundamental assumptions concerning God, the cosmos and the moral order. And these assumptions betray an approach to reality that is comparable to other portions of Scripture.

The wisdom literature's vision of anthropology is dependent upon its vision of cosmology. In the same way, its vision of cosmology assumes a particular anthropology. The two cannot be separated; in Leo Perdue's terms, they

---

35. Fox, 'Epistemology of the Book of Proverbs', pp. 670–684, esp. pp. 670–676. Also see Michael V. Fox, 'Qohelet's Epistemology', *HUCA* 58 (1987), pp. 145–147; E. L. Greenstein, '"On My Skin and in My Flesh": Personal Experience as a Source of Knowledge in the Book of Job', in K. F. Kravitz et al. (eds.), *Bringing the Hidden to Light: Studies in Honor of Stephen A. Geller* (Winona Lake: Eisenbrauns, 2007), pp. 72–75.
36. Fox, 'Epistemology of the Book of Proverbs', p. 673.
37. Ibid.
38. Ibid., p. 674.
39. See Christopher B. Ansberry, '"The Revealed Things": Deuteronomy and the Epistemology of Job', in J. DeRouchie et al. (eds.), *For Our Good Always: Studies on the Message and Influence of Deuteronomy in Honor of Daniel I. Block* (Winona Lake: Eisenbrauns, 2013), pp. 307–325.

are 'true dialectic'.[40] The poles of this dialectic and the biblical-theological contribution of the wisdom literature converge, so it seems, in a particular issue: ethics.

Wisdom, ethics and biblical theology

The discipline of ethics provides a category within which to relate the wisdom literature's cosmology and anthropology and to understand its contribution to biblical theology.[41] Among the wisdom literature's contributions to biblical theology, its vision of normative character, virtue and the good life may be the most significant. The concern with the formation of character through the inculcation of wisdom and virtue is fundamental to the purpose and agenda of Proverbs (1:1–7). In addition to the perseverance of Job (Jas 5:11), the sufferer's oath of innocence projects an exemplary ethical vision (Job 31:1–40), the Old Testament equivalent to the Sermon on the Mount.[42] And despite the frustration that characterizes all human endeavours, Qoheleth recognizes the value of reverence for God (Eccl. 7:18; 8:12; cf. 5:7), joy and contentment (Eccl. 2:24–25; 5:18–20; 9:7–9), diligence (Eccl. 9:10; 11:1–6), as well as responsibility for others (Eccl. 4:1–16). The voices and perspectives within these documents are diverse and distinct. Their characterization of normative character is multifaceted; and their vision of the good life differs in several respects. They do not play the same notes, but they participate in the same symphony and perform different movements within the same ethical score. This score presents variations on a theme, the theme of biblical ethics.

When the wisdom literature is viewed through the prism of ethics, it appears that the moral vision of the corpus is in harmony with covenant, prophetic and New Testament ethics. Far from representing documents 'near the pagan source of wisdom',[43] the wisdom literature reiterates and recasts ethical principles delineated elsewhere in Christian Scripture. The absence of explicit attention to Israel's covenantal and historical traditions in the wisdom literature may reveal 'sounds of silence', the sages' lack of concern with or disdain for Israel's

---

40. Perdue, *Wisdom and Creation*, p. 48.
41. Brown, *Character in Crisis*, p. 4.
42. See A. Weiser, *Das Buch Hiob*, ATD (Göttingen: Vandenhoeck & Ruprecht, 1974), p. 214.
43. Wright, *God Who Acts*, p. 104, who uses this expression in his discussion of Proverbs.

formative traditions.⁴⁴ However, if one listens closely, it appears the sages play ethical melodies characteristic of the moral vision sounded in the diverse sections of the Christian canon.

These ethical melodies are not conveyed through the same forms or in the same manner as the Torah, the Prophets or the documents of the New Testament. The 'underlying system of assumptions' and the fundamental ethical principles expressed throughout the wisdom literature, however, indicate that the 'sounds of silence' are more apparent than real.⁴⁵ Similar to other corpora in the canon, the wisdom literature assumes that God is the wise, sovereign, inscrutable creator of the cosmos, who has woven the basic threads of his will into the very fabric of the universe (Pss 19; 147; Isa. 40:28; 45:18; 55:8–9; Jer. 10:12; Rom. 11:33–34). Similar to other corpora in the canon, the wisdom literature seeks to orient readers to a way of life that is pleasing to Yahweh.⁴⁶ And similar to other corpora in the canon, the wisdom literature identifies a common *telos*: life and human flourishing (Deut. 28:1–14; 30:15–20; Prov. 1:33; 4:4; 7:2; 9:6; Isa. 55:3; Ezek. 37:1–14; John 3:36).⁴⁷ While the wisdom literature's posture and modes of discourse are distinct, these common assumptions and goals intimate that the wisdom literature approaches *reality* in a manner comparable to other portions of Scripture.⁴⁸

This does not mean, however, that the wisdom literature approaches *morality* in the same way as other portions of Scripture. In contrast to the deontological approach to ethics that characterizes Israel's covenant and prophetic materials, the wisdom literature is characterized by a consequentialist or virtue-based approach to ethics. Rather than dictating moral laws, the wisdom literature seeks to form the dispositions, hone the desires, shape the worldview and instil the kinds of discipline necessary to act in accord with the moral law and develop into a wise person.⁴⁹ Rather than operating on the basis of divine authority, the

---

44. See David Penchansky, *Understanding Wisdom Literature: Conflict and Dissonance in the Hebrew Text* (Grand Rapids: Eerdmans, 2012), pp. 64–85.
45. Fox, 'Epistemology of the Book of Proverbs', p. 675.
46. See Bartholomew and O'Dowd, *Old Testament Wisdom Literature*, p. 286; David VanDrunen, *Divine Covenants and Moral Order: A Biblical Theology of Natural Law* (Grand Rapids: Eerdmans, 2014), p. 375.
47. See J. Richard Middleton, *A New Heaven and a New Earth: Reclaiming Biblical Eschatology* (Grand Rapids: Baker Academic, 2014), pp. 95–107.
48. Murphy, 'Wisdom: Theses and Hypotheses', p. 39.
49. See Christine McKinnon, *Character, Virtue Theories, and the Vices* (Ontario: Broadview Press, 1999), p. 230.

wisdom literature operates on the basis of observation, experience and prudence, each of which is directed by particular theological assumptions. And rather than appealing to salvation history to motivate ethical behaviour, the wisdom literature appeals to the created order and a vision of the good life. The wisdom literature's approach to ethics and morality differs from the approach of Israel's covenant and prophetic materials. These approaches, however, are not incompatible. Since God is the source of both the moral order revealed in creation and the ethical principles delineated in Israel's covenant and prophetic corpora, it appears the sharp distinction between covenant and prophetic ethics, on the one hand, and wisdom ethics, on the other, is a modern imposition.[50] The wisdom literature does not traffic in a brand of natural law that stands in opposition to the revelation of God's will in the Torah, the Prophets or the New Testament. As noted above, the wisdom literature views the created order from a theological perspective and under certain theological assumptions. The order embedded in creation by the divine architect and concretized in the observations and admonitions of the wisdom literature mirrors the moral vision and divine order delineated in the Torah, the Prophets and the New Testament. God is the source and foundation of all of these ethical materials; and, in different ways, all these materials bear witness to the moral order established by God.

The confluence of covenant, prophetic, wisdom and New Testament ethics extends far beyond a common divine source and a foundational moral order. Each of these corpora reflects on the fundamental dimensions of social life: personal, familial, social, political, economic and cultic. And each addresses common ethical matters, ranging from justice in general (Deut. 16:19; 24:17; Prov. 17:15, 23; 18:5; Job 31:13–15; Isa. 1:17; 1 Tim. 5:21; Jas 2:9) to economic practices (Lev. 19:14, 35–36; Deut. 24:14–15; 25:13–16; Prov. 20:11; Job 31:28–40b; Rom. 13:8; Jas 5:4), interpersonal relationships (Lev. 19:13, 18; Ps. 15:3; Prov. 3:29; 14:21; 27:10; Job 31:29–30; Eccl. 4:9–12; Rom. 12:20–21; 13:9; Gal. 5:14), ethics of power (Deut. 17:14–20; Prov. 31:8–9; Job 31:13–15; Jer. 23:1; Ezek. 22:6; Matt. 20:24–28), treatment of the marginalized (Deut. 24:14–22; Prov. 14:21, 31; 19:17; 29:7; Job 31:13–15; Amos 4:1; Zech. 7:9–10; Jas 1:27), speech ethics (Exod. 20:16; Pss 15:3; 34:13; Prov. 6:19; 25:18; Jer. 9:4–9; Matt. 15:17–20; Jas 3:2–12), cultic activities (Deut. 26:1–11; Ps. 50:23; Prov. 3:9–10; 15:8; 21:27; Job 31:26–28; Eccl. 9:2; Isa. 1:12–15) and domestic values in particular (Deut. 5:16; 21:18–21; Prov. 20:20; 23:22; Mic. 7:6; Ezek. 22:7; Eph. 6:1–4). The hortatory rhetoric and educational philosophy enshrined in Deuteronomy is comparable to the pedagogical rhetoric and educational programme of

---

50. Bartholomew and O'Dowd, *Old Testament Wisdom Literature*, p. 286.

Proverbs.[51] The 'good neighbourhood' projected by the Decalogue corresponds to the ethos of the good neighbourhoods sketched in Proverbs 3:27–35; Ezekiel 18:5–9; and Matthew 5:1 – 7:29.[52] The internal and external dimensions of the righteous life scattered throughout Israel's covenant regulations (Lev. 19:17–18), crystallized in certain prophetic and psalmic catalogues (Isa. 33:15; 58:6–12; Pss 15; 24:4) and distilled in Job 31 are reiterated and developed in the Sermon on the Mount. And in the light of the canonical witness, it appears that the fear of Yahweh is not only an attitude that serves as the prerequisite for acquiring wisdom (Prov. 1:7; 9:10; Job 28:28; Eccl. 12:13); it is also a moral posture that serves as the precondition for covenant obedience (Deut. 4:10–14; 5:29; 10:12–13; 17:19–20; 28:58; 31:12), an attitude that is encouraged by the prophets (Isa. 50:10; 59:19; Mal. 3:5, 16; 4:2 [3:20]) and a disposition that shaped and motivated Paul's cruciform ministry of reconciliation (2 Cor. 5:11–21).

These general similarities regarding the source, goal, rhetoric and ethics of the Torah, Prophets, wisdom literature and New Testament writings represent the tip of the iceberg. The ethical correspondence among these corpora, combined with the wisdom literature's dialogue with prominent theological themes (e.g. retribution) and specific texts elsewhere in the canon (e.g. Prov. 30:5/2 Sam. 22:31; Prov. 30:6/Deut. 4:2; 13:1; Job 31:26–27/Deut. 4:19; Eccl. 5:3–5[4–6]/Deut. 23:22–24[21–23]), suggests that the wisdom literature does not exist in a canonical twilight zone. Its vision of cosmology and anthropology fuels its moral vision. And this moral vision is consonant with covenant, prophetic and New Testament ethics. While the individual wisdom books articulate and contextualize their ethical visions in distinctive ways, together with the other corpora in the canon, these documents assume a fundamental moral order and seek to inscribe one into this order through the promotion of

---

51. See William P. Brown, 'The Law and the Sages: A Reexamination of Tôrâ in Proverbs', in J. T. Strong et al. (eds.), *Constituting the Community: Studies on the Polity of Ancient Israel in Honor of S. Dean McBride Jr.* (Winona Lake: Eisenbrauns, 2005), pp. 251–280. Whereas Proverbs' pedagogical programme is expressed through the paradigm fear (1:7) – hear (1:5) – increase instruction (1:5) – acquire guidance (1:5), Deuteronomy exhibits a comparable but more comprehensive philosophy of education: read/hear – learn – fear – obey – live (Deut. 31:9–13). See Daniel I. Block, *Deuteronomy*, NIV Application Commentary (Grand Rapids: Zondervan, 2012), p. 35.

52. See Patrick D. Miller, 'The Good Neighborhood: Identity and Community through the Commandments', in W. P. Brown (ed.), *Character and Scripture: Moral Formation, Community, and Biblical Interpretation* (Grand Rapids: Eerdmans), pp. 55–72.

common ethical principles so that one may live rightly in relation to God, others, the creatures and the created world. They provide one with a moral vision as well as the moral capacity to fulfil the creation mandate (Gen. 1:26–28) by accurately representing or imaging God's character, will and order within his creation.

Conclusion

This sketch of cosmology, anthropology and ethics cannot do justice to the variety of ways in which the wisdom literature contributes to biblical theology. While cosmology, anthropology and ethics are the dominant notes within the corpus, the wisdom literature sounds many other tunes that contribute to the canonical symphony. Wisdom provided many of the New Testament writers with a theological category through which to describe the identity and deity of Jesus, the nature of his redemptive work and its implications for the church's life. As the 'wisdom of God' (1 Cor. 1:24; cf. 1:30; Col. 2:3), Jesus is the human embodiment of God's wisdom as well as the key to unlocking the mystery of God's redemption and kingdom order. As the wise man par excellence, Jesus is a sage who employs aphoristic speech to undermine the traditional wisdom of his opponents and to communicate the eschatological realities that have broken into the present age and anticipate the new order to come.[53] For Paul, the cosmology of Proverbs 8 serves as the lexicon for describing Jesus' protology in Colossians 1. And for many of the epistles, the proper response of Christian communities to the crucified Christ is a life of obedience and wholeness that mirrors the ethics and agenda of the wisdom literature (see esp. Jas 1:2–4, 22–26; 2:12–13; 3:13–18; 4:11–12; 5:7–11, 16, 19–20).[54] Wisdom in general and the wisdom literature in particular play an important role in New Testament conceptions of Jesus' identity, Christ's redemptive work, as well as kingdom ethics. More than this, however, the wisdom literature provides a worldview, anthropology and ethical vision through which to understand the goodness,

---

53. See Ben Witherington III, *Jesus the Sage: The Pilgrimage of Wisdom* (Minneapolis: Fortress, 1994), pp. 155–183; Stephen C. Barton, 'Gospel Wisdom', in S. C. Barton (ed.), *Where Shall Wisdom Be Found? Wisdom in the Bible, the Church and the Contemporary World* (Edinburgh: T&T Clark, 1999), pp. 93–110.
54. See Richard Bauckham, *James: Wisdom of James, Disciple of Jesus the Sage* (New York: Routledge, 1999), pp. 177–185, 203–205; Bartholomew and O'Dowd, *Old Testament Wisdom Literature*, pp. 256–259.

beauty and order of the created world as well as one's place in creation and moral obligations to the Creator. The wisdom literature's posture is distinct and its perspective is inclusive, but it is neither an alien body nor an orphan in the biblical household; rather it is a native member of the canonical house and a valuable contributor to its theological economy.

© Christopher B. Ansberry, 2016

10. 'CHILDREN, LISTEN TO ME': THE VOICING OF WISDOM IN THE PSALMS

Simon P. Stocks

'Wisdom in the Psalms' or 'wisdom psalms'?

'Wisdom psalms'
The idea of 'wisdom psalms' is contentious. Form-critical categorizations of the psalms have followed a variety of criteria, resulting in a range of conclusions about the identification of 'wisdom psalms'.[1] There is no agreement on the results despite common ground in the criteria used. These have typically been a combination of formal and thematic criteria. Formal identifiers might include: *'ašrê* formulas, numerical sayings, 'better' sayings, the address of a teacher to a 'son', alphabetic structure, simple comparisons and admonition. Thematic identifiers are typically regarded as: the contrast between righteous and wicked, the problem of retribution, practical advice as regards conduct, and fear of Yhwh.[2] All these

---

1. E.g. P. S. Johnston, 'Index of Form-Critical Categorizations', in P. S. Johnston and D. G. Firth (eds.), *Interpreting the Psalms: Issues and Approaches* (Leicester: Apollos, 2005), pp. 295–300.
2. For examples see R. E. Murphy, 'A Consideration of the Classification of "Wisdom Psalms"', in G. W. Anderson, P. A. H. de Boer et al. (eds.), *Congress Volume: Bonn 1962*, VTSup 9 (Leiden: Brill, 1963), pp. 156–167; R. N. Whybray, 'The Wisdom Psalms', in J. Day, R. P. Gordon and H. G. M. Williamson (eds.), *Wisdom in Ancient Israel: Essays in Honour of J. A. Emerton* (Cambridge: Cambridge University Press, 1995), pp. 152–160.

identifiers are derived from characterization of wisdom literature (Proverbs, Ecclesiastes and Job), resemblance to which is the determining factor.

In this context, it is instructive to turn back to Gunkel's pioneering work on form-critical classification of the psalms, to find that he did not identify 'wisdom psalms' as a specific *Gattung*. Rather he took a more nuanced approach in which he explored the various ways in which the wisdom poetry penetrated the Psalter over a period of time. He identified three manifestations of such influence: short wisdom sayings, wisdom poetry and elements of instruction. These can appear in a variety of other psalm genres, often resulting in a mixed genre and so accounting for the difficulty of identifying a 'wisdom psalm'.[3] The exploration of wisdom in the Psalter should not, therefore, be concerned with identification of specific psalms as 'wisdom psalms', but needs to identify the places where the influence of wisdom poetry is most evident, whether in a whole psalm or only a part. This begs the question of how to identify the influence of wisdom.

Finding wisdom in the Psalter

There is a variety of opinions regarding how to identify the influence of wisdom, but with considerable overlap between them. The criteria mentioned above are typical, and indeed were used by Gunkel, but are not unambiguous. Some psalms have an alphabetic structure without any other characteristics of wisdom (e.g. Pss 9 – 10; 111; 145); others emphasize the contrast between righteous and wicked living, but with the focus on Torah rather than on practical advice (e.g. 1; 119).

Taking account of both form and content, Crenshaw suggests that wisdom may be characterized as 'the reasoned search for specific ways to ensure personal well-being in everyday life . . . and to transmit this hard-earned knowledge'.[4] It is this search and desire to communicate that gives rise to forms and themes of wisdom literature. Therefore, in looking for wisdom in the Psalter, the approach adopted here is to identify texts with a mode of thought that matches

---

3. H. Gunkel, *Introduction to Psalms: The Genres of the Religious Lyric of Israel* (completed by J. Begrich), tr. J. D. Nogalski (Macon: Mercer University Press, 1998), pp. 21, 293–305.

4. J. L. Crenshaw, *Old Testament Wisdom: An Introduction*, rev. and enlarged edn (Louisville: Westminster John Knox, 1998), p. 3. See also the discussions in N. Whybray, *Reading the Psalms as a Book*, JSOTSup 222 (Sheffield: Sheffield Academic Press, 2002), pp. 36–37; and K. Dell, *'Get Wisdom, Get Insight': An Introduction to Israel's Wisdom Literature* (London: DLT, 2000), pp. 64–75.

wisdom books in respect to an *address to other people arising out of reflection on personal experience*. Since the psalms generally are hymns and prayers expressed to God, this provides a clear distinguishing factor for the identification of wisdom thinking: texts that are addressed to other people, rather than to God, and which make minimal reference to God (i.e. God or God's action is not the topic).[5] Psalms in this category are: 37; 49; 112; 127; 128. A related category is of psalms presented in the third person, with little or no address at all: 1; 14/53; 34; 73:1–20.[6]

These psalms provide a clearly identified body of texts in which to explore the expression of the wisdom tradition. Their shared characteristic of being addressed to other people (explicitly or implicitly) throws the spotlight onto their didactic function. Before exploring that, however, it will be helpful to identify and summarize their key themes and theological perspectives.

Wisdom themes and theology in selected psalms

Righteousness and blessing
Most of the psalms under consideration make a contrast between the ways of righteousness and wickedness. The righteous are described as those who delight in Torah (1:2), fear Yhwh (112:1), are generous (37:21; 112:5, 9) and speak wisdom and justice (37:30). In contrast, the wicked are those who borrow and do not repay (37:21), plot against the righteous (37:12) and oppress the poor (37:14). Note how these characteristics mainly relate to practical outward living. There is notably less description of the wicked; they are identified principally as those who will suffer calamity. This is depicted variously as being blown away (1:4), being in great terror (14:5), perishing/vanishing (37:20) and being cut off (37:9).

There is a general implication that Yhwh will be behind such consequences for the wicked, but this is not always made explicit, and the way in which such calamity will come about is tantalizingly ambiguous.[7] The wicked are 'like chaff

---

5. A similar line of argument is followed by D. Jacobson, 'Wisdom Language in the Psalms', in W. P. Brown (ed.), *The Oxford Handbook of the Psalms* (Oxford: Oxford University Press, 2014), pp. 147–157. The criterion need not imply that these texts are anthropocentric, merely that God is not foregrounded. The wisdom being expressed may implicitly be regarded as a gift from God. See Dell, *'Get Wisdom'*, pp. 6–7.
6. Crenshaw, *Wisdom*, p. 171, identifies some of these as 'discussion literature'.
7. See the discussion (pp. 278–279) in R. E. Clements, 'Wisdom and Old Testament Theology', in Day, Gordon and Williamson, *Essays*, pp. 269–286.

that the wind drives away' (1:4) and will 'wither like the green herb' (37:2);[8] the question lingers whether there is any active agency behind such eventualities. Yhwh's involvement is occasionally made explicit (34:16; 53:5; 73:18); but Yhwh is also depicted as somewhat remote (14:2) and uninvolved (37:13). The disappearance of the wicked is portrayed as somewhat mysterious (37:35–36) rather than as evidence of Yhwh's action.

The contrast with the righteous is not only in the blessing and prosperity that they will experience (1:3; 112:2–9) but in the way in which blessing will come about through the direct action of Yhwh (34:4, 17; 37:4). Such contrast is epitomized in 34:15–16:

The eyes of the LORD are on the righteous,
   and his ears are open to their cry.
The face of the LORD is against evildoers,
   to cut off the remembrance of them from the earth.

Psalm 73 is the exception that proves the rule. The apparent subversion of conventional wisdom thinking, wherein the wicked are described in terms normally used of the righteous, turns out to be a rhetorical device. A shocking (and yet plausible) alternative point of view is established in verses 4–12, only for its deceitfulness to be exposed and ridiculed following the revelatory turning point of the psalm in verse 17. Indeed, lest this dynamic should not be completely obvious, the psalm is set up in verses 1–2 to make explicit that it was the *perception* of the psalmist that was at fault, not the reality of existence.

Prosperity, trust and poverty
The enactment of prosperity is one of the principal ways in which Yhwh both blesses those who are righteous and works through them. That prosperity can be a blessing from Yhwh is clear in the expression of the desire that Yhwh restore the fortunes of his people (14:7). Such prosperity is particularly associated with those who fear/seek Yhwh (34:9–10; 112:1–3) such that the righteous are claimed never to be destitute (37:25). However, once again there is ambiguity in the degree of agency Yhwh has. Prosperity is often presented as a natural consequence of righteousness, without any agency. Only occasionally is a claim made that Yhwh acts directly to secure the prosperity of the righteous (37:5–6). At other times the needs of the poor are met through the actions of the righteous in being willing to lend and share (112:9). In contrast, the cause of

---

8. All Bible quotes in this chapter, unless stated otherwise, are from the NRSV.

poverty is directly attributed to the wicked, who are unwilling to lend and who oppress others (14:6; 37:14, 21).

The ambiguity in the origin of wealth is matched by an ambivalence about its effects. Whilst it is a good thing, it is also recognized as a threat to trusting dependence upon Yhwh. Anxiety and fretting are seen as sources of evil; their counterpoints are quiet trust and dependence upon Yhwh (37:7–11). For this reason:

> Better is a little that the righteous person has,
>   than the abundance of many wicked.
>
> (37:16)

The same sentiment is evident in Psalm 127, along with yet more ambiguity about exactly how Yhwh might build the house or guard the city. The clear blessings of progeny (vv. 3–5) typify those sources of security that cannot be laboured for but depend upon Yhwh. Psalm 128 similarly develops this theme, implying that, for anyone who seeks to live life well, walking in the ways of Yhwh is a far more important goal than is seeking after prosperity for its own sake.

Living in the light of mortality

Psalm 49 takes the topic of prosperity and develops it into a meditation upon mortality. Opinions differ as to whether the psalmist held any understanding of an afterlife.[9] What is clear, however, is that the prospect of mortal death is held up as a factor that should influence the way life is lived. The extent of a person's wealth makes no difference to whether or when he or she will die (v. 10). Therefore it is foolish indeed to trust in riches (vv. 6–9) or to be envious of the riches of others (vv. 5, 16–20).

It is implicit in Psalm 49 that Yhwh alone is the creator and sustainer of life (see vv. 7–9, 15). Therefore it is not surprising that the motif of life (and death) is used in other psalm wisdom texts. The image in Psalm 1 of the righteous as a tree 'planted by streams of water' depicts Yhwh's sustenance of life, with the tree's 'fruit in its season' a further image of fecundity. By contrast the wicked are 'chaff': dried up, dead and barren. Fruitfulness recurs as a familial image in Psalms 127 and 128, with the promise of progeny (128:6) typifying the blessings for the righteous. And again, in Psalm 34 Yhwh rescues the righteous and 'keeps

---

9. See e.g. P. S. Johnston, *Shades of Sheol: Death and Afterlife in the Old Testament* (Leicester: Apollos, 2002); J. Smith, *Dust or Dew: Immortality in the Ancient Near East and in Psalm 49* (Cambridge: James Clarke, 2012). Verse 15 of the psalm is an interpretative crux.

all their bones; not one of them will be broken', whereas 'Evil brings death to the wicked' (vv. 19–22). Finally, a similar use of the motif is in Psalm 37: there is 'posterity for the peaceable' (v. 37) whereas 'the wicked will be no more' (v. 10) – another striking contrast of life and death (cf. vv. 28–29), although whether it is meant in a literal or a figurative sense is not entirely clear.

'Come, O children, listen to me'

Having examined the theological content of the wisdom tradition in the psalms, attention now turns to its characteristic form of address to other people, in conjunction with minimal reference to God. This characteristic is represented most clearly by the address in 34:11:

> Come, O children, listen to me;
> I will teach you the fear of the LORD.[10]

Such an imperative is, of course, most characteristic of the wisdom tradition, being extensively used in Proverbs.[11] It highlights the didactic intent of such texts, assuming (as made explicit in this verse) that the hearing/listening is for the purposes of learning and instruction. What is to be made of this imperative to listen/hear? For the purposes of this analysis, three distinct voices, and therefore distinct listeners, may be considered. The first is the voice of the original psalmist. Without attempting to specify the original setting or context of a psalm, it may be read as the personal expression of a particular composer. An analysis of this voice will explore how the psalmists sought to offer instruction through their spoken words. The second voice is that of a 'contemporary' recitation of the psalm. The context may be any, from ancient Jerusalem to the present day, in which the person voicing the psalm is using a previously written text. The third voice is labelled 'canonical' and seeks to explore the implications of the psalm being part of the canon of Scripture and therefore in some sense representing the words of God.

The 'original' voice
When the writers of the psalms adopted elements of the wisdom tradition, they clearly wanted to instruct their hearers. They did this by at least three different

---

10. See also 34:2; 49:1.
11. E.g. Prov. 1:5, 8; 4:1, 10; 8:6, 33.

means: by giving personal testimony to their experiences (as in Ps. 73); by offering admonition based on existing theological ideas (as in Pss 37 and 49); and by making observations about life that might provoke the hearer into reflection on them (as in Ps. 1).[12] Testimony invites listeners to reflect on the genuine experience of the psalmist and to consider whether this might in turn become their own experience too. Admonition exhorts listeners to live according to the principles and priorities that have been determined by the experience of life – noting that wisdom is often expressed by an elder to younger people. Observations about life offer a more subtle invitation to reflect on those observations and work towards the listeners' own conclusions. In these three ways, the original psalmists can be seen to offer teaching about life and how to live well. This teaching is based on their own understanding and experience, and is offered to any who might listen to them.

The analysis of speech-act theory can offer an additional layer of insight into the functioning of these forms of address.[13] Speech-act theory distinguishes between the words spoken (the locution), the intended function of the speech (the illocutionary act) and the effect of the words on the hearer (the perlocution). The illocution of the speech in consideration here (the words of the original psalmist) is almost entirely 'assertive' – a description of the way the world is – or 'directive' – a call to heed the advice of the psalmist.[14] This is typical of wisdom teaching. An additional dimension of the speech can be construed if the psalmist is considered to want to construct reality based on his understanding and experience of life. In other words, the performative aspect of the original expression of the psalm may have a 'declarative' illocution that is bringing about genuine reality simply through the act of speaking.

Indeed, the performative and declarative aspects of the psalmist's speech are plainly evident in the command to 'listen' or 'hear'. The very act of telling others to 'listen' or 'hear' results in them doing so. What, then, is happening when the

---

12. D. G. Firth, 'The Teaching of the Psalms', in Johnston and Firth, *Interpreting*, pp. 159–174. This analysis reinforces the view that a didactic function is not dependent upon a form-critical psalm category (p. 164). On the 'didactic voice' in the psalms of lament, see C. Mandolfo, *God in the Dock: Dialogic Tension in the Psalms of Lament*, JSOTSup 357 (Sheffield: Sheffield Academic Press, 2002).
13. For an introduction to speech-act theory, see R. S. Briggs, 'Speech-act Theory', in D. G. Firth and J. A. Grant (eds.), *Words and the Word* (Nottingham: Apollos, 2005), pp. 75–110.
14. The distinction is not exclusive; an assertive illocution, 'The wicked shall perish', may also be construed as directive, 'Don't be wicked'.

words of the psalmist are included in a collection of written prayers and used by other people in another time and place?

The 'contemporary' voice

When speech is fixed in writing, does its recitation constitute the same illocutionary act as the original speech? In the case of the assertions of testimony, the expression loses its impact since the speaker is not recounting a genuine personal experience. Nevertheless, the illocutionary act of assertion is still the same, if the speaker is identifying with the original psalmists and testifying on their behalf. As regards the directives of admonition, there is even more reason for the illocutionary act to remain the same, since the same direction is being offered. Vanhoozer addresses this issue and concludes clearly that the act of writing effectively fixes the illocutionary act.[15] Therefore the recitation of a psalm can have the same illocutionary act as would the original performance of the psalmist, and this extends to the performative and declarative aspects of the speech.

The performative aspect of the speech is more significant than has previously been realized. It is precisely the voicing of the call to hear that makes hearing possible. Furthermore, it is the process of hearing (and understanding) that can create a new perception of the world in the mind of the hearers. An example of this could be the unidentified experience of the psalmist in the 'sanctuary of God' that forms the turning point of Psalm 73. Many suggestions have been made regarding what the psalmist experienced, such as the observation of worship, participation in worship, a revelatory oracle or a theophanic experience. A new suggestion, in the context of the present argument, is that the psalmist heard words of wisdom being recited, perhaps in the guise of Psalm 14 or 37 or an earlier/related form of one of them. It was this hearing that changed his perception and effectively changed his world, so that he was then able to affirm the same perception in his own psalm.

A comparison could be made here to Brueggemann's analysis of expressions of praise, which characterizes them as 'generative'. More than describing the world, they generate an understanding of the world which is constitutive of the reality (as perceived by the hearer). As he puts it, 'The liturgic act is the moment of announcement in which old claims are made present realities.'[16] Note the direction of causation: announcement leads to reality. To apply this

---

15. K. J. Vanhoozer, *First Theology: God, Scripture and Hermeneutics* (Leicester: Apollos, 2002), pp. 180–181 and 189–190.
16. W. Brueggemann, *Israel's Praise: Doxology against Idolatry and Ideology* (Philadelphia: Fortress, 1988), p. 36.

to an example in the psalms, 37:25–26 makes an observation about the world that is quite striking in its absolute nature: 'I have not seen the righteous forsaken / or their children begging bread.' Whilst this is clearly assertive, it begs to be taken as declarative too, such that in believing it and in living in a way consistent with the principles espoused in the psalm, the world will be conformed to such a description.

What this says about the wisdom tradition is that it is not so much the ideas and concepts that are significant but the voicing of them. No doubt this is why so much of the wisdom tradition is presented in reported speech. The manifestation of wisdom within the psalms taps into this dynamic, inviting the ongoing recitation (in the context of prayer) that leads to hearing and hence to renewed reality. This explains the significance of the wisdom tradition in the psalms being manifested as speech addressed to people (rather than to God). It requires the hearers to act, rather than asking God to act or expressing a response to God's action.

Note also that this dynamic can be operative even when the only hearer is the reciter. Perhaps there is an argument here for praying the psalms aloud, even when alone!

The 'canonical' voice

An extra dimension is added to this analysis when the canonical context of the psalms is considered. Now the words are not merely the expression of a particular person, nor a formalized manner of prayer, but in some sense the 'word of God'. This creates an institutional context that reinforces the directive to 'hear' or 'listen'.[17] The canonical context of the psalms demands that the words be 'heard' precisely because they are 'God's words' (which can helpfully be understood as God's illocution rather than God's locution). Furthermore, it gives a reason to interpret the illocutionary act of wisdom texts as going beyond the assertive and having a commissive aspect – that is, being a promise. The texts are now not only the assertion of the psalmist, but, by implication of their canonical status, the promise of God: they describe the world as God intends it to be. Such promises are illocutionary acts which go beyond describing the world and seek to conform the world to the words.[18] Moreover, there is an added

---

17. On the necessity of an institutional context for certain illocutions to be effective, see A. C. Thiselton, *Thiselton on Hermeneutics: The Collected Works and New Essays of Anthony Thiselton* (Aldershot: Ashgate, 2006), pp. 132–135.
18. Thiselton, *Collected*, p. 138. For a fuller discussion, see A. C. Thiselton, *New Horizons in Hermeneutics* (London: Marshall Pickering, 1992), pp. 294–298.

perlocution – an effect on the hearers – not previously present in the original or contemporary voice. Since the speech sets out the promise of how God intends the world to be, committed hearers are necessarily reminded of their responsibility to enact such a world, where, for example, the righteous are not forsaken, nor do their children have to beg bread.

The voicing of wisdom in the psalms as the manifestation of the illocution of God begs a comparison with the personification of wisdom in Proverbs 8 – 9 and Wisdom of Solomon 6 – 9. The psalmist and Lady Wisdom both call others to hear, and there seems to be significance in the process of speaking and listening. Lady Wisdom addresses humanity on God's behalf, and so too certain psalms offer a medium for the recitation of wisdom on behalf of God, who is the progenitor of both. The expression of wisdom in the psalms is strongly tied to the particular experiences of the original psalmists, so that it is through testimony and observation that wisdom is expressed. In her analysis of the significance of wisdom being personified as a woman, Camp comments that

> the most fundamental point made by these poems is that wisdom is *not* an abstract concept but a way of being that is at its heart relational and holistic, underlying every important personal, social and religious experience familiar to the ancient Israelite.[19]

Thus the expression of wisdom in Psalms is both life-centred and life-affirming, 'life' meaning the practical realities of daily human existence. The effect of hearing the voice of wisdom as experienced through the recitation of psalms addressed to people (rather than to God) is to rouse hearers to commit themselves to enacting the 'good life' that wisdom espouses.

Conclusion

Wisdom as it is manifested in the psalms can be seen as a divinely mandated expression of the realities of life that through its voicing is generative of new life. Although making minimal reference to God and, remarkably in their context, being addressed to other people rather than to God, the texts considered here both convey and create God's intentions for a good life. They

---

19. C. V. Camp, 'Woman Wisdom as a Root Metaphor: A Theological Consideration', in K. G. Hoglund et al. (eds.), *The Listening Heart: Essays in Wisdom and the Psalms in Honour of Roland E. Murphy, O. Carm.*, JSOTSup 58 (Sheffield: JSOT Press, 1987), pp. 45–76, here p. 45.

illustrate the power and significance of performative speech as the means of that process, drawing the committed hearers of such speech to play their part in the enactment of God's promises. The recitation of wisdom in the psalms thus parallels the speech of personified Lady Wisdom as the epitome of how God's wisdom is rendered effective.

© Simon P. Stocks, 2016

11. 'OH, THAT I KNEW WHERE I MIGHT FIND HIM': ASPECTS OF DIVINE ABSENCE IN PROVERBS, JOB AND ECCLESIASTES

Brittany N. Melton

Where is God in the wisdom literature? In the whole of the traditional biblical wisdom corpus God appears and speaks in only one instance, at the end of Job.[1] Moreover, Proverbs speaks about God only sporadically and Ecclesiastes rarely mentions God, as they mostly address everyday human affairs. Proverbs, Job and Ecclesiastes relate their experience of God from the human perspective. For

> wisdom trains its focus on the realm of mundane existence, in which divine presence and absence are typically difficult to distinguish. Wisdom confronts the usual hiddenness of God's presence in the world and the need to search for it. From wisdom's perspective, divine presence often appears as divine absence. Wisdom is concerned with discerning the difference between the two.[2]

---

1. Although wisdom's influence extends beyond Proverbs, Job and Ecclesiastes, it is helpful to maintain wisdom literature as an identifiable literary genre of the Ancient Near East, concerned with the nature of God, humanity and the world. The present concern is with the first in relation to the second, thus excluding the speeches of God in the epilogue and prologue of Job, since therein God is not communicating with humanity.
2. Joel S. Burnett, *Where Is God? Divine Absence in the Hebrew Bible* (Minneapolis: Fortress, 2010), p. 86; see esp. ch. 5.

The assertion about the absence of God in wisdom literature results partially from canonical comparison.³ That being so, divine absence is predicated on the construal of divine presence in 'the memory of [Israel's] first encounters with its God'.⁴ Elsewhere God is portrayed as speaking, available, present and active on behalf of a particular people. The wisdom literature provides a counterbalance when God does not seem to be acting in accordance with this portrayal. The reason behind this atypical characterization of God is certainly a matter of genre and theological standpoint rather than secular derivation.⁵ The perspective of biblical wisdom literature on God results from its predominately empirical approach, which contrasts with the description of God upheld in other books of the Hebrew Bible that attend to God's action in history.

This chapter attends to divine absence by focusing on the hidden, silent and inscrutable God one finds in the wisdom books. The 'sceptical' or 'radical' tone some have ascribed to Qoheleth and Job is produced as they wrestle to hold what they *believe* in one hand versus what they *perceive* in the other. Wisdom literature assumes a distinct vantage point by focusing on God as the Creator of the world and the source and giver of wisdom (e.g. Prov. 2:6; Eccl. 2:26; Job 28:20, 23). The sages sought wisdom as a means to experience divine presence and favour over against answers or simply to obtain wisdom for wisdom's sake. As a result, at times, God and Wisdom are referred to interchangeably. Thus, a discussion on divine absence is necessarily bound up with the role of wisdom in general and personified Wisdom. Wisdom's intent is an attempt, without guarantee, to secure God's presence in each person's life.⁶ And yet, the presence of God hovers at the limits of attainable wisdom, shimmering with the unattainable allure of a siren.

God as absent

Before proceeding the term 'absence' should be clarified. 'Absence' has two connotations in *The New Oxford American Dictionary*: either 'the state of being

---

3. E.g. T. A. Perry, *God's Twilight Zone: Wisdom in the Hebrew Bible* (Peabody: Hendrickson, 2008), p. 116.
4. Burnett, *Where*, p. 5.
5. Lennart Boström, *The God of the Sages: The Portrayal of God in the Book of Proverbs*, ConBOT 29 (Stockholm: Almqvist & Wiksell International, 1990), pp. 9, 32–33. The remaining *Megilloth* also portray a similar atypical characterization of God.
6. James L. Crenshaw, 'In Search of Divine Presence (Some Remarks Preliminary to a Theology of Wisdom)', *RevExp* 74 (1977), pp. 353–369.

away from a place or person' (i.e. the locative sense) or 'the lack of' something (i.e. the sense of being deficient). Both senses of 'absence', locative and deficient, have implications for the present discussion. To speak of God as absent in the locative sense means to assert that an individual or community is alienated or estranged from God. Absence in the deficient sense allows for discussion of a lack of or infrequent reference to the deity in general, including non-mention of the divine name (Yhwh) in particular texts (i.e. literary absence).

In Proverbs

God is absent in Proverbs in the sense of intermittent reference. Whybray proposed that God was redactionally inserted into the book of Proverbs, due to the sporadic positioning of the Yhwh sayings and a belief in the progression from secular to religious.[7] Inversely, the current trend maintains that theological conceptions are integral to or presupposed in the message of the book.[8] Regardless of these positions, the final form of Proverbs leaves the reader wondering why certain sections reference God frequently while others reference God hardly at all. For example, chapters 4–7 and 25–27 contain just two references to God per section, whilst chapters 15–16 contain many.[9] God appears removed from the sphere of human wisdom. However, one could argue that the more concentrated mention of God in the prologue (chs. 1–9) prepares the reader to assume God behind the quest for wisdom (noted by the phrase 'fear of the Lord'), thus making the whole book more God-centred.

In Ecclesiastes

God's absence has been asserted in Ecclesiastes in the locative sense as well as in the deficient sense, due to Qoheleth's emphasis on God's transcendence,

---

7. First asserted in R. Norman Whybray's *Wisdom in Proverbs*, SBT 45 (London: SCM, 1965), but later mitigated in *Proverbs*, NCB (London: Marshall Pickering, 1994), p. 152.
8. Boström, *God*, pp. 36–41; and Katharine J. Dell, *The Book of Proverbs in Social and Theological Context* (Cambridge: Cambridge University Press, 2006), chs. 4, 5. For presupposed covenant God see F. Derek Kidner, 'The Relationship between God and Man in Proverbs', *TynB* 7/8 (1961), pp. 4–9.
9. Boström (*God*, p. 34) calculates the distribution of God-references in Proverbs, demonstrating the scarcity of references, particularly in certain sections. Dell (*Proverbs*, p. 106) notes the prevalence of God-talk in chs. 15–16.

paucity of references to God, and lack of reference to God as Yhwh. Crenshaw and Boström understand Qoheleth's God to be distant and remote.[10] However, transcendence need not exclude structural divine presence (i.e. 'God's presence in the created order').[11] Some question whether Qoheleth's God can even be Yhwh, in part resulting from Qoheleth's exclusive employment of *'ĕlōhîm* rather than the Tetragrammaton. It seems prudent to understand this more general designation for God as an emphasis on God as Creator. Qoheleth has a different experience, not a different God. For him, God remains transcendent and mysterious. He emphasizes the distinction between God, the Creator and humanity:

> Be not rash with your mouth, nor let your heart be hasty to utter a word before God, for God is in heaven and you are on earth. Therefore let your words be few.
> (5:1 [Eng. 5:2])[12]

If this is not a locative statement but rather a claim about the disparity between God and humankind, then nowhere in Ecclesiastes does Qoheleth explicitly address God's presence or absence in the world. He does speak of God's times (Eccl. 3) and activity in the world, leading one to envision God standing behind it all. However, the only ground for quantitatively addressing the absence of God in Ecclesiastes concerns the scarcity of references to the divine (in thirty-eight out of 222 verses, and not at all in chs. 4, 10).[13]

---

10. James L. Crenshaw, 'The Silence of Eternity: Ecclesiastes', in *A Whirlpool of Torment: Israelite Traditions of God as an Oppressive Presence*, OBT (Philadelphia: Fortress, 1984), pp. 77–92; Boström, *God*, p. 153.
11. Terence E. Fretheim ('God and World: Presence and Power', in *The Suffering of God: An Old Testament Perspective*, OBT [Philadelphia: Fortress, 1984], pp. 60–78 [61]) calls for transcendence to be 'stripped of its narrow spatial associations' (p. 70).
12. All Bible quotes in this chapter are from the esv.
13. This statistic is more striking in the genre of Ecclesiastes than it would be for narrative passages in the Hebrew Bible. T. A. Perry (*Dialogues with Kohelet: The Book of Ecclesiastes* [University Park: Pennsylvania State University Press, 1993], pp. 83, 97, 102, 104, 140) identifies five instances where the understood subject God has been grammatically omitted in Ecclesiastes (2:21; 4:1, 17; 5:3; and possibly 8:12).

In Job

Job is the only book in the wisdom corpus that addresses divine absence in an explicitly locative sense. Absence in Job is about Job's alienation from God. 'Job is the lonely, abandoned sufferer. God and man are estranged.'[14] Job wishes to appeal to God, before God's face, and make his case. He says,

> 'Oh, that I knew where I might find him,
>   that I might come even to his seat!'
>
> (23:3)

There also is a sense in which Job experiences a withdrawal of the presence of God. He recalls a former time 'when the Almighty was yet with me' (29:5). However, 'Job's God, as presented in his speeches within the dialogue, is paradoxically both present and absent, an oppressive presence and a hiding friend'.[15] In Job there is a less clear dichotomy of presence and absence. Even though God is with Job God cannot be perceived; only his oppression is felt. '"Behold, I go forwards, but he is not there, and backwards, but I do not perceive him; on the left hand when he is working, I do not behold him; he turns to the right hand, but I do not see him"' (23:8–9). As far as Job is concerned God remains silent and hidden until the theophany.

In conclusion, without these lenses of redactional criticism and canonical comparison the absence of God is not a prominent theme in the biblical wisdom corpus, in that God is an assumed (and sometimes experienced) presence. However, several aspects related to divine absence feature in Proverbs, Job and Ecclesiastes. For this reason strict definitions for absence will be set aside from this point forward in order to explore aspects of absence which are by their very nature dependent upon some notion of presence. My aim is to survey the language surrounding this theme, rather than attempt to offer reasons for aspects of divine absence. Attention will be given to the silence, hiddenness and inscrutability of God in the discussion that follows.

---

14. Samuel Terrien, *The Elusive Presence: Toward a New Biblical Theology* (San Francisco: Harper & Row, 1978), p. 354.
15. James L. Crenshaw, 'The Concept of God in Old Testament Wisdom', in Leo G. Perdue, Bernard Brandon Scott and William Johnston Wiseman (eds.), *In Search of Wisdom: Essays in Memory of John G. Gammie* (Louisville: Westminster John Knox, 1993), pp. 1–18 (12).

God as silent[16]

There is no direct speech from God within Proverbs or Ecclesiastes. Within the biblical wisdom corpus God speaks only in Job. Aside from Job 38 – 41, God is not the subject of verbs of discourse.[17] More poignantly, for the better part of Job God is non-responsive. Job calls out to God but receives no answer:

> 'Behold, I cry out, "Violence!" but I am not answered;
>   I call for help, but there is no justice.'
> (19:7)

> 'I cry to you for help and you do not answer me;
>   I stand, and you only look at me.'
> (30:20)

Job expresses his desire for God to answer him (13:22; 23:5; 31:35). His request is predicated on his experience of God speaking in the past (12:4). Rather than conjecturing about why God is silent, the more important contribution of Job on the matter is the observation that, contrary to the assertions of Job's friends and other parts of the Hebrew Bible, 'silence on God's part is not a symptom of his disfavour'.[18] It should be noted that even when God does finally speak he does not directly answer Job's questions.

This portrayal of a non-responsive God is also upheld in Proverbs (albeit mediated through the voice of Wisdom):

> 'Then they will call upon me, but I will not answer...'
> (1:28a)

If Wisdom will not reply, it must be inferred that neither will God, since Wisdom serves as God's mediator to humanity. While it is more typical for Wisdom to be

---

16. For God's silence in the Old Testament see Marjo Korpel and Johannes de Moor, *The Silent God* (Leiden/Boston: Brill, 2012).
17. See caveat in n. 1.
18. Matthijs J. de Jong, '"It Shall Be Night to You, Without Vision": The Theme of Divine Disfavour in the Biblical Prophetic Books', in Bob Becking (ed.), *Reflections on the Silence of God: A Discussion with Marjo Korpel and Johannes de Moor*, OTS 62 (Leiden/Boston: Brill, 2013), pp. 105–126 (126). Cf. Elihu's assertion that God's silence is caused by human pride (35:12).

calling out in the streets (8:1–4), this verse speaks to the possibility that Wisdom will not always reply. Here, the context (vv. 24–28) is one of reciprocation: because the people would not listen to Wisdom (who presumably speaks on God's behalf), Wisdom will no longer answer them. Thus, Proverbs seems to espouse the typical prophetic view of silence as an indication of divine displeasure.

Divine silence is not directly addressed in Ecclesiastes. One must infer Qoheleth's opinion on the matter. It is presented as a simple fact of reality.[19]

God as hidden[20]

The language of 'hide-and-seek' is used of God/wisdom in all three books. In Proverbs, Wisdom says:

'. . . they will seek me diligently but will not find me.'
(1:28b)

'For whoever finds me finds life
    and obtains favour from the LORD,
but he who fails to find me injures himself;
    all who hate me love death.'
(8:35–36)

The integral connection between finding Wisdom and finding God is evidenced by the gaining of life and favour from the Lord, things which only God can grant. Thus, if one finds wisdom, one gains a certain degree of access to God (2:6–8). While the wise person pursues wisdom, the foolish person neglects or rejects wisdom and concurrently the divine.

In Ecclesiastes God's presence is hidden, stitched into the very fabric of creation and mundane activity.[21] In other words, acknowledging structural

---

19. Paul Sanders, 'How Comprehensible Can Divine Silence Be? Reflections on the Biblical Evidence', in Becking, *Reflections*, pp. 127–138 (135).
20. See Lothar Perlitt, 'Die Verborgenheit Gottes', in Hans Walter Wolff (ed.), *Probleme biblischer Theologie: Gerhard von Rad zum 70. Geburtstag* (München: Chr. Kaiser, 1971), pp. 367–382 (373–374, n. 13); for the hiding of God more generally see Samuel E. Balentine, *The Hidden God: The Hiding of the Face of God in the Old Testament* (Oxford: Oxford University Press, 1983).
21. Burnett, *Where*, pp. 97–101.

divine presence does not preclude the coexistence of divine hiddenness. This explains why Qoheleth desires to understand the ways of God, because grasping the created order is a means of knowing God. However, in Ecclesiastes it says:

> then I saw all the work of God, that man cannot find out the work that is done under the sun. However much man may toil in seeking, he will not find it out. Even though a wise man claims to know, he cannot find it out.
> (8:17)

This verse encapsulates Qoheleth's experience of the limitations of wisdom; even from the wise God's ways remain hidden.[22]

In Job, the friends instruct Job to seek God (5:8; 8:5). Their 'wise' words resonate with the sense in Proverbs that wisdom is readily on offer; if you seek, then you will find (Prov. 2:4–5). And yet, throughout the book, Job expresses the sense that God is hiding from him. He says:

> 'Why do you hide your face
>   and count me as your enemy?'
> (13:24)[23]

There is no guarantee of success. If God wishes to conceal himself, then he will not be found. Over and again Job comes up empty-handed in this endeavour.

> '[God] does great things beyond searching out,
>   and marvellous things beyond number.
> Behold, he passes by me, and I see him not;
>   he moves on, but I do not perceive him.'
> (9:10–11)[24]

Eliphaz suggests God is 'high in the heavens', veiled by clouds (22:12–14), and Elihu admits,

> '... When he hides his face, who can behold him,
>   whether it be a nation or a man?'
> (34:29)

---

22. James L. Crenshaw, *Defending God: Biblical Responses to the Problem of Evil* (Oxford: Oxford University Press, 2005), p. 166.
23. See 23:3 above.
24. See 23:8–9 above.

'The Almighty – we cannot find him.'
(37:23a)

Even when finally appearing to Job, God remains somewhat obscured by the whirlwind. In the words of O'Connor, 'the book of Job expresses an experience of a deity who remains veiled by the vastness of creation'.[25]

God's ways as inscrutable

Not only is God's presence in the world hidden, but the ways of God are inscrutable. Ecclesiastes speaks generally about the ways of God being beyond human comprehension:

> He has made everything beautiful in its time. Also, he has put eternity into man's heart, yet so that he cannot find out what God has done from the beginning to the end.
> (3:11)

> As you do not know the way the spirit comes to the bones in the womb of a woman with child, so you do not know the work of God who makes everything.
> (11:5)[26]

These examples demonstrate that attempting to comprehend the ways of God is a pervasive concern in Ecclesiastes. Qoheleth is seeking but not finding. Proverbs 20:24 validates the claims of Qoheleth regarding the limits of human comprehension. The words of Agur (Prov. 30:3f.) also attest to the inscrutable ways of God. In Job God's inscrutability is explored through Job's complaints that God is not acting justly (34:5–6). Life does not seem fair, and the system of just reward is not working as it should. Although Job has continually pursued righteousness he has received affliction.[27] Job voices this complaint on his own behalf, while Qoheleth offers various generalizations of injustice in the world (Eccl. 4:1–2; 6:1–2; 7:15; 8:14; 9:2–3). Qoheleth employs wisdom in order to

---

25. Kathleen M. O' Connor, 'Wisdom Literature and Experience of the Divine', in *Biblical Theology: Problems and Perspectives in Honor of J. Christian Beker* (Nashville: Abingdon, 1995), pp. 183–195, 320–22 (187).
26. See also Eccl. 7:14; 8:17.
27. See also Job 36:26, 29; 37:15–16; 38:18.

make sense of the ways of God, and Job seeks out God to demand an answer directly; but the ways of God are hidden beyond wisdom's reach, preserving the mysteriousness of God.

Understanding the relationship between God and Wisdom

Personified Wisdom was birthed in the poetic imagination as a literary figure to express the alluring yet elusive nature of God which the sages experienced. She is both a symbol of God's elusiveness as expressed in Job as well as a response to it in Proverbs. By the latter I mean that, as a result of the sages' inability to perceive God, coupled with a faith in God as sole Creator and Determiner of events, personified Wisdom as described in Proverbs serves as a mediator between humanity and God.[28] Wisdom functions as a means of God's presence to humanity.[29] The absence of God's tangible presence fuels the quest for Wisdom, for the chance to get as close as possible to the divine. Obtaining wisdom is a fairly straightforward endeavour in Proverbs, but this is not the case in Job and Ecclesiastes. The last two readily acknowledge the limitations of wisdom.[30] It is as if Qoheleth takes on the advice of Proverbs to find wisdom in order to gain the knowledge of God, but he comes up empty-handed. For Qoheleth, wisdom has its benefits, but there is no guarantee of obtaining it. 'All this I have tested by wisdom. I said, "I will be wise", but it was far from me. That which has been is far off, and deep, very deep; who can find it out?' (7:23–24).[31] In Job the descriptions of Wisdom and God appear to be interchangeable. For example, the hymn to wisdom parallels the speeches of God, in which the hiddenness of precious metals is

---

28. For Wisdom as a mediator see Dell, *Proverbs*, p. 129; and Boström, *God*, p. 166; *contra* those who equate Wisdom and God (e.g. O'Connor, 'Wisdom'), or regard Wisdom as a hypostasis (e.g. Helmer Ringgren, *Word and Wisdom: Studies in the Hypostatization of Divine Qualities and Functions in the Ancient Near East* [Lund: Ohlssons, 1947]), or as deriving from a goddess (Bernhard Lang, *Frau Weisheit: Deutung einer biblischen Gestalt* [Düsseldorf: Patmos-Verlag, 1975]).
29. Alice M. Sinnott, *The Personification of Wisdom*, SOTSM (Aldershot: Ashgate, 2005), pp. 166–167.
30. Richard L. Schultz, 'Unity or Diversity in Wisdom Theology? A Canonical and Covenantal Perspective', *TynB* 48 (1997), pp. 271–306 (281–285).
31. See also Eccl. 8:16–17.

a metaphor for 'unattainable' wisdom.[32] Wisdom seems just as elusive as God. Job asks:

'But where shall wisdom be found?
    And where is the place of understanding?
    ... it is not found in the land of the living.'
(28:12–13)

'From where, then, does wisdom come?
    And where is the place of understanding?
It is hidden from the eyes of all living
    and concealed from the birds of the air.'
(28:20–21)

Crenshaw recapitulates that in Job, '[t]rue wisdom, the poem insists, cannot be found in the land of the living, for it resides with God'.[33] Job never claims to find wisdom, even though he finally encounters God.

In each book the conception of wisdom mirrors the conception of God. Perhaps the writers cannot help but transfer their conception of God onto wisdom because the two are so entangled. This explains why the portrayals of God and wisdom are similar to one another in each book, but they differ from one book to the next. Although all three books proceed from a foundational belief in God and an experience of the divine as hidden and silent, each takes a distinct approach in order to find God and make sense of God's ways in the world. Proverbs pursues God's presence through Wisdom and order, and these become a mediated way of knowing God; thus God is hidden behind Wisdom and the created order. For Qoheleth both God and wisdom are inscrutable; 'humans ... are destined to knock at the door of wisdom, only to be barred from entering by divine decree'.[34] Job searches high and low for God and Wisdom; he finally encounters the presence of God in the whirlwind. God and wisdom are accessible in Proverbs, beyond grasp in Ecclesiastes, and elusive in Job.

---

32. Katharine J. Dell, *Job: Where Shall Wisdom Be Found?*, PGOT (Sheffield: Sheffield Phoenix, 2013), pp. 28–29.
33. Crenshaw, *Defending*, p. 166. Job 11:5–7; 12:13; 28:23; 38:36–37.
34. Ibid., p. 168.

Conclusion

From wisdom's perspective God at times seems absent, silent, hidden, inscrutable. It proclaims these things from experience, with a desire to recover God's presence via wisdom. Wisdom is the way to God, but is not always attainable. As such, the determination to find wisdom was fuelled by the sages' search for divine presence. And yet, even if wisdom is found, the mystery of God is preserved. In the wisdom literature we have a prime example of the tension between divine presence and absence. Insofar as wisdom is personified and takes on a much larger literary presence than God in these books, this speaks to divine absence. Where is God? He is hidden behind Wisdom. In equal tension, we may recognize that the conception of wisdom portrayed in each of these books individually cannot be divorced from the conception of God held by each book. Is God perhaps lurking somewhere behind the conception of wisdom? This speaks to divine presence in wisdom literature; even though it is somewhat obscured or backgrounded, it is inextricably intertwined with the presence of wisdom. One can behold Wisdom's beauty in part, but never grasp her fullness. One can know God in part, but never grasp him fully.

© Brittany N. Melton, 2016

INDEX OF AUTHORS

Ackerman, S. 117
Adams, S. L. 131
Albright, W. F. 45
Allen W. A. 79
Alter, R. 14
Andersen, F. I. 61, 64, 68, 130
Anderson, W. 99
Ansberry, C. B. 187
Ash, C. 68
Athanasius 182
Atkinson, D. 65–66

Balentine, S. E. 211
Bänziger, T. 171
Barbour, J. 97
Barth, K. 4, 27, 30
Bartholomew, C. G. 4, 5, 14, 21, 22, 25, 26, 27, 29, 30, 31, 32, 138, 139, 175, 180, 186, 189, 190, 192
Barton, G. A. 82
Barton, J. 15, 177
Barton, S. C. 192

Bauckham, R. 192
Bauer, J. B. 120
Beckwith, R. 119
Bellis, A. O. 51, 54
Benjamin, R. 95
Bergant, D. 29, 64
Berlin, A. 117, 129
Beyer, A. 116, 127, 128, 129
Biddle, M. E. 185
Blenkinsopp, J. 24, 49
Block, D. I. 158, 191
Boström, G. 49
Boström, L. 131, 141, 206, 207, 208
Boulton, M. 63
Bovell, C. 128
Brandt, P. 119
Braun, R. 86
Brenner, A. 29, 51, 120
Briggs, R. S. 200
Brown, S. A. and P. D. Miller 63
Brown, W. P. 182, 188, 191
Brueggemann, W. 149, 181, 201

Budde, K. 10
Bundvad, M. 88
Burnett, J. S. 205, 206, 211
Bush, F. W. 120, 125, 130
Byrne, P. H. 66

Camp, C. 29, 47–48, 52, 127, 168, 203
Campbell, A. 72–73
Campbell, E. F. 120, 125, 129
Capps, D. 65
Card, M. 63
Carson, D. A. 67, 69
Childs, B. S. 4, 13, 30, 102
Chisolm, R. B. 156, 162
Christianson, E. 27, 84, 92–93
Clements, R. E. 3, 13, 174, 196
Clifford, R. J. 46, 56, 57, 72, 73, 75, 76, 77, 78, 130
Clines, D. J. A. 28, 61, 69, 134, 147, 149
Cooper, J. S. 101
Cox, D. 63
Crenshaw, J. L. 5, 6, 7, 14, 22, 82, 89, 121, 141, 174, 195, 196, 206, 208, 209, 212, 215
Crüsemann, F. 12
Culp, A. J. 162

Daube, D. 120
Davies, G. I. 7
Davis, E. 33, 125
Davy, T. J. 79
Day, J. 6
Delitzsch, F. 9
Dell, K. J. 7, 22, 61, 71–72, 84, 92, 94, 96, 97, 98, 101, 103, 105, 110, 131, 195, 196, 207, 214, 215
Dhorme, E. 10–11
van Dijk-Hemmes, C. 51
Dillard, R. B. 171
Doak, B. R. 184

Douglas, J. N. 86
Duhm, B. 10
Dukan, M. 119
Dunn, J. D. G. 59

Ehrlich, C. S. 21
Eising, H. 124
Eskenazi, T. C. and T. Frymer-Kensky 129
Estes, D. J. 61
Exum, C. 106

Fahlgren, K. 135
Fevel, Ch. 22
Fewell, D. N. and D. M. Gunn 131, 160
Fingarette, H. 32
Firth, D. G. 157, 164, 166, 167, 200
Fischer, I. 120
Fohrer, G. 9
Fokkelman, J. P. 14, 18
Fontaine, C. 29, 166
Forman, C. C. 98
Fox, M. V. 19, 20–21, 40–41, 45, 51, 52, 81, 83, 95, 103, 121, 126, 128, 130, 131, 152, 175, 183, 185, 187, 189
Frankfort, H. et al. 22
Fretheim, T. E. 208
Frydrych, T. 183, 184
Frye, N. 26

Gammie, J. G. 7
Genette, G. 115, 159
Gese, H. 144, 163, 174, 181
Ginsburg, C. D. 91, 118, 119
Gladson, J. A. 18, 138, 154
Glover, N. 128
Goetz, S. 32
Goh, S. T. S. 122, 124
Goldingay, J. 175
Goldsworthy, G. L. xiii

INDEX OF AUTHORS

Goodman, M. 91
Gordis, R. 84, 151, 172
Gordon, R. P. 121, 164, 167
Goshen-Gottstein, M. H. 119
Goswell, G. 118
Grant, C. A. 85
Grant, J. 8, 12
Grätz, S. 171
Greenberg, M. 147
Greenstein, E. L. 187
Gregory the Great 91
Greidanus, S. 31
Gressmann, H. 8
Gunkel, H. 3, 195
Gutiérrez, G. 61, 68

Habel, N. C. 61, 63, 69, 72, 74, 76, 147, 150
Hahn, H. F. 8–9, 28
Hallo, W. W. 8, 176
Hals, R. M. 129
Hartley, J. E. 61, 65
Harrison, C. R. 86
Harvey, D. 28
Hatton, P. T. H. 42, 44
Heim, K. M. 18, 38, 39–41, 42
Hempel, C. et al. 22
Hess, R. S. 101
Hildebrandt, T. A. 38
den Hollander, A. et al. 115
Holm-Nielsen, S. 92
Hopkins, D. D. and M. S. Koppel 66, 67
Hornung, E. 176
Hubbard, R. L. 120, 131, 132
Hughes, R. A. 63
Hulme, W. E. 65–66

Jacobson, D. 196
Janzen J. G. 31, 61
Janzen, W. 165

Jarick, J. 99
Jerome 27, 92
Johnston, P. S. 194, 198
de Jong, M. J. 210
de Jong, S. 84, 184

Kalmonofsky, A. 129
Kalugila, L. 177
Kartje, J. 6
Kautzsch, K. 10
Kayatz, C. 44
Keller, C.-A. 146
Keys, G. 169
Kidner, D. 58, 207
Klein, L. R. 117
Klein, R. W. 164
Knierim, R. P. 180
Knox, W. L. 45
Koch, K. 42, 135–136
Koh, Y.-V. 85
Koosed, J. L. 92, 120
Korpel, M. C. A. 129, 210
Kosmala, H. 124
Kramer, S. N. 176
Kreeft, P. 31
Krüger, T. 26, 82
Kwon, J. S. 124
Kynes, W. 22, 61, 98

LaCocque, A. 104
Lambert, W. G. 177
Lang, B. 45, 46, 127, 214
Lapsley, J. E. 182
Larrimore, M. 27
Lau, P. H. W. 131
Leahy, F. S. 105
Lee, B. 161
Lee, E. P. 89–90
Lee, N. C. 63
Levenson, J. D. 166

Levine, E. 88
Levinson, B. 98–99
Levy, S. 26
Lichtenstein, M. H. 124
Lichtheim, M. 141
Lincoln, A. T. 59
Lindars, B. 160
Lipinski, E. 149
Lo, A. 14
Loader, J. A. 6, 15, 91
Lohfink, N. 13, 15, 23, 86
Longman, T. 32, 41–42, 120, 126
Lucas, E. C. 39, 42
Lundbom, J. R. 158
Luther, M. 84, 91, 92

McCreesh, T. P. 120, 124
McDonald, L. M. and J. A. Sanders 101
McGrath, A. E. 76
McKane, W. 10, 41, 141
McKenna, J. 30
McKeough, K. M. 172
McKibben, B. 33
McKinnon, C. 189
MacLachlan G. and I. Reid 115–116
Maclean, M. 115
McNeile, A. H. 82
Maier, C. 52, 128
Mandolfo, C. 200
Martini, C. M. 31
Masenya, M. 53
Meinhold, J. 8
Mettinger, T. N. D. 74, 75, 148
Middleton, J. R. 189
Miller, P. D. 131, 191
de Moor, J. 210
Morgan, D. F. 7
Morrow, W. S. 63
Munro, J. M. 105

Murphy, R. E. xiv, 10, 11, 12, 24, 42, 65, 88, 95, 103, 124, 137, 175, 180, 189, 194

Nam, D. W. 74, 75, 76, 77
Nel, P. J. 138, 163
Nemo, P. 32
Newsom, C. A. 10, 28, 182
Nicholas of Lyra 91
Noegel, S. B. 11

O'Connell, R. H. 109
O'Connor, D. J. 71
O'Connor, K. M. 213
O'Dowd, R. P. 4, 31, 139, 180, 189, 190, 192
Oeming, M. 6
Oeste, G. K. 162–163
Ogden, G. S. 11
Orr, M. 22

Park, S.-M. 168
Parry, R. A. 63
Parsons, G. W. 75
Patmor, H. 103
Paul, M. 109
Penchansky, D. 151, 189
Perdue, L. G. 7, 11, 86–87, 123, 141, 181, 188
Perlitt, L. 211
Perry, T. A. 84, 206, 208
Pigott, S. M. 117
Pinçon, B. 90
Plantinga, A. 32
Plumptre, E. H. 15
Polzin, R. M. 16–17
Pope, M. H. 11, 101, 118
Porter, J. R. 163
Preuss, H.-D. 174
Provan, I. 156

INDEX OF AUTHORS

von Rad, G. 13, 54, 100, 121, 137, 186
Ramsey, J. L. 66
Rashbam 91
Reitman, J. S. 66
Rendtorff, R. 118, 171
Ringgren, H. H. 44, 214
Rohr, R. 31
Roper, L. 71
Rowold, H. L. 71

Sadgrove, M. 102, 103
Sakenfeld, K. D. 123, 129
Sanders, P. 211
Sandoval, T. J. 18
Saysell, C. 171
Schipper, J. 163
Schmid, H. H. 12, 176, 177, 181
Scholnick, S. 71
Schroer, S. 53
Schultz, R. L. 214
Schwáb, Z. 41
Scott, R. B. Y. 122, 124
Seachris, J. W. 32
Seow, C.-L. 14–15, 61, 85–86
Shakespeare, W. 155
Shead, A. 83
Sheppard, G. T. 23, 82, 108
Siegfried, S. 12, 82
Simon, R. 10
Simundson, D. J. 64
Sinnott, A. M. 46, 214
Sloane, A. 63
Smend, R. 9
Smith, J. 198
Smith, J. K. A. 182
Sneed, M. R. 184, 185
Snell, D. C. 9
Sparks, K. L. 21, 104, 105
Spellman, C. 116

Steinberg, J. 118
Steinberg, M. 14
Stewart, A. W. 183
Stone, T. J. 116, 119, 124, 127, 128
Stump, E. 32
Szlos, M. B. 124

Talmon, S. 121, 172
Tamez, E. 92
Tan, N. N. H. 109
Tannen, D. 116
Tatu, S. 162
Terrien, S. 209
Thiselton A. C. 202
Thomas, H. A. 5, 30, 63
Ticciati, S. 27, 30
Toy, C. H. 10
Treier, D. J. 186
Trible, P. 128
Tromp, N. J. 102

Valler, S. 53
VanDrunen, D. 189
Vanhoozer, K. J. 201
Van Leeuwen, R. C. 5, 18, 19–20, 24–25, 38, 55, 132, 175, 179
Vatke, J. K. W. 9
de Villers, G. 171

Waltke, B. K. 38, 39, 42, 43, 55, 124, 128, 130, 142, 183
Walsh, J. T. 88
Walton, J. H. 61, 135
Waters, L. J. 79
Webb, B. G. 111, 160, 161
Weeks, S. 10, 27, 87, 97
Weiser, A. 188
Wellhausen, 3, 12
Westermann, C. 64, 174–175
White, J. B. 103

Whybray, R. N.   5, 7, 8, 9, 18, 45, 67, 82, 88, 121, 127, 164, 194, 195, 207
Williamson, H. G. M.   171
Wilson, G. H.   61, 83
Wilson, L.   61, 62, 63, 69, 70, 78, 155, 156
Witherington, B.   26, 192
Wolfe, L. M.   127
Wolfenson, L. B.   119, 120
Wolters, A.   27, 126
Wright, A. G.   15

Wright, C. J. H.   49–50, 79
Wright, G. E.   174, 188
Würthwein, E.   130

Yee, G. A.   51, 108
Yoder, C. R.   37, 50, 124, 127

Zakovitch, Y.   120
Zimmerli, W.   8, 181
van Zyl, D. C.   79

INDEX OF SCRIPTURE REFERENCES

OLD TESTAMENT

Genesis
1 *180*
1 – 2 *25*
1 – 11 *98*
4:1 *55–56*
12:1–3 *128*
14:19, 22 *55*
40:5–19 *161*
41:8 *157*
41:14–36 *161*
41:38–39 *157*

Exodus
1:14 *157*
1:15–17 *157*
7:11 *157*
20:16 *190*
20:19–21 *186*
28:3 *157*
31:1–6 *170*
31:3 *157, 179*
31:6 *170*
35:26 *157*
35:26–35 *170*
35:31 *157, 179*
35:35 *179*
36:1 *179*
36:1–2 *170*

Leviticus
19:13 *190*
19:14 *190*
19:17–18 *191*
19:18 *190*
19:35–36 *190*
23:15–21 *120*

Numbers
15:22–31 *23*
15:39 *98*
28:26–31 *120*

Deuteronomy
1:13–15 *158*
2:30 *158*
4:2 *191*
4:6 *157–158*
4:10–14 *191*
4:19 *191*
5:16 *190*
5:29 *191*
6:1–4 *26*
6:6 *26*
10:12–13 *191*
10:12–16 *186*
13:1 *191*
16:19 *158, 190*
17:14–20 *190*
17:19–20 *191*
20:10 *168*
21:18–21 *190*
23:22–24 *23, 98, 191*
24:14–22 *190*
24:15 *190*
24:17 *190*
25:13–16 *190*
26:1–11 *190*

Deuteronomy (*cont.*)
28:1–14   *189*
28:58   *191*
30:15–20   *189*
31:9–13   *191*
31:12   *191*
32:6   *55–56, 158, 160*
32:18   *56*
32:29   *158*
34:9   *158, 160*

Joshua
1:8   *160*
16:2   *168*
22:1–8   *160*
23:1–16   *160*
24:1–28   *160*

Judges
1:4–7   *160*
4–5   *117, 160*
5   *160*
7:13–14   *161*
8:19   *162*
8:21   *161, 162*
9:1–6   *162*
9:7–15   *161*
9:16–20   *162*
14:4   *163*
14:10–20   *161*
14:14–19   *163*

Ruth
1:1   *118*
1:1–5   *128*
1:3   *117, 129*
1:4   *127*
1:5   *117, 126, 129*
1:6   *117, 129*
1:8   *126*

1:8–9   *132*
1:9   *129*
1:15   *131*
1:16   *122*
1:16–17   *128, 129*
1:20   *129*
1:20–21   *129*
1:21   *117, 128*
1:22   *120, 127*
2   *120, 131*
2:1   *117, 125*
2:2   *122, 127*
2:3–4   *125*
2:4   *129*
2:6   *127*
2:7   *122*
2:8   *125*
2:10   *125, 127*
2:11   *126, 128*
2:11–12   *125, 132*
2:12   *122, 129*
2:13   *125*
2:15   *125*
2:17   *122*
2:18   *122*
2:19–20   *125*
2:20   *129, 130*
2:21   *125, 127*
2:23   *120, 122, 125*
3   *120*
3:1   *132*
3:4   *131*
3:9   *131, 132*
3:10   *122, 125, 129*
3:10–11   *122, 126*
3:11   *121, 125*
3:12   *130*
3:13   *129*
4   *121*
4:1   *129*

4:1–12   *117*
4:5   *127*
4:10   *127*
4:11–12   *121, 125, 129*
4:13   *129, 131*
4:13–17   *126*
4:14   *129*
4:15   *122, 126*
4:17   *117*

1 Samuel
1 Samuel 1 – 2 Samuel 8   *164*
2:1–10   *117*
9:1   *125*
13:13   *168*
18:20–29   *117*
23:17   *164–165*
24–26   *164, 166*
24:13   *165*
24:21   *164*
25   *47, 117, 165*
26   *165*

2 Samuel
6:6–11   *196*
9–20   *164, 166, 169*
9 – 1 Kings 2   *137*
9:8   *165*
12:1–15   *167*
13:3   *167*
14   *47, 105, 117, 167*
15–17   *168*
15:31   *168*
15:37   *167*
16:23   *xiii, 168*
17:14   *168*
20   *47, 105, 117, 167–168*
21:1–14   *168*
22:31   *191*

24:10 *168*
24:18–24 *168*

1 Kings
1 – 2 *169*
1 – 11 *169*
1 – 12 *85*
1:42 *125*
2:6 *169*
2:17 *105*
2:22 *105*
2:28–34 *169*
3:9 *170*
3:12–15 *169*
3:28 *169*
4:29–34 *128*
5:9–14 *169*
5:26 *169*
10:1 *163*
10:1–10 *170*
10:4–8 *169*
10:23–24 *169*
11 *xiii, 169*
11:41 *169*
12:8 *169*
21 *47*

2 Kings
14:9 *162*
14:9–10 *169*
15:20 *125*
22:11–20 *47*

1 Chronicles
22:15 *170*
28:21 *170*

2 Chronicles
1 – 9 *170*
2:7 *170*

2:13–14 *170*
9:1 *163*

Ezra
7:14 *171*
7:25 *171*
9 – 10 *49*

Nehemiah
13:23–27 *49*

Esther
1:10–12 *172*
1:13 *172*
5:13 *172*
5:14 *172*
6:13 *172*

Job
1:1 *60, 75, 186*
1 – 37 *17*
1:5 *75*
1:8 *60, 64, 147, 186*
1:9–12 *148*
1:12 *73*
1:13–19 *60, 78*
1:21 *75*
2:3 *60, 64, 73, 147, 186*
2:4–6 *148*
2:6 *73*
2:7 *60*
2:10 *75*
2:11 *66*
3 *66*
3:3–4 *75*
3:3–12 *63*
3:11–12 *67*
3:11–26 *63*
3:20 *67*
3:20–23 *63*

3:23 *75*
4:7–11 *66*
4:12–21 *161*
4:17 *60*
4:17–19 *66*
5:8 *67, 212*
5:9 *74*
5:10–16 *74*
5:17 *66, 74*
5:18–27 *74*
6:1–30 *65*
6:2 – 7:1 *63*
6:4 *62, 75, 76*
6:8–9 *75*
6:29 *65*
7:1–21 *65*
7:7 *65*
7:16 *65*
7:20 *62*
7:21 *76*
8:3 *66, 74*
8:3–6 *60*
8:4–6 *67*
8:5 *212*
8:8–10 *66*
8:20–22 *74*
9 – 10 *63*
9:3 *69*
9:10–11 *212*
9:14–16 *69*
9:14–20 *63*
9:17 *62, 69*
9:19 *69*
9:19–20 *76*
9:24 *148*
9:25–35 *76*
9:32–34 *69, 70*
9:33 *69, 70*
10:3 *62*
10:9 *65*

Job (*cont.*)
10:14–17 *76*
10:20 *65*
11:2–4 *66*
11:4–6 *60*
11:5–7 *215*
11:6 *67*
11:6–9 *74*
11:7 *67*
11:10 *74*
11:13–20 *74*
12:1 – 13:19 *65*
12:4 *210*
12:13 *215*
13:3 *69*
13:3 – 14:22 *63*
13:6 *69*
13:15 *63*
13:18 *69*
13:20 – 14:22 *65*
13:22 *69, 210*
13:23 *69*
13:24 *62, 69, 212*
13:24–28 *76*
14 *69*
14:3–4 *76*
14:6 *65*
14:13 *65*
14:13–17 *63*
14:15 *65*
15:7–8 *57*
16:1 – 17:16 *63*
16:7–16 *62*
16:9–14 *76*
16:17 *65*
16:19 *69, 70*
16:19–22 *70*
18:5–21 *74*
18:22 *127*
19 *63*

19:6–12 *76*
19:7 *210*
19:25 *69*
19:25–27 *63, 70*
20 *74*
20:6 *127*
21 *75*
22:5/6–9 *67, 147*
22:10 *147*
22:12–14 *212*
23 – 24 *63*
23:3 *209, 212*
23:5 *210*
23:8–9 *209, 212*
23:10–12 *65*
23:13–14 *75*
25:2–3 *74*
26:6 *75*
26:7–13 *75*
27:1–6 *65, 70*
27:2 *76, 129*
27:7–23 *75*
28 *156, 178, 183*
28:12–13 *215*
28:20 *206*
28:20–21 *215*
28:23 *206, 215*
28:28 *186, 191*
29 – 31 *70*
29:2 *70*
29:2–5 *76*
29:5 *209*
29:14 *70*
30 *63*
30:20 *210*
31 *65, 75, 187, 188, 191*
31:13–15 *190*
31:26–27 *191*
31:26–28 *190*
31:28–40 *190*

31:29–30 *190*
31:35 *69, 210*
34:5–6 *213*
34:29 *212*
35:5–8 *70*
35:10–11 *70*
35:12 *210*
35:13–14 *70*
36:26 *213*
36:29 *213*
37:15–16 *213*
37:23 *213*
38 – 41 *16, 17, 178, 183*
38:1 – 42:6 *17, 76*
38:2–4 *58*
38:4–21 *76*
38:18 *213*
38:22–38 *76*
38:26–27 *77, 215*
38:35 *77*
38:39 – 39:30 *76, 77*
40 – 41 *77*
40:8 *77, 148*
42:2 *75*
42:2–6 *183–184*
42:3 *71, 78, 184*
42:6 *71*
42:7–8 *16, 17, 64, 66, 67, 74, 78, 148, 150*
42:7–9 *60*
42:10–17 *17*

Psalms
1 *195, 196, 198, 200*
1:2 *196*
1:3 *197*
1:4 *196–197*
9 – 10 *195*
14 *196, 201*
14:2 *197*

INDEX OF SCRIPTURE REFERENCES

14:5 *196*
14:6 *198*
14:7 *197*
15 *191*
15:3 *190*
19 *189*
19:1–4 *180*
22:23 *186*
24:4 *191*
28:2–4 *136*
33:4–9 *180*
34 *196, 198–199*
34:4 *197*
34:9–10 *197*
34:13 *190*
34:15–16 *197*
34:16 *197*
34:17 *197*
37 *196, 200, 201*
37:2 *197*
37:4 *197*
37:5–6 *197*
37:7–11 *198*
37:9 *196*
37:12 *196*
37:13 *197*
37:14 *196, 198*
37:16 *198*
37:20 *196*
37:21 *196, 198*
37:25 *197*
37:25–26 *202*
37:35–36 *197*
49 *196, 198, 200*
49:1 *199*
49:4 *163*
50:23 *190*
53 *196*
53:5 *197*
65:5–13 *180*

73 *196, 197, 203*
73:18 *197*
74:12–17 *180*
78:2 *163*
89:5–18 *180*
90:3 *56*
104 *180*
104:9 *149*
111 *195*
112 *54, 126, 196*
112:1 *196*
112:1–3 *197*
112:2–9 *197*
112:5 *196*
112:9 *196, 197*
112:6 *151*
119 *195*
127 *196, 198*
128 *126, 196, 198*
128:6 *198*
136:4–9 *180*
139:13 *55–56*
145 *195*
147 *189*

Proverbs
1–9 *24, 25, 46, 47–48, 49, 50, 51, 52, 103, 106, 107, 108, 110, 126, 127, 138, 207*
1:1/2–7 *40, 188*
1:5 *55, 191, 199*
1:6 *163*
1:7 *6, 125, 191*
1:8 *47, 105, 199*
1:8–19 *52*
1:11–14 *52*
1:20–21 *107*
1:20–33 *44*
1:22 *107*
1:22–33 *107*

1:28 *210, 211*
1:32–33 *138*
1:33 *107, 189*
2 *156*
2:4 *111*
2:4–5 *212*
2:6 *206*
2:6–8 *211*
2:12–15 *52*
2:16 *49, 127*
2:16–19 *48*
2:16–22 *52*
2:17 *49, 50, 128*
3:3 *26*
3:7 *139*
3:9–10 *190*
3:13 *111*
3:13–18 *6, 54, 177*
3:13–26 *54–55*
3:14–15 *107*
3:17 *107*
3:19–20 *6, 55, 58, 177–179*
3:21–26 *55*
3:27–35 *191*
3:29 *190*
3:35 *140*
4–7 *207*
4:1 *199*
4:1–9 *156*
4:4 *189*
4:5–6 *111*
4:5–9 *48, 55*
4:9 *111*
4:10 *199*
4:14–19 *52*
5:1–23 *48, 52*
5:3 *49, 108*
5:3–14 *50*
5:5–6 *49*
5:15–19 *50, 51, 107*

Proverbs (*cont.*)
5:15–20   *106*
5:20   *49, 128*
5:20/21–23   *50, 131, 142*
6:6 – 11   *122, 131, 140*
6:12–15   *52*
6:19   *190*
6:20   *47*
6:20–35   *48*
6:24   *49, 128*
6:24–35   *52*
6:25   *49*
6:26   *49*
6:29   *49*
6:32–35   *146*
7:1–27   *26, 48, 51, 109*
7:2   *189*
7:4   *111*
7:5   *49, 128*
7:6–12   *108*
7:6–23   *107*
7:11   *49*
7:13   *49*
7:18–20   *109*
7:19–20   *49*
7:21   *49*
8   *44–45, 48, 54, 55–58, 107, 177, 192*
8 – 9   *45, 203*
8:1–3   *107*
8:1–4   *211*
8:6   *199*
8:6–11   *107*
8:11   *107*
8:12–16   *177*
8:13   *186*
8:15   *111*
8:17   *111*
8:18–19   *107*
8:22   *55*

8:22–31   *6, 46, 142, 178*
8:24–28   *211*
8:29   *149*
8:33   *199*
8:35–36   *211*
9   *6, 27, 48, 189*
9:1–6   *44*
9:3   *107*
9:5–6   *107*
9:5–9   *107*
9:10   *43, 46, 125, 186, 191*
9:17   *109*
10   *38, 39*
10 – 13   *42*
10:1 – 22:16   *38, 40, 47*
10 – 29   *16, 37, 138*
10:3   *143*
10:4   *139, 146*
10:7   *151*
10:8   *139, 140*
10:14   *139*
10:26   *122*
11:10   *143*
11:16   *43*
11:22   *166*
11:23   *143*
11:26   *146*
11:29   *139*
12:4   *121*
12:7   *27*
12:15   *139*
13:4   *146*
13:14   *122*
13:23   *43*
14:3   *139*
14:12   *43*
14:16   *139*
14:21   *190*
14:24   *139*
14:31   *190*

15 – 16   *207*
15:1   *166*
15:2   *139*
15:7   *139*
15:8   *190*
15:16–17   *19*
15:20   *47, 139*
15:25   *145*
15:33 – 16:9   *130*
16:1   *144*
16:1–2   *128, 183*
16:6   *186*
16:8   *43*
16:9   *128, 144*
16:16   *19, 43*
16:19   *19*
16:33   *130*
17:7   *43*
17:14   *167*
17:15   *190*
17:23   *190*
17:28   *139*
18:5   *190*
18:18   *130*
18:23   *43*
19:3   *142*
19:10   *43*
19:14   *128*
19:17   *190*
19:21   *43, 128, 169, 183*
20:4   *146*
20:11   *190*
20:14   *55*
20:20   *190*
20:24   *128, 183*
20:28   *130*
21:20   *139*
21:21   *130*
21:23   *132*
21:27   *190*

INDEX OF SCRIPTURE REFERENCES

21:30 *43, 183*
21:30–31 *43, 128*
22:22 *132*
22:24–25 *38*
23:10–11 *131*
23:13–14 *38*
23:20 *146*
23:22 *190*
23:22–25 *47*
23:27 *128*
24:3–4 *27, 179*
24:5–6 *43*
24:11 *138*
24:11–12 *131*
24:16 *138, 143*
24:30–34 *131*
25 – 27 *38, 207*
25:18 *190*
26:4–5 *43*
26:5 *139*
26:12 *139*
26:20–21 *38*
26:27 *132*
27:1 *43, 183*
27:10 *190*
28:27 *132*
28:28 *143*
29:2 *143*
29:7 *190*
29:9 *139*
29:16 *143*
29:18 *160*
29:26 *131*
30:1 *128*
30:1–6 *186*
30:2–4 *183*
30:3–4 *213*
30:5 *191*
30:6 *191*
30:18–19 *100*

30:18–21 *162*
30:21–23 *43*
31 *27, 117, 120, 121, 122, 123, 124, 126, 127, 130, 131, 132, 166*
31:1 *128*
31:1–9 *47*
31:3 *124*
31:6–9 *130*
31:8–9 *190*
31:10 *121, 124*
31:10–31 *47, 50, 121, 186*
31:13 *122, 131*
31:15 *122, 131*
31:18–19 *131*
31:20 *122, 130*
31:21 *122*
31:23 *53, 121*
31:26 *122, 130*
31:27 *122, 126, 131*
31:28–29 *122, 124*
31:29 *125*
31:30 *122, 124*
31:31 *121, 125*

Ecclesiastes

1:1 *85*
1:2 *20, 82, 90*
1:4 *184*
1:4–11 *178*
1:8 *93*
1:9–11 *184*
1:11 *93*
1:12 *85*
1:12–18 *21*
1:12 – 2:24 *83, 85*
1:13 *111*
1:17 *111*
2:12 *111*
2:16 *93, 151*

2:17 *82*
2:18–19 *184*
2:21 *208*
2:24–25/26 *89, 188*
2:26 *23, 206*
3 *208*
3:1–8 *94, 178*
3:9–14 *94*
3:10–22 *86*
3:11 *213*
3:12 *187*
3:12 – 13 *89*
3:14 *186, 187*
3:16 *184*
3:17 *23, 88, 151*
3:18 *184*
3:22 *89*
4 *208*
4:1 *184, 208*
4:1–2 *213*
4:1–3 *93*
4:1–16 *188*
4:5–6 *96*
4:7–8 *184*
4:8 *184*
4:9–12 *96, 190*
4:13–16 *184*
4:17 *208*
4:17 – 5:6 *23*
5:2 *208*
5:3 *96, 208*
5:3–4 *98–99*
5:3–5 *191*
5:5 *98*
5:6 *23, 88*
5:7 *186, 188*
5:8–9 *184*
5:10 *184*
5:17–19 *89*
5:18/19–20 *93, 188*

Ecclesiastes (*cont.*)
6:1–2 *213*
6:7 *184*
6:10 *184*
6:10 – 7:14 *90*
7:1–10 *86*
7:1–12 *96*
7:14 *184, 213*
7:15 *151, 184, 213*
7:15–18 *93*
7:18 *188*
7:19 *156*
7:20 *184*
7:23–24 *184, 214*
7:23–29 *156*
7:25 *111*
7:27 *20, 82*
7:29 *184*
8:6–9 *93*
8:9 *184*
8:11 *151, 184*
8:12 *23, 187, 188, 208*
8:12–13 *82, 96, 151*
8:14 *151, 213*
8:16 *111*
8:16–17 *214*
8:17 *184, 212, 213*
8:18 *184*
9:1–10 *86*
9:2 *190*
9:2–3 *213*
9:4 *82*
9:7–10 *89, 188*
9:11–12 *184*
9:13–16 *96*
9:15 *156*
10 *208*
11:1–6 *188*
11:5 *184, 213*
11:7 – 12:1 *89*

11:9 *23, 88, 98, 187*
12 *26*
12:8 *20, 82*
12:9–14 *82*
12:11 *156*
12:13 *23, 83, 186, 191*
12:13–14 *152*

Song of Solomon
1:1–5 *47*
1:2 *111*
1:4–6 *103*
1:5 *110, 111*
1:6 *102*
1:7 *106*
2:7 *102, 103, 107*
2:8–9 *111*
2:8 – 3:5 *109, 111*
2:15 *107*
2:16 *106*
3:1–5 *106, 107, 108*
3:4 *107*
3:5 *102, 103, 106, 107*
3:6 *112*
3:6–11 *110, 111*
3:11 *103, 111*
3:14 *184*
4:8 *108*
4:8–16 *111*
4:11 *108*
4:12 *108*
4:15 *108*
4:16 *107, 108*
4:16 – 5:1 *107, 108*
5:1 *103, 111*
5:1–8 *107*
5:2–8 *106, 108*
5:8 *102, 107*
5:8–16 *103*
5:10–16 *107*

6:1–3 *103*
6:3 *106*
6:8–9 *110*
6:9 *106, 110*
6:10 *107*
6:13 *105*
7:1 *56*
7:2 *107*
7:6 *111*
7:10 *106*
7:11–12 *107, 109*
7:13 *107, 109*
8:1–2 *107*
8:2 *109*
8:2–3 *107*
8:4 *102, 103, 107*
8:6–12 *102, 106*
8:7 *107*
8:8–10 *47*
8:10 *105, 107*
8:11–12 *106, 110, 111, 112*

Isaiah
1:12–15 *190*
1:17 *190*
3:3 *157*
5:21 *156–157*
10:5–19 *146*
10:13 *157*
11:1–9 *157*
13:8 *56*
23:4 *56*
29:14 *157*
31:2 *157*
33:5–6 *157*
33:15 *191*
40:25–26 *180*
40:28 *189*
45:18 *189*

46:3–4 *56*
50:10 *191*
55:3 *189*
55:8–9 *189*
58:6–12 *191*
59:19 *191*
66:13 *56*

Jeremiah
5:22 *149*
9:4–9 *190*
10:12 *179, 180, 189*
18:18 *xiii*
23:1 *190*
33:25–26 *180*
51:15 *179, 180*

Lamentations
1:1 *129*
2:1–8 *129*
5:3 *129*

Ezekiel
18:5–9 *191*
22:6 *190*
22:7 *190*
37:1–14 *189*

Daniel
2:24–45 *161*
4:19–27 *161*

Hosea
2:21–22 *180*

Amos
4:1 *190*

Micah
7:6 *190*

Habakkuk
3:2 *186*

Zechariah
7:9–10 *190*

Malachi
2:10–16 *49*
3:5 *191*
3:16 *191*
4:2 *191*

NEW TESTAMENT

Matthew
5 – 7 *191*
7:24–27 *27*
15:17–20 *190*
20:24–28 *190*

John
1:1–18 *59*
3:36 *189*
9:1–2 *153*

Acts
14:15–17 *180*
17:24 *180*

Romans
1:20 *180, 185*
11:33–34 *189*
12:20–21 *190*
13:8 *190*
13:9 *190*

1 Corinthians
1:24 *xv, 192*
1:30 *192*

2 Corinthians
5:11–21 *191*

Galatians
5:14 *190*

Ephesians
1:17 *180*
3:10 *180*
6:1–4 *190*

Philippians
1:9 *180*

Colossians
1 *192*
1:9–10 *180*
1:15–20 *59*
1:28 *180*
2:2–3 *180*
2:3 *192*
3:16 *180*

1 Timothy
5:21 *190*

Philemon
6 *180*

Hebrews
1:1–4 *58*

James
1:2–4 *192*
1:5 *xv*
1:22–26 *192*
1:27 *190*
2:9 *190*
2:12–13 *192*

James (*cont.*)
3:2–12   *190*
3:13–18 *192*

4:11–12 *192*
5:4   *190*
5:7–11   *192*

5:11   *65, 188*
5:16   *192*
5:19–20 *192*